Bringing Down Goliath

Bringing Down Goliath

Jolyon Maugham KC

WH
ALLEN

2 4 6 8 10 9 7 5 3

WH Allen, an imprint of Ebury Publishing
20 Vauxhall Bridge Road
London SW1V 2SA

WH Allen is part of the Penguin Random House group of companies
whose addresses can be found at global.penguinrandomhouse.com

Penguin
Random House
UK

First published by WH Allen in 2023

www.penguin.co.uk

A CIP catalogue record for this book is available from the British Library

ISBN 9780753559789

Typeset in 13.5/16.25pt Garamond MT Std by Jouve (UK), Milton Keynes
Printed and bound in Great Britain by Clays Ltd, Elcograf S.p.A.

The authorised representative in the EEA is Penguin Random House Ireland,
Morrison Chambers, 32 Nassau Street, Dublin D02 YH68

Penguin Random House is committed to a sustainable future
for our business, our readers and our planet. This book is made
from Forest Stewardship Council® certified paper.

For Claire, who makes everything possible.

'What we allow the mark of our suffering to become
is in our own hands.'

— bell hooks, *All About Love*

Contents

Introduction

The law, backed by the power of the State, is how lawmakers shape the world. It rewards the conduct they like and punishes the conduct they don't. Our lives are shaped and changed by the law, it is the sluice gate through which the river of humanity flows.

The law is a slingshot to bring down Goliath.

Rich and poor, weak and strong, all are subject to it and equal before it. With it, any of us can take on a global corporation, or a mighty government, and win. It is blind to power and it is blind to identity. Lady Justice atop the Old Bailey does not see who appears before her. And no one can put their thumb on the scales she holds because we can always see that justice is done.

At least, that's the idea.

The reality, I have to tell you, is more complicated. Judges don't wear blindfolds and their ears catch your vowels. Judging is a negotiation between what the law says and the judge's perception, often founded in their social class, of what value-laden concepts like morality and fairness require.

Governments – especially in a country, like ours, that lacks a written constitution – do place their thumb on the scales. Sometimes the combination of explicit public bullying and private patronage suggests a heavier body part than the thumb.

And the cost of asking whether all are equal before the law is an exercise too expensive for most of us. As the

nineteenth-century Irish judge, James Mathew, put it: 'In England, justice is open to all – like the Ritz Hotel.'

For most of us the law touches our life gently. Along with
other social mores it conditions the behaviour of those who
interact with us. Landlords, employers and retailers tend to
treat us as the law requires. But mostly because they choose to.
The practical reality, for most of us, is that the law cannot be
wielded to compel them to. It's a tool too expensive to buy.

But that's not true of everyone. Make an enemy who has
money – speak an uncomfortable truth or threaten their
interests – and you will quickly learn how the law can be
used as a weapon to deliver injustice, to bend the weak to the
will of the strong.

The law should, and it can, protect the weak from the
strong. Literally. It must discourage employers from abus-
ing interns desperate to enter a profession. It must re-tilt the
scales so Instagram is not financially rewarded for serving up
harmful content to children. It must deter the rape of women
by men. (It fails when it does not. And the unequivocal story
told by the statistics is that it is failing.)

These are real, profound problems. But they should not
disguise what good the law can do.

The hand of a good lawyer holds the mightiest pen. Its
stroke can enlist the power of the State. If your arguments
do persuade a judge that a global tech behemoth has broken
the law, you can rely on the State to coerce it to comply.

It is how far-off corporations are prevented from freeload-
ing on the public infrastructure their businesses need. And,
if eventually they do pay their taxes, it is the principal deter-
rent to venal politicians diverting those taxes from the public
coffers into the pockets of their friends.

It should police the dividing line between what is for the public good and what is for private benefit. If water companies dump sewage into our rivers and onto our beaches rather than invest in infrastructure it is because the law fails to discourage them from preferring their shareholders. When Government gets to buy the votes of MPs in Parliament with constituency boondoggles from public funds it is because the law has not played its part.

Law can help protect democracy. It can prevent a man selected by tens of thousands of voters from suspending a Parliament elected by tens of millions. And it can compel him to do what that Parliament has explicitly commanded him to do.

All of these things, I have enlisted the power of the law to attempt or do.

The stories of how – and of whether I succeeded – make up most of this book. Through Good Law Project I have tried to collectivise the power of tens of thousands of regular people – who cannot by themselves afford the hundreds or thousands of pounds an hour that top lawyers charge – to use the law for a better world.

The law should mean justice – but it too rarely does. It's into that gap between the 'should' and the 'does' that Good Law Project has sought to step. This means we have to work with what the law is – but I also want it to be better. I want it to work for everyone like it works for the rich. It must work for people of colour like it works for those who are white. It has enormous power to do good – but far too often that power is abused or unused.

The law can also help us to engage in the world.

Our lives are shaped by decisions that feel more and more remote from us, which are deaf to our cries to be heard, that reveal power to be wielded in ways we know to be wrong and which insulate the wicked from consequence. And we sense this is getting worse.

The temptation is to disengage from it all, to become an acid commentator from the sidelines, rather than a player in the highest stakes game there is.

The law cannot be the main agent of democratic change – the fruits of winning control of Parliament are rightly greater than the law can ever offer – but it can be an understudy when Parliament fails to function. It provides some answers to the question, 'How do I live in this world that is full of things that are wrong and that I want to change?' It can hold out the promise of making the things you care about better. It can improve things from how they are.

And this is what, as the following pages will tell, I have tried, and will try, to do.

PART ONE

How the System Works

1. Getting to Now

The life I have is hard, but I got to choose it, and the road that brought me here I did not.

Even before university, I had seen a lot of the world.

My mother had me in 1971. She had grown up in Romford and moved to London to study sociology at North London Poly. No one in her family had previously studied for a degree. A mutual friend had introduced her to a novelist called David Benedictus, then famous as the author of an exposé about Eton, the school he had attended, called *The Fourth of June*.

The relationship was a casual one. He was of a different social class and, although she didn't know it, already engaged to someone else. I have the letter she wrote to him: 'What this letter is trying to say is that I'm pregnant and you are the father . . . This is not meant as any sort of tragic declaration – I can't feel tragic. All there is are words on a page from me to you.' And I have some of the carbon-copy responses from his lawyers and an eventual agreement recording that in return for a payment of £5 per week until she married she would not 'allow the child to bear his surname nor in any way represent to any person that the child is the child of Mr Benedictus'.

When my mother finished her sociology course in 1972, she moved to New Zealand, following in the footsteps of her parents who had moved there when her father had lost his job working as office manager for an electrician. There she went to teacher training college and met and married Alan. They had a child together in 1975 and, around that time, he adopted me. But I grew towards adulthood believing him to be my biological father.

To parent is to fail, as every child, and in their heart every parent, knows. I could not see it then – the only lens available to a child through which to view their parents is whether their needs are met – but I am sure he tried. When I was 16, still at school and vulnerable, they asked me to leave their house. They paid a very small sum of money into my bank account, not nearly enough to live on, until I finished school. I worked cleaning up after my peers at the girls' secondary school but did not make enough to live independently.

I moved in with a teacher from the school – a man who took an interest in troubled boys my age. Several times I shared his bed. I then moved to the flat of a depressed bachelor in his fifties who alternated between unsuccessful – from his perspective – transactions with sex workers and similarly impotent passes at me.

In real life, poverty and dignity don't make comfortable bedfellows. Darning and well-scrubbed kitchen floors are all well and good. But Victorian ideals of virtue are easier to hold to when you rise every morning from a safe and warm bed. The lawyer in me now cannot defend a legal system that criminalises those who steal because they are hungry.

It seems remarkable now – with the distance of the many years since I was 16 – that I managed to emerge from this period of my life unbowed. But I also know how I grasped and hustled for chances to improve my financial situation. The way I then behaved to those around me falls short of the standards that I now, more prosperous, set for myself. But I also understand that ideals of morality are something I can afford now, but could not afford then. Sometimes you just survive.

Those events have left me with a deep suspicion of ethical standards set by those whose lives have been of unbroken wealth. The cost of dignity, of the high moral ground, is not fixed. If you are brought up in money, and at the best public schools, maybe you mediate your expectations of the biggest prizes society has to offer. The stakes are rather higher, and the compromises uglier and more demeaning, if you are a single mother struggling to provide for her children.

I survived those years, but I hated them. Now, they mean I have some ability to imagine my way into the lives of those who lack what I now have. I know that there are some things you cannot learn in books.

After finishing school, with mediocre grades, I took what I had planned to be a year out in England. I moved in with 'Aunty' Betty, who my mother's parents had helped to bring up when they lived in High Spen, near Rowlands Gill in the north east. She was in the next village down the hill, in Highfield, built near a former cokeworks. Several weeks before I had left New Zealand, I learned from my mother that Alan was not my biological father; that he had adopted me. That fresh fact set me on a long path that continued into middle adulthood of making sense of what up to then had been my life. I met David Benedictus for the first time and with his help I got a clerical job at the BBC.

I gratefully, and gracelessly, chucked in what had been my life living with Betty. From selling stereos at Fenwick's department store in Newcastle, I moved to London, living successively in Morden, Muswell Hill and, five of us in a one-bedroom flat, in Fitzrovia. I was promoted to radio production assistant at the BBC and wrote, in quick succession, a feature for Radio 3 about a New Zealand poet called James K. Baxter and a Western for Radio 4's *Afternoon Play* slot. Across the half landing of our flat in Fitzrovia lived two sex workers and, from time to time, I would have awkward meetings with BBC colleagues on the stairs.

The writing persuaded Durham University to offer me a place to study law, despite my mediocre grades from school.

Those years before university, living in London, awkward and unhappy, I survived with the help of my biological father's lover, a woman called Karen Ross. David's motives were fine, and he was generous and sometimes loving, but he had a deteriorating marriage and two children of his own. Karen had not had children and I needed a mother and she took me under her wing.

And then university, at Hatfield College in Durham.

It's a strange process, learning the law. It is, you come to understand, your job to know the law and apply it. But changing it is for politicians and questioning it is for vicars and other philosophers. So you learn to dissect the human condition but, less even than surgeons, you never engage with the corpse.

It's worth pausing, briefly, to surface an embedded assumption in the model we choose to train lawyers.

Our training encourages us to put aside our personal views on what our clients do. Instead, we are a weapon they get to deploy, a prized commander in the private militias they engage. Our job, we are taught, is to help clients navigate the law in ways that advance their personal and commercial interests. If this is your job it is, indeed, enough to know the law. If you think of the job of a lawyer in this way, the tools to interrogate the difference between right and wrong become more than superfluous – they become positively unhelpful. They get in the way.

In recent times, legal regulators, and in particular the Solicitors Regulation Authority (SRA), have begun to tug at some of these threads.

Can a lawyer draft a clause that binds the victim of a sexual assault not to report it to the police in return for money? Or a contract which misrepresents the law so as to fool a worker into believing they lack protections, protections that Parliament has given them, from bad employers? Or create documents which reflect a false reality, on which the tax liability is less than that the true reality would bear?

These things might all be in clients' interests but they also thwart legal rights and obligations that Parliament and judges have created. They undermine the law.

Nevertheless, the assumption that lawyers must put aside their personal views continues to be embedded in the way they are trained. The purpose of the training is to enculturalise you to be a lawyer; to perform a service for your clients. You begin by being trained to understand that law is different from good, and your job is to apply the law. But as you practise the law you lose interest in what is good. Many, many lawyers take a dangerous step further and come to believe that because it is the law it is good.

Not so long ago, a retired senior judge spoke about her professional shame that of the 15 Nazi officials at the infamous Wannsee Conference that planned the final solution to the Jewish problem, nine had law degrees. But a training that causes lawyers to see behaviour through a narrow prism of whether a thing is lawful might make lawyers particularly vulnerable to doing, or facilitating, things which are wrong.

These issues have increasingly stark resonances if you are a lawyer in a country like the United Kingdom, where the constitutional orthodoxy is that Parliament can make any law it wants, that there are no checks on its law-making power, and that a judge's job is simply to apply the law that Parliament has made.

Most countries have a higher law to protect human rights – as much as the law can – from how a particular government fancies treating its opponents or its scapegoats. But we do not. We have a Human Rights Act which enables judges to declare legislation incompatible with human rights, but which also allows ministers to ignore that declaration. And even that flimsy protection – a scold and on-your-way – Government periodically threatens to throw out by abolishing the Human Rights Act. It is a rich irony that in 2022 the charge is led by the so-called Justice Secretary, Dominic Raab, as he faces many claims that he has mistreated his junior colleagues.

I have spent the later years of my professional life unlearning or interrogating the cultural lessons from my early exposure to the law. Only one of my teachers, a young lecturer called Tamara Hervey, ever fed any (in her case feminist) critical theory into their teaching of the law. But had I had more teaching like that, would it have helped me succeed as a lawyer?

After university, in October 1996, I began pupillage at the fashionable set of 11 King's Bench Walk, where Tony Blair had started out as a barrister and Lord Irvine of Lairg was Lord Chancellor in waiting. 'Young man,' I still remember

'Derry' Irvine booming at me, 'there is one thing that will stop you being taken on at this set of chambers – and that is your appalling manners.' When his prediction came true, I looked around for an alternative and was lucky enough to be offered a place at the specialist tax set of 11 New Square.

At no stage in my life had I contemplated that I might become a tax lawyer. But it was a good life by the usual metrics.

It was not particularly stressful. Unlike other areas of practice, no one calls you up late on a Friday night with an urgent tax query. And it was extremely well paid – almost always when there are tax disputes there is lots of money, and therefore little downward pressure on fees. I worked almost exclusively as a litigator, but it was never especially engaging.

You can divide tax work in half. There is the advice you give before a future transaction is entered into, on what its tax consequences will be. And there is the scrap you sometimes have after a transaction takes place, if HMRC happens to disagree with that advice. Lawyers would describe this as a divide between non-contentious and contentious work.

In tax it was the non-contentious work that attracted the enormous fees. If you were a senior tax barrister, the act of saying a structure 'worked', in other words that it successfully attracted a lower tax treatment than some alternative, gave the 'promoter' who had devised that transaction a valuable thing to sell. And so promoters came to offer – and many tax barristers came to accept – higher fees as an inducement to bless transactions. These conflicts of interest carried horrible financial consequences for wealthy transactors who should have known better. But they also carried similarly grim consequences for low-paid agency workers who lacked any ability to interrogate what they were told to do.

I also worked almost exclusively for taxpayers.

Throughout my career – from the very earliest moments – I had wanted to work for HMRC. But it was not until 2013, after many rejected applications to join the various Government 'panels', that I was finally accepted on to the A Panel, the most prestigious one. But even then the overwhelming majority of my work continued to be for taxpayers. By that stage I think HMRC saw me as tainted.

Tax was my job for about fifteen years. The work was relatively easy, easier by far than what I do now. And I enjoyed the income – which was considerable even though it is only when you become a 'silk', a King's Counsel, that it really takes off – without ever being motivated by money. But I was never going to be truly top-drawer – I never found it interesting enough to really engage with it.

I think I stuck at it for a few reasons.

Like so many lawyers who start asking questions about whether they want the life they have, I felt a bit stuck for alternatives. And the easiness, and the money, are powerful disincentives to changing. Why turn off cruise control on the endless highway of life? No one encourages you to change the world. No one reminds you of – or even knows – the stories you told your younger self about what you would be.

It takes a serious itch, a pathology, to wrest back the steering wheel. And it was in 2013 that I began to scratch.

Margaret Hodge was Chair of the Public Accounts Committee and was asking all the right questions about whether corporations were paying their fair share of taxes. Her questions resonated with the media, and a public that was hurting from austerity's bite. Here was a project I could contribute to.

I started writing a blog, called Waiting for Tax, with an inaugural piece called 'How do you solve a problem like tax avoidance'.[1] I had some technical knowledge, I was a decent writer and, rarest of all, I was happy to talk to the media.

Most of the tax profession didn't speak about the issues at all. Those who did spoke mostly to the clients' media to deliver the message – appreciated by the class who paid their bills – that any attempt to tackle tax avoidance, to get the wealthy to pay their share, would spark a capital flight. They would pull their kids out of public school, sell their stuccos in Belgravia, and move to the Channel Islands. This idea lacked any evidence to support it, and was more than a little ridiculous, but it was nevertheless treated with great deference, mostly because of who it was convenient to.

It wasn't just lawyers whose training and then self-interest caused them to forget, or jettison, their curiosity about how their work resonated in the broader world.

Within the tax profession, the predominant emotion during those years was an often quite explicit contempt for what was seen as the ignorance of those politicians and journalists who tried to talk about the relationship tax had with the larger world. A few pushed back – Richard Murphy and the Institute for Chartered Accountants in England and Wales deserve particular credit. But there was very little interest inside the profession in examining whether the status quo, which so appalled the public, served the broader interests of society.

Of course, neither tax nor the law are closed systems. They exist to serve the world around them. And Margaret Hodge and the Public Accounts Committee created space for those who wanted the system to serve society and to work alongside journalists and politicians to build political pressure for change.

It's easy to forget how grim it was, that 2010–2015 Parliament.

The big political story was austerity – Chancellor George Osborne and Prime Minister David Cameron's response to the global financial crisis caused by the hubris of bankers. Rather than the orthodox economic response of increasing public spending, the Government set about slashing the benefits and public services of those who had neither caused the financial crisis nor benefited from the boom that preceded it. They cut taxes for the rich: they brought in a lower rate of income tax for the highest earners, cut inheritance tax and capital gains tax, and cut corporation tax for shareholders.

But it was worse even than that.

Floating around at the time was the idea of a 20 per cent windfall wealth tax on the global elite. It was difficult to deliver, lacked mainstream political advocacy, and so was never taken up seriously. What we got instead was a decade of cheap money which delivered massive asset price inflation for the haves and raised the costs of acquiring housing for the have nots. In relative terms, the effect of cheap money was to impose a huge wealth tax on the less wealthy, who would have to commit an even greater proportion of their income to housing.

My blog slowly grew in influence. I started to be invited to meet policymakers at HMRC and the Treasury, and to give intermittent advice to the Labour Party. Indeed, the then Financial Secretary to the Treasury, David Gauke, let it be known that he was a fan. But my breakthrough piece was about how some barristers at the tax bar were taking advantage of structural weaknesses in the regulatory, legal and insurance environment to make vast sums giving advice they knew to be wildly over-optimistic.

The post was called 'Weak transmission mechanisms – and boys who won't say no' and begins:

I have on my desk an Opinion – a piece of formal tax advice – from a prominent QC at the Tax Bar. In it, he expresses a view on the law that is so far removed from legal reality that I do not believe he can genuinely hold the view he says he has. At best he is incompetent. But at worst, he is criminally fraudulent: he is obtaining his fee by deception. And this is not the first such Opinion I have seen. Such pass my desk All The Time.

The 'he' in question, I shall not name. But the brief description in the above paragraph will be sufficient to enable that part of the tax profession that regularly uses tax Counsel to narrow the possibilities down to slightly under half a dozen names. These are the Boys Who Won't Say No – the 'Boys' for short – and we all know who they are.

***

Assume you are a seller of tax planning ideas – a 'House'. You have developed a planning idea that you wish to sell to taxpayers. But your customers will typically want independent corroboration – from a member of the Bar – that your idea 'works', that is to say that it delivers a beneficial tax treatment. Or, to use the preferred euphemism, that it 'mitigates' your tax liability.

The fees that can be generated from bringing a planning idea to market are substantial: I am aware of instances where a single planning idea has generated fees of about

£100 million for the House. But without barrister sign-off, you have nothing to sell.

This fact creates predictable temptations for the Bar. If you are prepared to sign off a planning idea, the House will pay you handsomely. In some instances hundreds of thousands of pounds for a few days' work. But the tax code is not made of Swiss cheese. Planning ideas that actually deliver are rare. Their supply is constrained – constrained far beyond demand.

All of this is trite.

It is what happens if you allow your independence to be swayed by your desire to collect the fee that I wish to explore. And the answer is, not enough.[2]

And I was away. Margaret Hodge took advantage of parliamentary privilege to read out a list of QCs who she thought were particular offenders and all of a sudden I was working alongside a bank of journalists to try and find ways to report on what was really happening.

I was ready for this campaigning to have a substantial negative impact on my income. One of the great privileges, which was so very important to me, of working as a barrister is that your practice is your own. If you want to blow it up, well, that's up to you and no one can tell you not to.

They couldn't tell me not to, my colleagues, but they also couldn't understand it. What did I hope to gain; what was the 'play'? They would quip that my blog was the longest suicide note in history, at least for my practice. But it didn't really work out like that. I learned that having a small group of clients who were very keen to support me was enough to sustain a viable practice and more than compensated for the shift from indifference to hostility of the majority. I had not foreseen this, but it was a lesson of wide application.

And, happily, my work began to resonate more broadly.

An issue particularly (and rightly) troubling to the public was the grotesquely small sums of tax being paid by the huge tech giants, in particular Facebook and Google. I remember the former releasing its accounts one morning. I wrote a quick blog about what was really going on and immediately got a call from Radio 4's *World at One* asking me to come into the studio and talk through it. I hopped into a cab and, on the way to the studio, fielded calls from Facebook's public affairs team and then the Labour Party about what a particular paragraph in my blog meant. Both were pushing me to clarify the blog text to make it clear their interpretation was the right one.

In the middle of all of this, early in 2015, I was appointed Queen's Counsel.

For a barrister, the only external validation of your quality you can get is to be appointed (now) King's Counsel or 'silk'. Applying involves gathering together a large number of referees – judges, opponents, clients – and the need to have their good wishes if you wish your application to succeed creates a powerful incentive not to rock the boat.

For a tax barrister, becoming a silk is the gateway to serious money. The one thing that is consistently true about tax cases is that they all involve large sums of money. One consequence is that there is very little incentive to economise by using a junior barrister. All the money chases a relatively small number of KCs who can charge what they like in consequence.

But in my heart, I had already left that world behind.

Becoming a QC was important to me, for very different reasons. If I got that external mark of success I didn't have to stay: I no longer had to prove anything. And it liberated me to say what I wanted to say – I no longer needed to fear being black-balled by referees. For most people, taking silk is an on-ramp to a higher income, but for me taking silk was an off-ramp to something I cared about more.

Having silk also made me much more valuable to the Labour Party, who I was then advising on tax policy.

My blog had become very influential in policy circles and I had started to write about the non-dom rule, an especially egregious expression of the welfare for the wealthy that runs through our tax system. The non-dom tax break rewards wealthy individuals with foreign connections who choose to live in the UK and keep their money abroad, with a lower effective tax rate.

I'd been writing about it for some time and its existence then was only slightly less remarkable than its persistence now. Even if you think it's a good idea to bestow upon wealthy individuals with vague foreign connections a hugely valuable tax break, why would you do so in a way that encourages them to keep their assets *outside* the United Kingdom? It's just bananas – it rewards the wealthy for behaving in ways that undermine the national interest and punishes them if they support it by bringing their wealth onshore.

Shortly before the 2015 general election, I got a call from my Labour Party 'handler', Ed Miliband's Director of Economic Policy, John Wrathmell. Shadow Chancellor Ed Balls, he told me, was going to announce that a new Labour government would abolish the tax break. Would I work up some figures showing how much money abolishing non-dom status would raise?

As it turned out, Labour smartly decided not to major on how much money would be raised but on the fact that abolishing the break was fair. The job of my blog was to cover the financial flank. This was smart politics – as the Leave campaign later proved before the 2016 Brexit referendum, there were things people could be persuaded they cared about more than their wallets – and Labour enjoyed its only real poll lead whilst majoring on non-dom status.

On the day the policy was announced, I was sent out to do media interviews. I had had no media training at all – remember this was a centrepiece of Labour's manifesto during a general election campaign. And I also didn't have a brief – no one had explained to me whether my job was to be an independent expert or an advocate for the policy. Welcome to politics, young man: if you can't ride two horses at once you shouldn't be at the circus, as James Maxton quipped.

Labour thought it had the 2015 election locked up. In preparing for government, it put together a detailed legislative programme for its first hundred days in office. I had been asked to go into Number 10 and run tax policy – and was also being touted by some in the Shadow Cabinet as a prospective Attorney General from the Lords.

But we parked that discussion until the election result came through, either with the exit poll on 7 May or early the following day. But the electorate, it seemed, had taken fright at the prospect of 'chaos with Ed Miliband', to recall David Cameron's now immortal tweet.

It's a brutal business, politics.

A number of Labour advisers had put other careers on hold and left young families around the country to live in

London, where the political action was. The huge personal sacrifices only made sense if you hoped to win a general election. Losing meant that sacrifice was in vain – it tossed those years onto the scrapheap. And it also left you unemployed – typically contracts with the party end the day after a general election. Deliver – or else.

My investment, luckily for me, had been lower. No one then knew quite what the years after 2015 would bring and my mood had begun to lift by the evening of Sunday 10 May when I went with my wife Claire for an early evening drink in Brixton. 'Don't worry, my love,' I said, lifting my head from the second glass, 'the Good Ship Maugham will rise again.' This drew a stern response: 'You do know, Jolyon, don't you, that you were never *actually* Attorney General?'

What I had gained, however, was a platform on social media and with it a route to the public, along with good name recognition with senior journalists and a small foothold in the world of politics.

I was quickly animated by the Brexit referendum campaign that followed.

I had spent a glorious year at Katholieke Universiteit Leuven as an Erasmus student, studying not just with academics, who make up the law faculties in England, but with practitioners and judges, including a slender, rather bookish man called Koen Lenaerts who we will meet again in Chapter Six as President of the Court of Justice. I also studied under the most brilliant lawyer I have met, the then Belgian Advocate General to the Court of Justice, Walter van Gerven. Being taught by lawyers of their calibre broadened my intellectual and philosophical horizons.

But it was much more than that.

It was a wonderfully optimistic project, the Erasmus scheme, a conscious piece of European nation-building. It wasn't formally in the curriculum that we should fraternise closely with other promising young students from around Europe and dream of what together we might build, but the demands of academia were easily held at bay.

I felt more comfortable amongst that community, together away from home, than I had before – and perhaps have since. I felt European and I felt at home.

Whilst I had been campaigning about tax avoidance I had begun to attract instructions from NGOs who wanted to litigate to tackle it. They did not know, but I did, that the very thing that caused them to send me cases was also the very thing that made me ill-equipped to take them on. I no longer had the necessary intellectual distance.

Fortunately, none of the ideas the NGOs came to me with quite worked. A campaigner's idea of a good piece of litigation is only very occasionally the same as a lawyer's. But those NGOs did introduce me to the idea of strategic litigation. What if, rather than waiting around for clients to come to me with their ideas, I swapped roles and became the client myself?

Several days after the June 2016 referendum, Nick Barber, Tom Hickman and Jeff King published a blog post called 'Pulling the Article 50 "Trigger": Parliament's Indispensable Role', arguing that:

> Our membership of the European Union has conferred a host of legal rights on British citizens . . . Applying the common law . . . the Government cannot remove or nullify these rights without parliamentary approval.[3]

Sometimes as a lawyer you just *know*.

I had that sense about the prorogation challenge (see Chapter Seven) despite the fact that the legal cognoscenti had written off its chances, and I had it about this argument too. I put up my first ever crowdfunding page on 29 June, less than a week after the referendum, capping donations at £100 each to reach a target of £10,000. The crowdfunding platform had never been asked to do this before – and to the best of my knowledge never has since – but I wanted the case to be people-powered and was happy to gamble that we would still raise the money. With the help of 406 donations, we were funded within a day. It morphed into the so-called People's Challenge, which was one of the other claimants before the Supreme Court in Gina Miller's 2016 case that established that it was for Parliament not Theresa May to decide what to do with the referendum.

Later that year, in October, I was contacted by a man I didn't know called Rupert Evans. And his email to me, it turned out, was the genesis of Good Law Project.

Rupert had wanted to do something about Brexit and had been following what I'd said about overspending by the official 'Vote Leave' campaign. Steve Baker MP – a prominent figure in that campaign – had boasted in an email about having found a loophole that enabled him to ignore the law around spending limits: 'Vote Leave will be able to spend as much money as is necessary to win the referendum.'[4] (We later forced the Electoral Commission to investigate exactly this practice, after which Vote Leave accepted it had broken the law.[5])

Rupert was interested in whether Vote Leave's far-right sister campaign – Leave.EU – had committed similar breaches of spending limits (it later transpired it had).[6] Over a series of emails and conversations, I explained why Leave.EU did not seem like a good target. Brexit, it seemed to me, was a political event which could only be undone by another political event – a second referendum or another general election. I thought that exposing how the *official* Vote Leave campaign had overspent might have some influence on the politics but I could see how easy it would be to shrug off accountability for overspending by the unofficial Leave.EU campaign.

Nevertheless, we met a few times, and eventually Rupert persuaded me to take £10,000 to help with the Brexit work I was doing.

This wasn't a hugely material sum to me at the time, and I was incredibly reluctant to take his money. I wrote to explain that 'basically the only thing I have is my reputation. That makes me incredibly nervous about accepting money from someone I don't know especially well,' but eventually I got comfortable. 'You and I have an explicit understanding – verbal or written at your choice – that I've supported you because I want to support what you're doing, not encourage you to my agenda. You do as you choose and are not beholden in any way whatsoever,' he wrote to me, and I couldn't think of a good enough reason to say 'no'.

The money hit my account in late November 2016, and I immediately regretted having taken it. I felt as though it had imposed upon me all sorts of moral obligations to spend it fruitfully. And I didn't really have a plan as to how.

But I advertised for some legal interns and with their help put up a website for Good Law Project, a name I had hatched over dinner with a friend. You can still find it on the internet archive – although I'd rather you didn't. There wasn't much there beyond a sense that we might litigate across a series of themes around fairness. More interesting was the impulse that had driven its creation – more about this in Chapter Six.

The Conservative Party was trying to untie a great Gordian knot: how to deliver Brexit. Theresa May gave an interview in which she said that God would guide her – inspiring a brilliant cartoon by Martin Rowson in the *Guardian* with God looking down from His cloud at Theresa with the line 'Brexit!?! What th' fuck do I know??!' The Labour Party, meanwhile, was trying to figure out how to sell the pro-Brexit instincts of Jeremy Corbyn and John McDonnell to an overwhelmingly Remain membership.

Neither of the main political parties was making any attempt to speak to the half of the country that had wanted to remain in the EU. 'Parliament without Opposition is mere ceremony' was the first line of our website. And this way of being, of looking at where there are gaps that we can usefully fill, has become a big part of our success.

As Good Law Project became more successful, in 2017 and 2018, and I became more politically prominent, I began to feel more and more uncomfortable with my dual life running it and practising tax law.

Part of this was the huge pressure my activities placed on my colleagues at Devereux Chambers. I had been able to choose whether to involve myself in politics, and all that came with it. They had not.

What politics came with was a heavy burden.

There was an occasion where someone managed to breach the heavy security and multiple locked doors to get into my room at Devereux Chambers. Nothing appeared to have been taken but I was left with the clear impression that it was a warning. Leaked emails later showed that Richard Dearlove, formerly head of the Secret Intelligence Service, had been asked to procure 'MI5 intel on key remainiac agitprop agents like Jolyon Maugham QC – their financials etc to put the frighteners on them.'[7]

I also received a series of evocative emails from someone describing how he planned to arrange a professional meeting with me in chambers and beat me to death. Colleagues were forced to introduce additional security measures and I was politely asked to stay away from our offices. I later learned that several large men had turned up at the entrance to the Inns of Court on Tudor Street, asking whether this was where I worked, and I was pleased I had listened to the request to stay away.

I don't think it would be quite right to say that I had signed up for this – certainly I hadn't given informed consent – but I was keenly aware that my colleagues hadn't given any consent at all.

I was also struggling with whether I could continue to act as a barrister. All of my colleagues and clients knew about my not-so-secret double life as a political campaigner. But I worried about whether I could still do what they were paying me for to a high enough standard whilst distracted by everything else.

It just didn't feel right.

I had planned to leave chambers at the end of 2019. But my plans were delayed by events that bled from my private into my professional life, and into the public eye.

It was a good Christmas, 2019. We were joined by our friends – the campaigner Sue Wixley and her partner, the wine writer

Tim Atkin. Other family friends, Deb Nagan and Michael Johnson, brought their son and Luka, their lurcher.

At some late stage in the afternoon, I opened the door to let in a breath of air and Luka, as was his wont, bolted into the garden and made straight for our chickens. They were doubly guarded, by the Fort Knox of coops, an Eglu, and an outer perimeter of electrified poultry netting. Not seeing the netting in the gloom, Luka bowled into it, knocking the gate open. Luka was recovered. But, fatefully, the gate was not replaced.

At some cheerfully late hour, the guests having departed, we settled into bed. Early on Boxing Day morning, I was awoken by my very anxious hens. I got out of bed, looked out the window, and saw a fox racing around the Eglu. This was not the first such raid – hence the double perimeter – but it was the first time a fox had breached the poultry netting. It was now trying to work out how to breach the Eglu. I got out of bed and put on one of the unisex traditional cotton dressing robes we had acquired on a visit to my wife's family in Java, the Indonesian word for which is 'kimono'.

Things then began to move quickly. I went downstairs, let myself out the door, and approached the Eglu. Seeing me coming, the fox dived for one of the loops in the netting and discovered, to its and my alarm, that it was too small. So there we were. The chickens in a state of high distress, me underprepared, and a very anxious fox trapped in the netting. I grabbed the baseball bat I kept to hand and despatched it.

Whether I would have acted differently on another morning is a counterfactual I will never get to explore. But I went back to bed and reflected on a fairly tooth and claw start to Boxing Day.

I grew up in Gisborne, in rural New Zealand, amongst farmers whose attitude to animals that troubled their flocks would be aptly described with words shorter than 'unsentimental'. And we had lots of pets – dogs, chickens, goats, hamsters, cats and (albeit briefly) mice. But I hadn't learned, even after thirty years of living in the UK, quite how different attitudes to animals are here.

Over the preceding months, I had kept my Twitter following abreast of our intermittently successful efforts to keep chickens in central London. I tweeted about how one had been missing, presumed dead, and then made a miraculous reappearance. And of how another, scratching around in the dust, had fallen dead with a strangely cricked neck. They are wonderful pets, despite not being conspicuously brilliant or easy to keep alive, and you can always use the eggs.

My attempt to continue the theme read as follows: 'Already this morning I have killed a fox with a baseball bat. How's your Boxing Day going?'

I added that it 'Wasn't a great deal of fun. Got caught up in the protective netting around the chickens and I wasn't sure what else to do. Not looking forward to untangling it . . .' And I referred to the fact I had worn the 'kimono'.

Within the hour, I had received a phone call from the *New York Times*. But it took me a little longer to understand quite how wide of the mark my tweet had been, and how angry so many were, and not just those who were serial haters. Later that morning, I reported myself to the RSPCA, who came and collected the fox and took my statement. I also went on social media to apologise, and referred myself to my professional regulator. But it was too late.

That evening I received a call from the *Daily Mail* – whose owner, Jonathan Harmsworth, Viscount Rothermere, hosts hunting parties at his lavish family estate from which his guests kill animals for fun – saying that they were going to carry the story with 'some prominence', a phrase I now know to mean 'on the front page'. The story quickly went global.

The *Mail* was not the only newspaper to pick it up. A number of others carried the story in a somewhat wry tone. But over the following weeks any number of columnists at other newspapers – and especially at the *Guardian* – took their chance to settle some scores. One *Guardian* journalist in particular both ignored what I understood to be our agreement that a conversation was off the record and misreported what I had told them.

The story ran for several weeks. My strong advice, if you are going to get something wrong, is to do so at a time of the year where there is lively competition for media space. Christmas and the New Year I would not recommend.

And I found the attention very, very hard.

It wasn't just the weeks of media coverage. Allen & Overy, a multi-billion-pound law firm, sought to force me out of the profession on the basis of the newspaper coverage, by writing to say they would not instruct any of my (self-employed) colleagues at Devereux Chambers whilst I remained a tenant. And the RSPCA, not for the first time, took to social media to condemn me – a job which made it very difficult for them to arrive at the inevitable conclusion that although I had tweeted stupidly there was no basis for a private prosecution.

Perhaps the least forgivable conduct was that of the BBC. After the suicide, several months later, of the television presenter Caroline Flack, I was texted by a producer: 'I was wondering whether you'd consider doing an interview with us tomorrow morning. Less about what happened but more about events after reaction on social media.' I arranged to speak to her and discuss what she had in mind. When we spoke, I made it clear I would appear only to talk about the aftermath, because I thought it was important that people understood how it was to be in the eye of a storm. She agreed.

The interview opened with the presenter asking why I had beaten a fox to death. And she asked whether I had learned to be less rude on social media. The BBC, it seemed, was also intent on settling some scores.

If you listen to the interview you can hear how close to tears I came, but from somewhere came the answer I wanted to give: that it was important for someone to try to hold the Government to account, a task I had often criticised the BBC for failing even to aspire to. It strikes me, even now, as remarkable how much more aggressive in tone is the BBC when it interviews those without power.

I also talked, thinking of poor Caroline Flack, who had taken her own life in the aftermath of a media storm, about how, but for a loving family, I might not have made it. I never contemplated suicide, but I could certainly understand how someone without a support network would have found the onslaught impossible to withstand.

Sitting next to me in the studio was a rabbi; I think he was the next guest on. I remember his shock at the questions – I could feel him tensing in the seat next to mine – and he hugged me as I left the studio. It remains the only broadcast interview I have ever done on the subject. The presenter, I should say in fairness to her, has subsequently apologised.

Several years on, the pain of it all has faded somewhat.

But there was no good reason then – as there is none now – why ministers and newspaper proprietors should be free to kill animals for sport but it is front-page news and a matter for a criminal investigation by the RSPCA for me to kill a trapped fox to save my chickens. Jacob Rees-Mogg, who supports the killing of foxes for sport, used the privilege from defamation proceedings given to those speaking in the Commons repeatedly to attack me. The point was made best of all by a Tory friend, who WhatsApped me after Boxing Day: 'Tories are all v grateful for Jolyon allowing them to go on Boxing Day hunts without hassle for the first time in years.'

Whatever you think about what I did – and I am genuinely sorry to those I upset – a huge amount of the reaction had nothing to do with what I did to that unfortunate fox.

Three years on, the BBC, along with the more transparently right-wing press, continue to include the episode in much reporting of my work. It is, I suppose, an easy way to try and diminish me and the work I do. But I only really began to understand it when a friend compared it to the misogynistic trope ('crazy cat lady') used by the right-wing journalist Andrew Neil, whilst working at the BBC, which was and is routinely used to belittle the work of another anti-corruption campaigner, the journalist Carole Cadwalladr.[8]

I am fortunate to be able to say that it was the worst thing to happen to me in my adult life and it was not without moments of amusement. The New Zealand press, which had celebrated the Brexit exploits of an expatriate Kiwi, downgraded me to 'British barrister' in its coverage of the incident. Anne Widdecombe, bless her, refused 'to join the witch hunt over . . . the smug lawyer who along with Gina Miller has sought to frustrate the will of 17.4 million Britons.'[9] And I enjoyed, for reasons too obvious to require explanation, the coverage in Fox News.

But the clearest truth is my wife's: that she doesn't need to look at the date to tell a 'before' from an 'after' photo. Those months will always remain written on my face.

On 5 March 2020, the RSPCA announced that 'An independent post-mortem and forensic veterinary assessment of the fox's body was carried out and the findings indicate that the fox was killed swiftly' and that they would not prosecute. I issued a statement in response:

I welcome the RSPCA's decision, embedded in their press release, that there is no basis on which they can properly bring a private prosecution.

I note what the RSPCA says about killing a fox. Their advice differs from the Government's advice to householders which says one 'must' – in other words you have no choice but to – humanely kill any fox caught on your property and that you 'shouldn't release captured foxes.'

I know that some were genuinely upset by my actions on Boxing Day and the tone of my tweets. I am profoundly sorry for that upset. It was my intention to convey in a gently self-deprecating manner the incongruity of my Boxing Day morning. I got that wrong.

As to my actions, in the situation in which I found myself – needing to act in great haste to save the chickens my family keeps – I did not have the luxury of time to reflect on the competing ethical approaches of the RSPCA and Natural England. Of course, I respect the different assessments others might, equally reasonably, have made.[10]

It is a mighty creature, the British establishment. It coddles its defenders with baubles and applause and it is brutal in its treatment of those who pick at its hegemony. But I'm still here. And the episode reminded me of where I should stand in relation to it.

The other transformative experience of my adult life has also taken me back to where I started. It has prompted me to reflect on what I have lost, as well as gained, in the years I have lived in England since arriving in 1989. It has reconnected me with how power works and what power does. And that is the work I have done with Good Law Project on trans rights.

I came to this work because someone I love is trans. Because they 'pass' – only those who they choose to tell know they are trans – and the decision whether to 'out' themselves is theirs and not mine, I will not identify them. For present purposes, their identity is irrelevant. What changed how I saw the world was not who they are; but the obligation that loving them imposed upon me to see the world through new eyes.

Those eyes are not the eyes of my tribe. My natural tribe are the winners. White, university-educated, well-paid, sometimes with family money and culturally sophisticated; skilled at negotiating passage through the world for themselves and their children. Their experience of the world was my recent experience of the world. My tribe's experience doesn't come without (mostly trivial) frustrations, but the institutions whose role is to usher us smoothly through life – schools, hospitals, the justice system – make good on their implicit promises. Those institutions understand very well how it is to serve us that they exist.

Our experience is also of being treated respectfully in public discourse. If institutions failed us, their leaders would be held to account in the press; and our representatives would be invited on to the BBC to talk about what those failures meant for us. Some presenter on the *Today* programme – I remember when I lived on the same street as Justin Webb and I bumped into him at social events and discussed the issues of the day – could be relied upon to put the points of my tribe to government ministers.

We are heard.

And because we were the people who subscribed to *The Times* or the *Guardian* our views would be represented in those newspapers. And if, for variety, those media outlets carried a column from outside our tribe, we might congratulate ourselves on the pluralism to which we were exposed. We see that we are treated, more or less, respectfully and fairly.

It is perfectly natural, if this is your experience of institutions and discourse and media, to assume that its treatment of you is universal. As an adult, I had never really asked whether my experience was mirrored in the lives of others.

I have two adopted sisters in New Zealand, both women of colour, but I have not lived with them as an adult, and I cannot speak to how they experience the world. My wife has Jewish and Indonesian grandparents and is usually read by others as South-East Asian or mixed-race, but moves through the world as a Cambridge graduate living a prosperous life in a hugely diverse city.

I did have some sense that going to university and becoming a barrister and living in central London had shaped – perhaps it would be more accurate to say 'distorted' – how I looked at the world. And I also knew it was a problem. When in 2016 I briefly discussed with the then Shadow Chancellor John McDonnell the prospect of becoming a Labour MP – I was then but have not for many years been a party member – I was keenly aware that I would not be able to be the MP I wanted to be unless my constituency life was outside London.

Knowing you are wearing blinkers is better than not knowing. But it does not show you what you cannot see.

The conceptions you have about how the world works if you are one of its winners – more particularly the misconception that your experience is universal – are not easily unlearned. They are deeply rooted, the internal reflection of what manifests outwardly as privilege.

But, as I learned, they are inimical to understanding how the world works for those whose experiences are different.

Our newspapers, and many of our politicians, speak of trans people in a manner that recalls pernicious racist stereotypes of the past. The reporting is intellectually dishonest and crafted to incite fear and loathing. Trans people are depicted as ugly, sexually predatory, mentally disturbed. The relentless focus on their genitals is intended to reduce them to objects and deny their humanity. Wrongs committed by individuals who are trans are presented as representative of the tendencies of trans people as a whole – the very essence of bigotry.

Although I hold a different view, there is a minority strand of feminist thought that is uncomfortable with aspects of transness. But it is not their advocacy that has made the issue so salient in the right-wing press. It is not for the sisterhood that those with real power have donned the clothing of feminism. The right and the far right – Putin, Johnson, Trump, Orbán, Murdoch, Rothermere, Bannon: their conduct speaks of who these men are and what they are for, and it is not feminism. They work to destroy those who challenge the status quo in which power continues to be held by, and in service of, white men like them.

Perhaps most striking (to me) of all is how the media systematically excludes 'dissenting' voices, both of trans people and other strands of mainstream feminist thought. The voices of what the evidence suggests is a consistent majority of cis women who support trans people are rarely heard, rarely read. It is remarkable how the lives of trans people have become, in the pages and the airwaves of our national media, a conversation in which they are rarely if ever invited to participate as equals. And this is not just true of the media, as I explain in Chapter Four.

Watching the media foster and curate an orthodoxy – that there is an antagonistic debate between cis women and trans people – that bears so little relationship to reality has fostered a deep scepticism in me of for whom and for what these media really speak.

As a way of radicalising people, pushing them to extremes, it is astonishingly effective, and destructive. The pattern is both particular to trans people – and it is also universal. How do these same actors shape our perceptions of others: of single mothers, of working-class families, of people of colour, of Muslims or Jews? Of those who are disabled? Of past and present leaders of the Labour Party?

The reverberations of what they have fostered echo along the corridors of all our institutions.

My memory of hearing a culturally privileged parent of a trans child explaining how she struggled to fulfil her obligation to ensure her child could access health care remains very fresh. It is bafflement – and then disbelief – that what they had understood from their own past, that the system functions fairly and properly, is not universal.

You might readily imagine that accessing health care will be difficult and involve waiting. But this does not capture the reality.

Health-care provision for trans adolescents which is internationally orthodox, a human right and essential for their well-being is simply not available in the United Kingdom. To describe the process for accessing it on the NHS as a 'waiting list' is a misdescription. The treatment is only useful if you can access it in time and you cannot.[11] It is like being asked to wait ten months for an abortion.

Meanwhile, a child is in need. And, if their parents are fortunate enough to be able to find the money, they might think, what private provision is available?

The answer, again, is none. Those who once offered private provision in England were subject to a barrage of regulatory harassment and shut up shop or moved abroad. So parents can consult with a doctor overseas and pay for private prescriptions to be dispensed by UK pharmacists. But because they too have been threatened not every pharmacist will dispense these perfectly legal prescriptions, and if they contain injectable medication then no one will agree to administer it in the UK because it hasn't been prescribed by a British doctor. So the parents might go on YouTube to try and work out how to give an intramuscular injection themselves.

And what about monitoring? If you smoke, or use heroin, your GP will give you blood tests to help you manage your treatment. But if you are taking hormones because you are trans? Many GPs will simply refuse.

Loving and responsible parents are forced to cobble together health-care provision from a patchwork of sources for no better reason than that the political orthodoxy does not cater to families like theirs.

Things are no better for adult trans people.

One Saturday morning I received a distraught phone call from a friend. A trans woman, S, who my friend had arranged for me to interview for a case Good Law Project was bringing was dead. It was believed that S had chosen to take her life, after being shunted to the bottom of lengthy NHS waiting lists. 'You should go and see her family,' the friend said. 'They are big fans of you and your work and I know they would appreciate it.'

Several days later I visited. The family she lived with was one that she had made to replace her hostile biological family. I sat with them and I embraced them and thought of the power I had, the difference that Good Law Project might make, and the choices we had where they had none.

We have worked on case after case. We have helped individuals bullied by meritless defamation threats, trauma centres sued for helping trans women who have been raped, those seeking fertility preservation, those denied health care, those discriminated against, and more, and more. The forces arrayed against us are powerful and the advocacy is gruelling, expensive, often fruitless and desperate, because if you are trans the stakes are so high. I believe I will soon have to stop doing this work because no one will fund it and the community is impoverished, including by the need to pay for its own health care.

I feel hugely optimistic about the future for the trans community. The vast majority of people in this country are accepting and kind – especially those who are younger, and especially the cis women who we are told by newspaper columnists are 'in conflict' with their trans sisters. Huge global brands spend heavily on understanding what the future looks like, and only prosper if they get these calls right. And they all scramble to signal trans inclusivity. I should say that I do not offer this up as proof of the moral quality of those brands – I offer it up only as the best available evidence of what the future holds.

The meantime is, for the trans community, a disaster. But standing alongside them, for me, is not. I have gained a much more sophisticated understanding of how power operates. And learned that there is something that is universal – across social class, race, gender – of being outside. Outsiders have always understood this – it's why if you go on a Black Trans Lives Matter march you will be joined by both people of colour and trans people – and I am grateful to have learned it.

Many of my natural tribe – the people I described several pages back – have not had my opportunity to see the world afresh. But I believe it has given me a skeleton key to a whole new moral universe.

My adult life is blessed by a wonderful marriage and three children who are reasonably forgiving of my failings as a father, more forgiving than I have any right to expect. We live a prosperous life, not rich by the standards of my colleagues who continue to work at the Bar, but comfortable enough that my life would not be made meaningfully better by more money. That is another blessing.

The work that I choose to do is hard. There was a month in 2021 where Good Law Project had two cases and I also had two tax cases to argue left over from my tax practice. The tax cases felt like doing the crossword on the way home from the office – the Good Law Project cases were like wrestling an octopus.

It also asks of me that I find a way to be at peace with the daily publication in national and social media of revolting allegations about my financial and other motivations. It requires, on occasion, that I use close security. It means I have made plans for a time when I will no longer feel safe living in England.

There is no real impediment to me returning to my previous life. 'Let me know,' the Global Head of Tax at one of the Big Four accounting firms told me once, 'when you decide to give all of this up. Let me know, and we'll make some real money together.'

Giving a speech on receiving the Praeses Elit in Dublin, a prize awarded to those who have advanced the discourse in their line of work and are a source of inspiration to young people, I reflected on Gandalf standing on the bridge at Khazad-dûm in *The Lord of the Rings*. The fiery twin-horned Balrog approaches. And, although Gandalf knows the Balrog is too much for him, he plants his staff on the bridge and he says: 'You shall not pass.' The work is relentless and I know full well how modest will be my impact. Sometimes, often, I feel I can't go on. But trying gives meaning to my life.

These are the dictates, choosing to live this way, of my childhood.

I have put down the anger. But I hold on to the pain and it is a flame I fuel because it powers me to take up arms for others. Whose lives have not been as blessed as mine is. Whose pleas for better are unheard. This is a choice. As bell hooks wrote in *All About Love*: 'What we allow the mark of our suffering to become is in our own hands.'

2. Winner Takes All

We did not get this world by chance. It was shaped, socially as much as physically, by the forces acting upon it, including those of the past. From this point follows another, equally obvious. Our constitution and our legal system are the victory dance of power. To engage with them is to bless or curse them, to join the dance. You cannot stand by.

The dominant feature of our constitutional landscape in the United Kingdom is parliamentary sovereignty. The idea it expresses is that there is a single superior source of power which is legitimate in a democracy; the Parliament elected by the people. It is the one ring to rule them all.

Parliament's own website describes it like this:

> Parliamentary sovereignty is a principle of the UK constitution. It makes Parliament the supreme legal authority in the UK which can create or end any law. Generally, the courts cannot overrule its legislation and no Parliament can pass laws that future Parliaments cannot change. Parliamentary sovereignty is the most important part of the UK constitution.[1]

In principle it's an attractive idea. The House of Commons is made up of MPs who are elected by the people. If you live in a democracy, who else might legitimately hinder their power? Unelected judges?

But then you begin to reflect a little.

Should a Parliament elected by, on some occasions, barely a third of the vote have supreme and unchallengable power? Even if the prime minister it chooses uses that power for something never put to the people in a manifesto? Should it hold supreme power for five years even if support in the country for the policies of the ruling party has slumped? Even if much of that power is wrested from Parliament by a prime minister neither they nor even MPs got to choose? And, at a more fundamental level, does it really make sense for anyone to have unlimited power?

Other systems, in other countries, recognise that power must come from the people. They find ways to distribute that power over temporally different electorates. They have multiple elected houses, each of which can clog the other and which are elected at different times. They elect representatives in tranches rather than all at once. They have an elected head of state who has his or her own democratic legitimacy. And, most important of all, they have a higher law restraining their elected house or houses which it takes a super-majority of the electorate or its representatives to change.

In the United Kingdom, we have no written constitution, no higher rule to define or restrain the power wielded by a government. To describe parliamentary sovereignty (or 'supremacy', the two are used interchangeably) as the 'dominant' feature is to understate it. We are ruled by what Lord Hailsham described as an 'elective dictatorship' and parliamentary sovereignty might more accurately be described as the only feature of our constitution. All else is mere memories and good manners.

What if Parliament wanted to do a bad thing? What about if it decided to criminalise political dissent or to imprison writers who expressed views the Government deemed unpatriotic? Could Parliament do that?

Here is what Tom Bingham, described in one obituary as 'the greatest judge of our time – arguably the most significant judicial figure among the long line of notables in the history of the Anglo-Saxon legal systems',[2] had to say about that in his book *The Rule of Law*:

> Critics of parliamentary sovereignty have no difficulty conceiving of flagrantly unjust and objectionable statutes: to deprive Jews of the nationality, to prohibit Christians from marrying non-Christians, to dissolve marriages between Blacks and whites, to confiscate the property of red-haired women, to require all blue-eyed babies to be killed, to deprive large sections of the population of the right to vote, to authorize officials to inflict punishment for whatever reason they might choose.
>
> No one thinks it at all likely that Parliament would enact legislation of this character, or that the public would accept it if it did . . .[3]

That coda – that Parliament can be relied upon not to do awful things – speaks to a particular understanding of how – or more particularly against whom – Parliament has used its power through the ages.

The description it gives of what Parliament can be relied on not to do is hard to reconcile with, to give one of many possible examples, the activities of the East India Company, which Parliament empowered to flagrantly exploit the people of India for its, and our, financial gain. The expanded powers of the British Nationality Act give the Government power to strip British citizenship from a Jew even if, in the case of a Jew who acquired their citizenship through naturalisation, the effect would be to leave them effectively stateless.[4] They will have a hugely disproportionate impact upon people who are not white. And it is no exaggeration to say that the Public Order Bill, which at the time of writing has passed the House of Commons, criminalises many expressions of political dissent.

I don't make those points to rain on Tom Bingham's parade. He was, by all accounts, a decent man and the views he expressed are entirely constitutionally orthodox. He also goes on to say that he doesn't like the conflict that parliamentary sovereignty sets up between judges and Parliament. I could have picked any one of numerous other constitutional grandees.

Still, the truth remains that our constitution is the construct of grand, privately educated, wealthy, white English men and reflects their perception of what the United Kingdom is in the world, what it has done and to whom, and what it is likely to do. It is a complacent constitution – a profound shortcoming in a thing whose main purpose is to be a safeguard – crafted by men who have not lived life on the sharp edge.

Most of the books about our constitution and system of government are written by those people and for those people. The world those books describe reflect their experiences of moving through the world but their experiences are not universal. The rule of law is a different thing for those with the wealth or social capital to engage lawyers – we are a powerful militia if you can afford us – to what it is for those who do not.

So, this isn't a chapter, and this isn't a book, for law students or constitutional scholars. They have enough books already. Most of them, to be fair, were written a few years ago, before public life in the United Kingdom became quite so volatile. Perhaps that volatility will open up space to ask some questions. But the volatility didn't create the problems; it just exposed them. The detailed, self-contained, internally consistent visions of a utopian England described in those books never existed, not for those outside the cultural milieu of those who wrote those books.

It is impossible to understand the role the law does play in the United Kingdom – and the role it plays in other countries, and the role it could play here, and the limits of its role – without understanding something about the powers and limits of other parts of government. To understand what the law can do to hold government to account you have to understand something about them as well as about the law.

Parliament

The way democracy operates in the United Kingdom is this. We divide the country up into 650 areas, which we call constituencies, and each of those constituencies votes in a general election on who it wants to be its representative in Parliament. The person who gets the most number of votes in that constituency gets to be the Member of Parliament – and they don't need to have the support of half the electorate. Indeed, general election records show that in 1922 several candidates became MPs despite only getting 26 per cent of the votes. More recently, in 2019, a candidate became an MP with only 29 per cent of the vote.

What this means is that it's perfectly possible to win a majority of seats in the House of Commons without having the support of a majority of voters. Indeed, it is possible to argue that never has a political party won the support of a majority of voters. And, in the period since the Second World War, that's quite clearly true. Parties with the support of a relatively small proportion of voters have often won the majority of seats in the House of Commons. In 2005, for example, the Labour Party was supported by only 35 per cent of voters but still won a majority, over 55 per cent, of the seats in the House of Commons.

I don't stress these points to make the argument for a system of proportional representation – although representation that is proportionate to votes would be a pretty good definition of democracy – because that isn't what this book is about. But they are important to hold in your mind when you come to consider other features of our system of government, like parliamentary supremacy.

The question of who should get to vote is also starting to become contested. In April 2022, the Conservative Party used its majority in Parliament to pass legislation – the Elections Act – which requires voters to show photo ID before being issued a ballot paper to vote in a general election. It's not clear what need there was for this legislation given that voter fraud is vanishingly small in the UK, but most researchers identified that it would be likely to have a detrimental effect on the propensity to vote of groups history shows to be less likely to vote Conservative.[5] And if you are wondering about motivation, you should ponder why acceptable forms of photo ID include types of concessionary travel pass available to over-sixties but not a 16–25 Railcard. (YouGov polling with fieldwork of 15–16 June 2022 showed that only 5 per cent of voters under the age of 25 planned to vote Conservative in a general election.[6]) Who would benefit most if some of that part of the electorate were to lose their votes?

Perhaps that will be it. Perhaps we will see no further attempts at voter suppression. But if you look at the facts it's hard to see that as anything other than complacent. If there was no good need for this attempt – which happened anyway – how can you be confident there will not be others?

We don't have a system of government by referendum – so-called 'direct democracy' – where you get a say in what your MP does after they get voted in. What we have instead, or tell ourselves we have instead, is a 'representative' democracy – a phrase associated with an Irish politician called Edmund Burke – which means that MPs do what they think is in the best interests of their constituents. But it's more of a bed-time story than a constitutional reality. MPs are a mixed bunch who act for a variety of reasons and none of them can be controlled by voters or the courts.

How your MP speaks and votes and acts will be shaped by how ambitious they are (broadly speaking, their ambitions are best served by doing what their party leader wants them to) and the size of their majority in their constituency (the larger their majority, the greater the freedom they have to ignore what their constituents want and support, instead, either what they think is right or what best serves their personal interests). Sometimes these features will be the yeast that leavens the dough of public interest. Sometimes they will be the dough itself.

We also have an unelected House of Lords, the so-called Upper Chamber, but its powers are very limited. They might best be characterised as 'nuisance' powers – they have the right to slow down, including by proposing amendments, some of what the House of Commons does. In theory, the Lords have some other powers, including a power to veto an extension to the five-year period at the end of which a general election has to be held, but quite how secure these powers are has never been tested.

My point is not that the way our democracy operates is dreadful. There are important respects in which it functions – recent history cautions that it would be safer to say that it *presently* functions – better than, for example, that of the United States. My point is that the foundation of our constitutional arrangements – the winner in Parliament takes all – rests on unsteady sands.

The Government

Parliament is where the people are, with some qualifications, represented. But it's the Government – or what is sometimes called the 'executive' – that holds the whip hand.

The prime minister is the person best able to command the confidence of a majority of the House of Commons. He (there have only ever been three 'she's, of whom only one was chosen in a general election) appoints ministers who serve for as long as he wants them to, and together they exercise the power of government to propose laws, direct civil servants, make or approve senior appointments including to regulators and law enforcement agencies, and so on.

The head of the Metropolitan Police is appointed by the Home Secretary who is appointed by the prime minister. Which, it hardly needs to be said, is relevant context to the disinclination of the Metropolitan Police to investigate wrongdoing by those in power. It may well explain why we had to sue the Met before it would investigate the prime minister's breach of lockdown rules in 2022. And it ultimately concluded that both the then prime minister Boris Johnson – and his eventual successor as prime minister, Rishi Sunak – had committed criminal offences.

The Government also has very real practical control over Parliament. Usually, it sets the agenda for what Parliament is to do – although for a short period under Theresa May Parliament briefly wrested it back. The so-called Benn Act – see Chapter Seven – was the first occasion in modern times where that had happened and many MPs weren't sure whether it was possible until they did it. Other than following a truly exceptional event, therefore, the Government gets to control what the House of Commons votes on and so can control its exercise of its powers to, for example, adopt or repeal Acts of Parliament. And although the prorogation case (see Chapter Seven) established that Boris Johnson's attempt to suspend Parliament was unlawful, other politically motivated prorogations of Parliament (and I know that others have been contemplated) could well succeed.

These are instances of how the prime minister, who controls the executive, exercises direct control over Parliament. But if he can influence, or persuade, or coerce his MPs, he can also exercise indirect control.

There are long-established forms of influence over MPs – such as the power of patronage. The prime minister can help or hinder the careers of MPs, including by giving or denying high office. If MPs are ambitious, if they want to get on, they'll listen. It's also often suggested that, via his internal enforcers at the 'Whip's Office', the PM can blackmail MPs by releasing to the press or other authorities stories, true or false, of personal misconduct. What is certainly true is that the prime minister can sack a representative of the people – by withdrawing from an MP the right to call themself a member of the PM's party – with the likely consequence that they will lose their seat at the next general election.

Our constitution means that MPs flip between Burke's snarling watchdog of their constituents' interests and whimpering lapdog to their party leadership.

Also demonstrably true is that there have been a series of credible reports of ministers bribing MPs by awarding, or withholding, public money to or from their constituencies. But, although Good Law Project has managed to extract a limited promise from ministers that it will not happen again, there was no denial that it has happened in the past. And we have no illusions. The practice will certainly continue – and indeed there is evidence that it has.[7] What makes this practice particularly objectionable is that it misappropriates public money and uses it for the private purposes of the Conservative Party: the enforcing of party discipline. It is very likely to be a criminal offence – which should matter but doesn't without a truly independent criminal investigation agency – and it undermines representative democracy.

Another striking feature of the landscape is that we often don't get any say about who gets to exercise this vast power of the executive. When Theresa May resigned as prime minister in 2019, there were Conservative Party leadership elections to choose who would replace her and become prime minister. Tory MPs in Parliament got to whittle the candidates down to two – but not to choose the winner.

The choosing was done by around 160,000 members of the Conservative Party who were eligible to vote. Fewer than

140,000 voted and of those who did 92,153 voted for Boris Johnson. That was the extent of Johnson's mandate to exercise the powers of prime minister. Yet he claimed a right to suspend the whole Parliament chosen in 2017 by 46 million people.

More recently, of course, Johnson has been replaced by first Liz Truss and then Rishi Sunak, neither of whom could claim any democratic mandate to exercise the vast powers of the executive. And Liz Truss planned to, and Rishi Sunak will, abandon promises that were made by the Conservative Party to voters in its 2019 manifesto.

From whence comes their democratic mandate?

There are no rules about any of this beyond an idea, all but unique to the United Kingdom, that our judges invented and now cleave to, about the only true source of power being a five-yearly Parliament and that its power should be unbridled.

That idea is contestable – and extremely dangerous – and most countries would conclude just flat wrong.

Judges and Judicial Review

The current president of the Supreme Court, the UK's highest court, is Lord Reed. In a case about whether the Government acted within the law in charging employees to sue their employer in an employment tribunal, he described the role of the Courts thus:

Courts exist in order to ensure that the laws made by Parliament, and the common law created by the courts themselves, are applied and enforced. That role includes ensuring that the executive branch of government carries out its functions in accordance with the law.[8]

This short passage highlights the role of the Courts in ensuring that the law – whether made by Parliament or by the Courts themselves in the form of the common law – is obeyed by everyone, including by the Government.

You think politicians are filling their pockets or those of their friends with public money? It's to judicial review that you must go. You think the Metropolitan Police are frightened of investigating apparent criminality in Number 10? It's to judicial review that you must go. You want to challenge a decision by Boris Johnson to suspend Parliament because it's inconvenient to him? It's to judicial review you must go. You think local authorities are dumping children in its care a long way from home to save money, and exposing them to additional risks of sexual exploitation? It's to judicial review you must go. (I brought all of these cases, by the way.)

Anyone with a sufficient interest – an idea which lawyers refer to as having 'standing' – can bring a case asking a court to determine whether a thing Government or some other public body has done or (sometimes) proposes to do is lawful. The procedure, no prizes for guessing why, is called a judicial review.

The underlying idea that judicial review expresses is that everyone is subject to the law – even ministers and the prime minister. Legal types often refer to this as being the rule of law, a notion with a nice ring to it but, like many things that ring nicely, the content is hollow.

The way judicial review works is this.

You start by sending a letter to the person whose actions you plan to challenge (I'm going to talk about Government but you can judicially review anyone exercising public powers) setting out what it is that you object to, what you think the relevant facts are, and why it is that you think they have broken the law. You also set out the details of any information you are seeking and why it is relevant.

You send this letter because there are non-binding rules (called a Pre-Action Protocol for Judicial Review, or PAP) which set out how judges would like you to act. They say you should send this letter, in normal circumstances at least. And that's why it's generally referred to as a PAP letter.

The Government is supposed to respond to your letter within 14 days, either conceding your claim (which is possible in theory) or setting out why your claim is wrong. It should also enclose any relevant document you've asked for or explain why it doesn't need to. You then review that letter with your lawyers and, if you still think Government's actions are unlawful, you continue.

You then get to file your claim, which should contain a statement of the facts you rely on, why you say the decision you are challenging is unlawful, and any written evidence you rely on. Time limits in judicial review proceedings are short – you generally have to file your claim no later than three months from the date of the decision you are challenging – because of the public interest in resolving quickly the lawfulness of Government's decisions. The part of Government you are suing (known as the defendant) then has 21 days to respond with a summary of its response to your claim.

To protect Government having to send detailed responses on claims with no realistic prospect of succeeding, you need the Court's permission to bring your judicial review. A judge will read your claim form and the defendant's response and decide, 'on the papers', whether your claim should have permission (whether it is 'arguable'). If they conclude it doesn't pass that threshold you can usually ask for a hearing to make your case in person.

Let's assume you do get permission. You can then apply for a 'costs cap'. In most important or big-ticket litigation in the UK the rule is that the loser pays the winner's costs ('adverse' costs, as they're known in the trade). To guard against this being too serious an impediment to important judicial review challenges it's sometimes possible to get a 'costs cap' – capping the amount you would have to pay if you lose – rather than obliging you to sign a blank cheque for your opponent's costs as the price for litigating.

You proceed to the main event where the defendant provides their detailed reasons why, they say, the claim is wrong. And, the rules say, they must identify any relevant facts, whether helpful or not, and supply the underlying documents. Unlike commercial litigation in England and Wales (Scotland and Northern Ireland have their own systems), defendants in judicial review proceedings don't usually have the more onerous obligations to disclose all relevant documents. And, again unlike in normal litigation, you don't usually get to cross-examine the defendant's witnesses.

When all of that is done, you have a hearing before a judge, usually in the High Court, and then a decision. If you win there are an array of possible remedies for the court. It might – it has a degree of discretion – declare the decision you have challenged to be unlawful. It might cancel (or 'quash') the decision. It might tell the defendant it cannot do a thing which is unlawful. And it might – albeit very rarely – tell the defendant what it needs to do.

That's the procedure.

But what's really going on? What does a good judicial review look like?

Courts proceed, rightly, from the notion that the best people to make decisions are those our system makes (and usually ministers appoints as) the decision-makers and it wouldn't be right for judges to get involved just because they don't like the decision. The circumstances in which they will interfere are very limited. Those circumstances include, in particular, where they can see that the decision-maker has acted outside a statutory power that Parliament has given to them; where the way in which the decision has been made is procedurally unfair (lawyers are much more comfortable as guardians of process than they are as guardians of outcome – and they tend to believe that good processes tend to deliver good outcomes); where a decision is conspicuously unfair because it involves the decision-maker going back on their word ('breaching a legitimate expectation'); or where a decision is so unreasonable that no reasonable decision-maker could have arrived at it.

If you are trying to assess whether a judicial review might succeed, a useful alternative to these rather intricate and apparently value-laden questions is to ask a different one. Given the expertise that lawyers have (which is in the law rather than in policy) and the expertise that the decision-maker has and the democratic mandate they have to make those decisions, is it still right for a judge to get involved? If you wrestle with this honestly, you've got a decent shot at landing in the general vicinity of the right answer.

That description sets out the theory.

But judicial review is built on the same shaky foundations of much of the rest of our constitution.

Take, for example, this passage from Lord Donaldson (delivered when he was a very senior judge) explaining (in essence) why it is that the judicial review procedure is hostile to the idea of Government being forced to provide documents or to be grilled on their contents:

> This development [i.e. the remedy of judicial review and the evolution of a specialist administrative or public law court] has created a new relationship between the courts and those who derive their authority from public law, one of partnership based on a common aim, namely the maintenance of the highest standards of public administration . . . The analogy is not exact, but just as the judges of the inferior courts when challenged on the exercise of their jurisdiction traditionally explain fully what they have done and why they have done it, but are not partisan in their own defence, so should be the public authorities. It is not discreditable to get it wrong. What is discreditable is a reluctance to explain fully what has occurred and why . . . Certainly it is for the applicant to satisfy the court of his entitlement to judicial review and it is for the respondent to resist his application, if it considers it to be unjustified. But it is a process which falls to be conducted with all the cards face upwards on the table and the vast majority of the cards will start in the authority's hands[.][9]

It warms the cockles, this passage, but it bears the same relationship to the reality of Government's conduct of judicial review proceedings as the Spanish Inquisition bears to the teachings of Christ.

Our experience of Government lawyers – supported by lots of Government lawyers who have interviewed for jobs with us – is that they can only mediate so far (some try harder than others) between the political instincts of their clients to avoid responsibility for lawbreaking and their desire to adhere to the words of Lord Donaldson. And it is not a criticism of the civil service to say that we do not live in times that reward those who are closely wedded to ethical conduct.

We have seen the disclosure of documents which have been carefully curated to give a misleading impression of the facts, frequent breaches by ministers of their duty to put their cards face up on the table – some amounting to deliberate attempts to mislead the court, and unethical attempts to use public money as a weapon to discourage scrutiny.

There is no real sense in which ministers are in 'partnership' with the Courts. Instead ministers treat judges as a challenge to be suppressed: threatening them with legislative oblivion and describing those who fail to do the Government's bidding as committing, in Rishi Sunak's words, 'judicial recidivism' – likening judges to repeat criminals.[10]

The notion, pushed by ministers and their newspapers, of judges as interventionist is a politically convenient fiction with absolutely no basis in reality. Judicial review cases are extremely hard to win. About one in twenty or one in twenty-five judicial reviews that are launched succeed in court – those at least were the figures in the last half-dozen or so years up to and including 2020. In 2021, after a period of sustained attack on what was asserted by right-wing think tanks to be over-reach by judges, the equivalent figure slumped to one in fifty. The last 20 years have also seen a change in the outcome of cases reaching a final hearing from the claimant being more likely to win to the defendant being more likely to win.[11]

And if you think, as the present Government has claimed, that its increased success in court speaks to its particular fidelity to the rule of law, well, I want what you're smoking.[12] This line defies everything we know about this Government – including the resignation of a succession of high-profile Government law officers on ethical grounds and the boast of a Government official, reported on Politico on 17 June 2022, that 'We're fucking breaking international law like it's one of our five a day.'[13]

The judiciary is not a monolith. Different judges think and do different things. Some do treat their oath – to act 'without fear or favour, affection or ill-will' – as . . . well, as an oath. Others take a rather more pragmatic approach to the exercise of an idea they no doubt like but which they perceive as having been made for less politically fractious times. I mean no criticism by this because different specialist public law judges can have different ideas about where the law ends and politics start.

Even the idea that it is right for judges to resist ministerial pressure is contested. I was told by a senior legal source of a prominent Court of Appeal judge who had said privately that claimants will lose a lot of cases because judges need to conserve their power in case of another 'prorogation-type' event (a direct attack on democracy). You might even have some sympathy for this point of view – difficult though it is for claimants.

It is also widely believed in the profession, including by judges, that judicial review cases which carry enhanced political risk for the Government are more likely to be placed before judges whose legal philosophy diminishes that risk. And it is undoubtedly true that formal power to allocate judges to cases is held by a judge, the Lord Chief Justice, who is appointed by a government minister, the Lord Chancellor.[14]

These perceptions, which I should also say are mine, are absolutely orthodox, and they pose very real questions about where and how what we call the law takes place. The problem is that for a practising lawyer to speak them in public would be heresy – quite possibly career-ending. The more thoughtful of our academic lawyers recognise this and seek to take more of the burden.

Nick Barber, a professor of Constitutional Law and Theory at the University of Oxford, recently suggested exactly this:

> I think our role should be to make the judges' life miserable. For most non-academic lawyers it is problematic to criticise judges because they might appear before them next week. So I think I would encourage academic lawyers to be more critical of judges and more willing to stand up and examine judicial reasoning on behalf of a public that perhaps lacks the skills to do that. We should act as the bridge between the public and the judges, and we should be willing to be critical of the judges when we're undertaking that task.
>
> The danger of the judiciary appeasing the Government is, of course, that it relieves them from the political consequences of their law-breaking. In the long run, because of our notion of Parliamentary supremacy, the only protection for judges from a marauding Executive is political.[15]

It is worth underscoring something from these polite paragraphs. Professor Barber thinks practising lawyers won't criticise judges because to do so will lead to the professional equivalent of punishment beatings. Of course, this cannot be squared with the judicial oath to 'do right to all manner of people after the laws and usages of this Realm without fear or favour, affection or ill will'.

Although I am a King's Counsel, and am still arguing several cases in the higher courts, I will not appear in the Administrative Court again. Nevertheless I am very keenly aware of what I consider to be the impact of speaking these words on cases Good Law Project brings.

The unfortunate truth is that judges in the United Kingdom are relatively feeble things. They are feeble because – unlike pretty much everywhere else – they have decided that they have no role beyond that which Parliament is content to leave to them.

In the United States, judges can and do strike down laws made by elected representatives because they conflict with the constitution. As we presently understand things in the UK, our judges cannot interfere with Acts of Parliament or anything done in Parliament.

And of all the Victorian follies of our constitutional landscape the absence of a higher law is the most striking. Along with Israel and New Zealand, we are one of only three democracies in the world without a written constitution.

Constitutions typically set out how the relationship between the various bits of the State – the legislature (or Parliament), the executive (or Government) and the judiciary – are supposed to work. They define and safeguard the ground that each can occupy, protecting judges from threats so they can do their vital job of ensuring the executive complies with the laws made by Parliament.

They also say something about how a State should treat its citizens, and people generally.

That we don't have one has for many years been argued to be a strength – 'in committing it to paper we would lose in flexibility more than we would gain in clarity and security' has been the line. That view would once have been a strong orthodoxy amongst constitutional scholars who held the happy view that the good common sense of the British chap would stop bad things from happening. It's certainly less clearly an orthodoxy now. The Brexit referendum and its aftermath revealed to ministers and their special advisers that there needn't be sanctions if you told those well-meaning chaps to get the hell out of the way and told civil servants – amongst whom those Good Chaps were meant to be found – that if they wanted a career they'd best do what they were told.

A constitution is an insurance policy. You can carry on for years oblivious to whether you have one – and only come to care if someone sets your house on fire. There are different accounts of how we are coping without one. One view is that the decision of the Supreme Court in the prorogation case shows that we're doing OK, and that what we are experiencing is not so much constitutional but political crisis or decay. I can understand that point of view – I wouldn't lightly dismiss it.

But I'd offer two reflections.

First, it's not clear we would have had a political crisis had we had a constitutional framework for the Brexit referendum. Would England's voters have been able so obviously to disregard the wishes of those in Scotland and Northern Ireland? Would it have allowed such a momentous change on a narrow majority of those voting? Would it have overlooked serious and deliberate overspending – and falsehoods?

That's not just wishful thinking. It also points to how a constitutional framework might help us manage other seismic political events in our future.

The other point is a very particular response to our very particular conception of how things work.

The leading judicial lights of the Supreme Court talk more and more of the importance of respecting the supremacy of Parliament with its unique democratic legitimacy.[16] Some of the value judgments embedded in that proposition can be interrogated – and this chapter tries to do exactly that. But the lawyer in me blanches at any notion of unlimited and unchallengeable power – which is what the idea of parliamentary supremacy represents.

Perhaps the judiciary will wake up. Perhaps it will come to reflect on the fact that parliamentary supremacy – or at least our conception of it – is not the only way one can think about the demands of democracy. Perhaps it will revisit the limits it has invented to its own competence – parliamentary sovereignty as a legal idea is one for judges to make and shape – before too many fundamental rights are lost. It is hard to feel optimistic at present – but things change in cycles. Or, as the conservative folk singer, Bob Roberts, put it in a film of the same name: 'The times they are a changing back.'

Ultimately, though, we must have a written constitution if democracy in the UK is to weather the tumult that lies ahead.

A higher law, entrenched by a super-majority in a referendum, or by the manifestos of successive governments, would allow the people to speak not just once, every five years, but over time. We would then have democracy as process, not event. Each day would be Valentine's Day.

3. What the Law Can Do

The law is those policy choices made over time which Parliament and judges have caused to be backed by the power of the State.

From that definition some useful themes emerge.

One is the notion of policy choices made *over time*. Laws, usually, respond to public demand rather than drive it. So, for example, the laws to allow gay people to marry were introduced in the United Kingdom from 2013 but only after a predominance of public support. And laws, once made, have an incumbency advantage: they remain the law unless steps are taken positively to change them. For example, rather incongruously given the debate on free speech that has come to occupy so much public discourse, blasphemy has been a crime in Northern Ireland and remains a crime now. So the law tends to be somewhat backward-looking.

Conceived of in this way, the law is not an obvious tool for driving social change. Think of a mountaineer attempting a peak who pauses to drive a piton into a cliff face. Legislation tends to consolidate social gains rather than drive them.

That having been said, if the social weather turns, legislation can help you defend territory you won in more enlightened times. The Equality Act – and the Human Rights Act – are important safeguards for the vulnerable against the regressive tendencies of an autocratic minister or press, at least so long as they remain the law. Should you lose your footing as a campaigner, legislation can break your fall.

Another important aspect of the law is that it is backed by the State, or, putting it more precisely, the State will play a part in ensuring that people comply with it. Sometimes the State will itself invest in ensuring that the law is adhered to – think of the police investigating crimes or HM Revenue and Customs checking that you've paid enough tax – and sometimes the State will provide the machinery with which you can ensure that the law is complied with. If you have a buy-to-let property and your tenant won't move out, the State will (subject to modest safeguards) provide for their removal by force.

This notion of sanction or punishment for breach helps to explain what the law is. It has to be more than just words on a page, sound and fury. Lawyers express the point by way of a Latin maxim (it's another way for us to feel cleverer than you, which we like) – '*Ubi jus ibi remedium*' – meaning where there is a right there has to be a remedy for its breach. But this only *helps* to explain what the law is.

The obligation to file your personal tax return by 31 January can be found in section 7 of the Taxes Management Act 1970. But if you happen to find that inconvenient you can simply choose to file late and the penalty, so long as you file within three months, is only £100. And you might sensibly regard the £100 as a fee to file late.

Similarly, during the course of the Brexit referendum, a number of material breaches of the complex law regarding spending were committed by both of the main Leave campaigns. But they paid their fines – some tens of thousands of pounds – and treated them as a cost of fighting the campaign the way they wanted.

And during the Covid pandemic, the then prime minister, Boris Johnson, failed to obey the lockdown laws his Government had created. Tens of thousands of families said goodbye to their dying parents and grandparents remotely but he continued to celebrate at drinks parties with his colleagues. Initially the police refused to investigate. We thought that decision was unlawful and so we sued and the police changed course and concluded that, on the evidence, Boris Johnson had broken the criminal law. But he took the opportunity given to him in the legislation to escape trial by paying a fixed penalty fee of £100.

Payment of those financial penalties is mandated by the State. If you don't pay them the law, eventually, will allow large men to come to your house, take your telly, sell it at auction, and apply the proceeds towards your debt. And, of course, occasionally the State can also utilise more persuasive types of enforcement than modest fines: it can impose upon you a term of imprisonment. It's this feature, of being backed by the power of the State, that separates the law, at least in the sense in which I've used the word, from, for example, the obligation imposed by some religions to eschew certain meats or other foodstuffs.

But, of course, as the examples I have given show, the law does not ordinarily punish lawbreakers with prison. The law also needs another quality to function: the quality of awe. We should come before it as a child instructed by a parent – fearful of its breaking.

The need for the law to inspire awe is coded into its performance: the wigs, the vellum, the robes and the ceremony. All of this is designed to position you, the public, in an obeisant position relative to it. Like a dad, the law needs to be experienced as powerful or it cannot function.

If the only means by which people are caused to comply with the law is fines, the awe dissipates. The law ceases to matter to those whose wealth makes the fines immaterial. It invites avoidance by those who do not believe they will be caught or punished. And so it can come to burden those who behave as the law encourages and, relatively speaking at any rate, assist those who do not.

This latter was very much a feature of campaigning in the Brexit referendum. Some would-be campaigners – typically those with reputational or regulatory capital who would be harmed by a finding that they had broken the law – adopted a 'safety first' approach to electoral law that impeded what they did and spent. Others – new organisations with no reputation to lose, like Leave.EU and Vote Leave – took highly aggressive positions on what the law meant. They were rewarded for it politically but the cost was born by all of us: it exposed that the law need not matter. And that is a consequence we are living with now.

If we want to live in a society with rules we have a duty to protect that majesty – or at least to engage thoughtfully with the cost if we do not. This obligation falls on lawmakers – to ensure that what the law demands is protected. It falls on law-performers – judges and lawyers – to behave in ways that uphold public perceptions of the value of the law.

And it also falls on Government, the most important subject of the law, to defer to what it represents.

But too often Government has not deferred. When it became clear to us that Matt Hancock, then Health Secretary, was breaching the law relating to the publication of vast Covid contracts, we sued. During the course of the litigation it became clear that some publications were deliberately being delayed to suit the prime minister's office. When the Court found in our favour – declaring that Matt Hancock had broken the law – he responded by saying loudly and publicly that he believed he had done the right thing.[1]

Primary Legislation

So where does the law come from?

The main source, the 'superior' source in the sense that it trumps all others in the event of inconsistency, is primary legislation.

Voters elect Members of Parliament to the House of Commons. The House of Commons, one of two Houses of Parliament with the other being the House of Lords, wield the democratic power of voters. It has democratic legitimacy and with that legitimacy it can pass laws which state or create or change the law in the area it covers. The books call this type of law primary legislation or Acts of Parliament or statutes.

The process of making legislation in Parliament starts with the Government tabling bills – legislation in its beta form. These bills then go through a series of what are called 'readings' and committee stages in which they receive some level of scrutiny from MPs. And what emerges at the other end is a detailed and thoughtful articulation of the policy preferences of the House of Commons of the day.

That's the idea anyway.

Those bills then go to the House of Lords for approval. Members of the House of Lords aren't elected by the public. Some were appointed by political parties. Some are there because they had an ancestor who received the kind of peerage that they could pass down to their children and they to theirs. Some are there because they are representatives of the Church of England. And some are there because they persuaded the House of Lords Appointments Commission that they had something to offer the nation.

However, because members of the House of Lords are unelected, their powers to interfere with what the House of Commons does are limited. Sometimes – depending on the type – they can make alterations to primary legislation. Some types they can delay. But some types, for example legislation for which the ruling party made a manifesto commitment, they understand they should not interfere with.

Formally, an Act of Parliament only becomes law when the monarch agrees to it – a process called royal assent. Probably this is just ceremony – for a monarch to do anything other than approve an Act of Parliament would generate a constitutional crisis. And that hasn't happened since the reign of Queen Anne more than three centuries ago. Parliament has a democratic legitimacy that the monarch does not. But what a monarch would do if there was already a moment of constitutional crisis remains a lively matter of political debate. We just don't know.

Secondary Legislation

Below primary legislation in the hierarchy is what we call 'secondary legislation', most usually to be found in the form of 'statutory instruments'.

An Act of Parliament can give permission for a minister to make statutory instruments. That permission will be contained in an 'enabling' provision in an Act which will or at least should tightly circumscribe the limits to the law-making power. Those limits should cover things like the purpose for which the law-making power can be exercised, the types of things it permits and the procedure, if any, which the minister's proposal must be subject to before it becomes law.

We don't talk much about secondary legislation but it's where much of the action happens. Over the last decade we have made an average of 33 Acts of Parliament and about 3,000 pieces of secondary legislation a year. Constitutional theory holds that this legislation – drawn up by civil servants and signed by ministers – is legitimate because MPs have a democratic mandate to make laws and there's nothing wrong with them delegating that power to ministers subject to certain limits.

But the secondary legislation contemplated by Acts of Parliament is increasingly powerful and without any meaningful limits. Government, which draws up the timetable for parliamentary consideration of legislation, increasingly acts to inhibit parliamentary scrutiny. And the enabling provisions are increasingly incredibly widely drawn – stretching to, on occasion, power for a minister to change the Act of Parliament in which the enabling power itself is contained. The effect is a massive transfer of power away from Parliament and into the hands of ministers, something to which Parliament consents only as a matter of legal form.

Case Law

The final source of law is case law – also known as common law. Case law is the law that judges express when they decide cases. Judges 'express' it either because they repeat principles they extract from other cases where other judges have decided analytically similar questions or, if a question is new before them, they say what the answer is. Central to this notion of case or common law is the idea of 'precedent', that if a judge has decided a question in the past, a later judge (certainly a later judge whose status is junior or equivalent to that earlier judge) should 'follow' what the earlier judge decided.

In practice, the common law is no easy thing to describe. It is too diffuse to be laid out in any book. It has no unifying subject matter. And it is drawn from many different places – earlier decisions of our own courts, foreign courts, international treaties, works of scholarship. Even its formal place in the hierarchy – below primary and secondary legislation, either of which can overrule the common law – is disputed around the edges. All that can be said of it that is universally true is that it is the law if a judge says it is and it remains the law until another judge says it isn't.

Judges make law for lots of different reasons. Sometimes they are working through how Parliament or a minister had intended for primary or secondary legislation to apply to a particular set of facts that the legislation did not tackle head on.

A good illustration of this point comes in the wry opening paragraph in the judgment of Lord Hoffman in a 2005 case about whether teacakes – those marshmallow domes deposited on biscuit and covered in a thin crackle of brown-said-to-be-chocolate – are 'standard rated' for VAT (i.e. the retailer has to charge you 20 per cent VAT) or are 'zero rated'.

The supply of food is in general zero-rated for VAT: see section 30 and Schedule 8, Part II, Group 1, item 1 of the Value

Added Tax Act 1994. But there are exceptions. One exception is confectionery: see item 2 of the Excepted Items. But there is an exception to that exception: cakes or biscuits are in general also zero-rated. There is however an exception to that exception to the exception, namely biscuits wholly or partly covered with chocolate. They are standard-rated.'[2]

It took a lot of civil servants to categorise the various exceptions to the exceptions to the exceptions to the rule that confectionery is not food. And yet it still took a large number of court hearings to resolve the question of which category teacakes fell into. It's all well and good for humanity to contain multitudes – but to some poor sod falls the task of describing them all. And when they fail in that impossible job one of the things that the common law does is plug the gaps.

The judge-made common law is also responsible for concepts of enormous materiality to our everyday lives.

The idea, for example, of 'employment' – a relationship an individual can have with someone to whom they supply their services – was made by judges. From it flows huge consequences for the public purse – income from employment is taxed much more heavily than income from self-employment and together the two make up more than half of all tax paid. And also huge consequences for individuals: employees are entitled to better treatment from the person to whom they sell their labour than are the self-employed from the person to whom they sell theirs.

It is barely an exaggeration to say that the judge-made notion of employment has shaped the structure of our economy. From it, and the regulatory arbitrage opportunities opened up as it has failed to adapt to changes in technology, has emerged the huge growth in platform businesses like Uber. I talk about this more in Chapter Eight.

Starting with the fact that the common law is subordinate to primary and secondary legislation – or putting it another way, that the law made by judges can be changed by the law made by legislators – also gives you a useful insight into where the common law operates. It charts those territories of human conduct that legislators have chosen (so far) to leave to judges. Those areas, in practice, are ones which are nuanced, complicated, evolving, important; where legislation can be too fixed an articulation of policy.

Of these, perhaps, the most important are tort and contract.

The law of 'torts' is the law of wrongs. Judges have decided that some types of wrongs, which give rise to harm to others, are 'actionable'. In other words, if you are a victim of one of those types of wrong you can sue. Usually the main question is, how culpable is the wrongdoer for the harm you have suffered?

But only if you have the money, of course. Pursuing these types of actions is contingent on you having the deep pockets necessary to pay lawyers. Or finding help from a collective set up for such a purpose – like a trade union. Or managing to find a decent no-win no-fee lawyer. Otherwise you have to lump it.

Other approaches are available. You might say, for example, that road traffic accidents are inevitable in modern society and whether you are compensated for the harm you suffer if you are on the bumpered end of one shouldn't depend on whether you can prove the driver breached a legal standard of culpability. Your needs are the same either way so all road users should pay into a collective insurance fund. This would be vastly more efficient, and fairer too.

The law of contract – of a binding promise between two parties enforced by the power of the State – is the foundation of how our economy works. The law dictates when a promise comes about, when the parties can walk away from it and what happens if they breach it. And it is primarily about encouraging a kind of paradigm of good economic decision-making in commerce.

It's very effective at achieving that ambition, of delivering that paradigm, because money is the law's happy place. If you enter into a contract from which you would have made a million were it not for a breach by your counterparty the law can make the counterparty give you a million quid. Job done. The law has imposed its magical order on the world. Or, as a lawyer would say, it has restored the status quo ante (Latin again; and you see why we don't get invited out much).

Outside of that domain, the law begins to struggle. It can compensate you for the diminution in family finances consequential on your husband being flattened by a drunk driver. But it can't compensate you for a forever-vacant left side of the bed. Or that your newborn son will never get the inside track on how to wee standing up.

Of course, that's not a criticism of the law – some things are beyond all who are mortal – but it is still useful to bear in mind as you contemplate what the law can do, and the terrain in which it is most comfortable.

What Does the Law Do?

Another way of answering the question 'What is the law?' is to look at what it does.

To ask for a cohering intellectual architecture is to conceive of the law as a purpose-built town, a Welwyn Garden City if you like, rather than the London that it is: old and new, planned and wanton, elegant and grotesque all at once. No existing legal system, in the common law world at least, was planned from scratch by a master builder. What we have developed haphazardly over time.

It follows that there is no internal logic that entitles you to make sense of it as a whole. The best you can hope for is to learn to think like a lawyer and develop the ability to make an educated guess about what the answer might be.

That being said, there are some ideas that are more rule than exception, just about.

The law's two concerns are the public good and private rights.

Under the banner of public good, the law identifies territory to occupy. Much of human interaction is not its concern – there are, for example, no legal consequences if you don't do your homework, you impress an impassioned kiss upon a consenting adult who is not your husband, or break a promise to your daughter. Your conduct might be, in some conceptions, wrong but, as a contract lawyer would say, there is no intention to create legal relations.

The 'territory' the law chooses to occupy, the areas it regulates, defies all sensible explanation. Adultery was until recently grounds for divorce – it had some legal consequences – but only certain types of adultery. Penetrative sex was grounds for divorce but you could blow your neighbour to your heart's content (assuming the heart to be the apposite organ).

Judges are not priests and the law does not aspire to be a moral code. But equally if it slips anchor and drifts too far from

popular conceptions of right and wrong it begins to jeopard-
ise its own legitimacy. Some things which are immoral – for
example avoiding your taxes – are legal. And some things
which are illegal – noisily protesting at the destruction of the
planet outside the offices of Big Oil – are moral.

It's also worth noting the uneasy temporal relationship
between the law and morality. A philosopher would say that
the moral quality of your actions is a function of what was
in your mind when you acted. What happens later is after
the event and irrelevant. But legal sanctions work very differently. You won't know until much later, if ever, whether the
law will punish your actions, whether the law will come to
bless or to curse what you did. But the moral quality of your
acts remains the same.

So the lines are very blurred, but if you do happen to cross
over into territory occupied by the law there are consequences.
You'd think that the most serious consequences attach to
conduct the law characterises as 'criminal'. And, indeed, that
is true up to a point: only conduct which is criminal in character can result in imprisonment. But criminal conduct can
result merely in a fine or not even that, just a 'convicted' stamp
against your name in a book we together keep. Whether those
marks matter depends on who gets to write in and who gets
to read the book. It's not hard to think of countries in which a
conviction for political dissidence might be a matter for pride
and the same is no less true of the UK. A range of opin-
ions might well be held in polite society in the UK towards
someone convicted of the crime of protesting against, for
example, ecocide.

The law books talk of criminal acts as being those which
are against the public interest – against public welfare or

morals – so that the public has an interest in stopping them. But it's not easy to find any real analytical substance to these assertions beyond that the lawmaker at the time perceived them to be sufficiently serious to merit the epithet 'criminal'.

The other key feature of the criminal law is the predicate that, because the stigma of conviction matters, it should only be imposed where it is certain that the person accused has committed a crime.

So in the criminal law (alone), the conduct which is said to be criminal has to be proven 'beyond reasonable doubt' before it attracts sanction. The level of confidence a judge must have before imposing a non-criminal sanction is much lower – just 'more likely than not' before finding against the defendant.

Beyond the criminal law, but still broadly under the banner of the public good, are a slew of obligations which individuals owe to the State and which they are encouraged to adhere to with civil penalties – fines to you and I – and which a lawyer might sweep up into a basket called 'regulatory law'.

Examples of these types of obligations include the duty to submit your tax returns on time, to pay minimum wage as an employer and to guard against money laundering. Breach of these can attract financial penalties – civil penalties as lawyers call them – without criminal sanction.

The intention – inasmuch as it is possible to discern one – is to deter certain types of misconduct which are insufficiently serious to merit criminal sanction: a kind of transitional regime, if you like, between acceptable and criminal. But conduct which is punishable by civil penalties can very often also attract criminal sanction. Knowingly failing to pay the minimum wage can be punished by civil penalties but is also a crime.

What's more, the State often seeks to attach the same reputational consequence to civil penalties as attach to criminal ones, for example by publishing with much fanfare a list of those who have attracted civil penalties. You're left with a lingering sense that the real motivation for civil penalties, with their lower burden of proof, is that they are an easier way to whack wrongdoers than are criminal penalties. And perhaps there's nothing wrong with that.

These are the tools that the law uses to encourage people to behave in ways that are considered from time to time to be consistent with the public good. And, being concerned with the public good, they are operated by the State as guardian of that public good. Only the State has the power to impose them.

When it comes to the second of the law's concerns, what I earlier called private rights – relationships between individuals – the law proceeds from a different premise. 'This stuff is not really about the public interest,' it says, 'it is for you to sort out.' What it does in this territory is create a framework which governs how we should behave towards one another, again in certain spheres. And it provides a mechanism whereby that framework might be enforced, again at the behest of individuals.

Contract and tort – which I have mentioned above – fall within this sphere. So does employment law, the law of landlord and tenant, and indeed the law of marriage.

Creating a framework through which you and I might compel the mightiest in the land is the law's great achievement. Governments may be captured by the interests of powerful global corporations but they remain subject to the law, just like you and I, and are compellable, just like you and I. That we are all equal before the law and subject to it is the law's great boast. It is the high-water mark of our universal human desire that life be fair.

All of this is true.

But the law cannot operate fairly without lawyers. And lawyers are expensive – hundreds or sometimes even thousands of pounds an hour – and they are only rarely available to those without immense wealth. In most spheres, legal aid, like the dodo, can only be seen in books. Draw back the curtain of rhetoric and you reveal a reality that is sometimes not merely empty of substance but worse.

The law can become just another means by which the wealthy and powerful – with lawyers – can enlist the enforcement power of the State to impose their unlawful will on those without power. Who are bullied for sums they do not owe; deprived of rights to which they are entitled; silenced and forced to apologise for speaking their truth.

The defining image of the law is Lady Justice, blindfolded to signal her indifference to who appears before her, holding in one hand scales representing the neutrality of the law, and in the other a sword signifying the power she wields. This is a lovely, comforting idea, but without equal access to the law, without equal enforcement of it, and equal treatment before it, the law is a mighty arsenal to which only the powerful incumbency has the keys.

The institutions of, and around, the law are not oblivious to these problems.

There are instances where it is still possible to tap the shrunken legal aid pot, in particular if you are charged with a criminal offence.

There are cases, especially those where the facts are self-contained, where it is possible to access high-quality and free legal representation provided by law firms. Those opportunities are in practice accessible mostly to those who are educated or have good networks. It also helps if your case raises issues that are attractive to the types of people who allocate the 'pro bono' resources of law firms. I don't want to be rude about pro bono programmes – but they can represent a kind of Victorian philanthropy for the 'good' poor which is antithetical to 'blind' justice.

And the rights the law gives to you have some real-life existence – they offer you some protection – even if you cannot afford to use them. The possibility of rights being enforced deters their breach and the fact of those rights existing conditions behaviour. Most employers will pay the minimum wage because they could be chased by a regulator or because they know it is 'right' even if the employee has no real-world way to take action for breach of the National Minimum Wage Act.

But access to justice remains an enormous problem – and not just in the abstract. It has real-life effects which, if you want to understand them properly, have to be examined through the prism of wealth and power. If you must be rich to use the law then, logically and necessarily, the law is an instrument for the advancement of the interests of the rich.

Those with money can use the law to beat down those without. I have seen a number of defamation cases threatened against individuals in the trans community, using hugely expensive lawyers, which they cannot afford to defend and so concede despite having all the legal merits on their side. We have funded the defence of a cis woman who suffered a sexual assault – and was then sued by her abuser for talking about it. And we have funded the defence of a local political party official who was sued by a transphobic lawyer who was unhappy with a report that inhibited her path to elected office.

The denial of access to justice means the denial of rights to those who lack money. It enables the wrongdoer to laugh at the law. What use to a tenant is the right to a habitable property if they cannot force their landlord to tackle black mould on the walls and ceiling? What use to an employee is the right not to be sacked for pregnancy if they have no way to claim compensation? What use is your right to be seen by an NHS consultant within 18 weeks if you cannot afford a lawyer to help you force the issue?

This delegitimises Parliament – which is reduced to legislating theoretical protections that are not available to those who need them – and it also brings the law into disrepute.

The issue also arises in judicial review.

Perhaps the most famous legal case on 'standing' – whether you pass the test for having a sufficient interest to bring a judicial review – is a case in which Lord Rees-Mogg, father of the present Member of Parliament for North East Somerset, challenged the Maastricht Treaty, which founded the European Union. He used a stellar team of four barristers, headed by David Pannick QC. The Court of Appeal said:

> It is suggested by Mr Kentridge [acting for the then Government] that these proceedings are no more than a continuation by other means of arguments ventilated in Parliament. Be that as it may, we accept without question that Lord Rees-Mogg brings the proceedings because of his sincere concern for constitutional issues.[3]

But he also brought the proceedings because he could afford to. It should not only be the wealthy whose 'sincere concerns' the Court gets to hear. In truth, those are the people who need the protection of the Courts the least and they should not get it the most. But a series of recent court decisions have refused standing for cases crowdfunded by thousands of everyday people whose 'sincere concerns', unlike those of Rees-Mogg, do not seem to matter. This is appalling, but judges say it, and because they do it is the law.

I have tried to put this issue at the heart of the work I do with Good Law Project. We work with communities who are the least able to access the law. We listen to them to identify the issues that matter most to them. The mechanics of crowdfunding enables us to collectivise individual interests to make the law accessible. It means that tens of thousands of people who alone could not access justice, together can. And, with my colleagues, I have set up a not-for-profit law firm, Good Law Practice, to bring costs down even more.

It is not nearly enough but it is what I can do. Broader solutions must come from reform of the rules on costs, from changes to civil procedure rules and common law rules on standing so as to protect rather than punish crowdfunded attempts to broaden access to justice. But the profession must also play its part – perhaps through a levy on the profits of those lawyers who do not voluntarily commit to ensuring access to justice.

Criticise a lawyer for choosing to act for a wealthy rogue – a dodgy oligarch, say – and large sections of the profession will lecture you on the importance of protecting access to justice. But the truth is, there is no access-to-justice problem for wealthy rogues. None goes without legal assistance – not so long as they can pay well. But as a profession we tolerate a world in which tens of millions will as readily grow wings as access justice.

What is the actual concern here – access to justice? Or protecting the right of lawyers to rinse the worst people in the world free of criticism?

Who knows what lies behind Lady Justice's blindfold; but if you choose to talk about the majesty of the law and you wish to avoid the accusation of hypocrisy you'd best do your bit to ensure that what is revealed is not a sly wink at the powerful.

Public Law

In Chapter Seven I write about the case I brought, along with the ecologist Dale Vince and the SNP politician Joanna Cherry MP, against then prime minister Boris Johnson after he swore, repeatedly, that he would not ask the EU to extend the date of the United Kingdom's departure despite the obligation on him in the so-called Benn Act to do exactly that.

Whilst the case was ongoing I was asked time and again by journalists: 'What happens if the Court orders him to send the letter and he doesn't?' Look in the pages of a legal textbook and the answer is relatively simple: he would be in contempt of court and go to prison. But I felt strangely awkward giving that answer to journalists – which is probably why they (quite rightly) asked me. Were the police really going to go to Downing Street, imprison the prime minister and leave him there until he signed? It did seem unlikely. But if, on the other hand, they wouldn't, what was left of the rule of law?

There are sensible, and difficult, questions to be asked about the relationship between the law and Government.

The law is most comfortable, as I have explained above, with money: that's its happy place. But the Courts can't fine Government. All that would do is shift money from its right to its left trouser pocket, with the lawyers collecting a transfer fee.

And had we, as we were often encouraged to, sued the Government for damages for mishandling the pandemic, who would foot the bill? The State would borrow the money to pay the damages so the burden would fall on our children when they repay the debts. Enriching today by burdening tomorrow? Leave aside that the case was legally hopeless – would you even want it to succeed? In judicial review proceedings, where Good Law Project is most active, public law can deliver hard-edged legal results. If you are about to be deported to a country you left as a toddler and have no memory of, a successful judicial review is transformational.

But most litigants in judicial review proceedings have as the pinnacle of their ambition the hope that a judge will 'quash' or cancel an unlawful act taken by a minister. The training judges have equips them to examine a thing a minister has done and determine whether it is compatible with the law. If it isn't compatible, they will say, in effect, that the minister was trying to exercise a power that they never really had. And so the thing that the minister thought they had done never actually happened.

For a judge to move beyond that, and tell a minister positively what to do, is much less common. It usually involves a making of choices, a weighing up of competing factors, and that is generally a job for a minister. Judges are rightly reluctant – except in the clearest of cases – to take that power for themselves.

So you might succeed in cancelling an act by a minister. But very often, even if you succeed, and the statistics show that only a bit over 2 per cent of all judicial reviews end with the

Government losing in Court, all you get is the Court declaring that the act you have challenged did not adhere to the law.

And what, you may wonder, is the point of that?

Well, there is the legal answer. And then there is the real answer.

The legal answer is that our system assumes someone will give a damn. And although a declaration can't change the past – unlike an award of damages it won't put you back into the position you would have been in had the law not been broken in the first place – that's not to say it does nothing.

If a court makes a declaration that a particular act is unlawful, civil servants and ministers hear that any deliberate repetition is in the realms of the criminal – misconduct in public office, for example – and they act accordingly. So a declaration can help to shape the future: the politicians of tomorrow learn that the acts that the politicians of yesterday found convenient were unlawful. In theory at least, they avoid repeating them. That's an important function.

But our constitution anticipates that the real impacts will take place in the political sphere.

You can see this assumption in our 'Ministerial Code', which sets out the so-called Nolan Principles of Public Life that ministers are 'expected' to adhere to. It talks of 'the overarching duty on ministers to comply with the law and to protect the integrity of public life'.

Well, expected by whom?

I might want them to adhere to the law. I might think, over time, society will cease to function if they don't. But who cares what I think? Who is the person who matters if those expectations that ministers will comply with the law are not met? The Ministerial Code answers that question too. It says that ministers are personally responsible for their own compliance with the code. Great. And it goes on to state that the only person who can punish breaches of it is the prime minister: it's the prime minister who expects ministers to comply with the law.

So the way the system is supposed to work is this.

Ministers are supposed to act within the law – and the prime minister is supposed to consider whether to punish them if they don't. Under that system, if a court says, in response to a legal challenge, that the minister broke the law, the prime minister ought to consider whether the breach is of such a nature as to justify punishing the minister. In that conception of the world, identifying whether the law has been broken so that the prime minister can take action is the function – or at least a function – of a declaration.

But self-evidently all of this depends on whether the prime minister regards compliance with the law as important.

The first Court judgment we obtained in our cases about pandemic procurement concerned the legal obligation on the part of the Government to publish Covid contracts within thirty days – no ifs and no buts.[4] The obligation existed to protect the public interest in transparency – that we should be able to scrutinise where public money is going. But this just wasn't happening. There were delays, sometimes of months approaching years, in publishing contracts.

Of course, in the real world, everyone understood that the number of public contracts being awarded had skyrocketed due to the pandemic. Not only were we having to buy the stuff we had to buy ordinarily, but we also had to buy the stuff we didn't: personal protective equipment, lateral flow tests, ventilators and so on. So there were enormous numbers of additional contracts to be published. What's more, because procurement was happening at pace, contracts weren't always documented as well as they might be in ordinary times. This made it difficult for those in charge of publishing the contracts to keep track of what was going on.

We understood all of this.

What we didn't understand was why the contracts that the Government was publishing slowly, or not at all, were the contracts that looked the fishiest. That wasn't something that could be explained by the pandemic. Triaging the contracts you are happy to publish and the contracts you're not imposes an extra burden. It slows things down further. It looked to us like something that could only be explained by a government that didn't fancy scrutiny. So we sued for breach of the thirty-day rule and we won.

The case had a very considerable impact on transparency. Contracts that seemed to be being held back from publication began to be published. And the desire of Government lawyers to have an explanation for the Court generated a strong impetus for publication of the remainder.

But what was the legal sanction?

Speaking in the aftermath of the judgment, and facing calls for his resignation, Matt Hancock, then the relevant minister, claimed that breaking the law was 'the right thing to do'. This was a remarkable response: the response of a man who considered himself above the law and above the Ministerial Code.

What about the prime minister? How did he react? Did he sanction the minister? There is no sign that he did. And, what's more, the documents disclosed in the litigation showed that it was, in part, the prime minister's own office that had caused, or at the very least exacerbated, the delays. The prime minister's people had asked for more time so the contracts came out at a moment convenient to the Number 10 media machine.[5]

The prime minister didn't just stand and watch Hancock's smash-and-grab raid on our constitution – he drove the get-away car and fenced the proceeds for a boost in the opinion polls.

And here's where the arm of the law does not reach. Long though it may be with petty criminals, it will not collar a prime minister who does not care whether the law is broken because he benefits from its breach.

Around the margins it has something to say. There is the theoretical threat of misconduct in public office – a serious criminal offence that could cover deliberate or reckless law-breaking that is serious in character. But the threat is little more than theoretical.

There are serious evidential hurdles in the way of bringing such a prosecution. You'd have to show not merely that the minister broke the law but that they did so deliberately or recklessly. It is very difficult to imagine how those hurdles might be crossed by a member of the public who lacked power to compel the production of evidence. That leaves public bodies who have a specific statutory responsibility for tackling criminality and have power to compel evidence – bodies like the police or the National Crime Agency or the Serious Fraud Office.

But there is nothing in how those bodies comport themselves that suggests any inclination to investigate criminality by those in power.

Indeed, the evidence is very much the opposite. The lock-downs imposed in 2020 and 2021 to try and limit the spread of coronavirus seem to have been regarded as an inconvenience by the then prime minister and much of the circle around him. The main thing was not to get caught: partying staff were told they should leave Number 10 by the back exit to avoid being photographed by the press.[6]

This conduct wasn't merely morally sub-optimal. It was criminal, and ought to have been investigated. But, despite the vast amounts of evidence of criminality – written party invitations, photographs – it wasn't. Good Law Project commissioned and published an opinion from a heavyweight legal team, Danny Friedman KC and Adam Wagner, which set out how the police's failure was likely to be unlawful.[7] It made no difference.

It was only after we began legal proceedings against the police force that the police opened an investigation. And the punishment of the then prime minister, Boris Johnson, and the present prime minister, Rishi Sunak, when it came, was a £100 fine. The cost of three or four glasses of Johnson's favourite plonk[8] and three-quarters of one per cent of what Sunak spends heating his swimming pool.[9]

Even where you force the police to investigate, and the evidence is so overwhelming as to compel the conclusion there was an offence, the legal remedy still does not matter. Johnson shrugged off the fine. Sunak shrugged it off. The notion that it is legal consequences that matter sits somewhere towards the winged end of a spectrum that begins at 'sensibly arguable' and ends with 'for the birds'.

The real sanction for a breach of public law is a political one.

It should hurt a government politically for a judge to declare that a minister has broken the law. The notional right-thinking citizen who casts her vote at the ballot box every five years should weigh in her mind, along with everything else, whether the Government treats itself as restrained by or above the law – and perhaps for the moment she does. But public anger at lawbreaking is not a currency with a fixed value. Presence makes the heart go wander. Eventually voters get bored.

Privately, I have challenged judges, politely of course because I do occasionally remember the side upon which my bread is buttered, to think about what it means for the rule of law if ministerial adherence to the law becomes a matter of choice, as Matt Hancock argued to the BBC. And we are not yet in a world where the well of public outrage has run dry.

But the dilemma I already face – how to explain to those who back our cases that it really does matter if Government breaks the law – will not be ours alone for ever. It lies in wait for judges too. It is hardly an exaggeration to say that, over time, they could be reduced to glorified newspaper columnists passing judgment on ministerial conduct, only in less elegant prose.

If we value the rule of law, if we want politicians to continue to adhere to it, they have to be incentivised to think it matters. The law provides no real mechanism through which that might be achieved. It can only be done in the arena of politics.

You have to turn up the political heat.

It's only when you get yourself comfortable with the messy truth that the law and politics can't really be disentangled that you begin to be able to assess, as a campaigner, what litigation can do.

When we think about whether or not to bring a case we absolutely have in mind whether there is an actual or latent public interest. Will the traditional media want to cover it? Will it generate interest on social media? Does it speak to something the public thinks is important? It's only if it does that we might be in business.

Of course, if, like ours, your litigation is crowdfunded, you don't have any choice. If people don't care – or can't be persuaded to care – about what you are litigating about you can't take the case. You won't be able to raise money to fund your own lawyers – and you won't be able to put cash aside to meet the other side's costs if you lose.

But, although needing to fund the litigation is part of the story, it's still only part of the story. No public interest means no real-life sanction for the lawbreaker. And although it can be hard to win a case if it catches the public mood – judges get uncomfortable when the barbarians of the press knock at their gates – you're guaranteed to lose a case that doesn't. Ministers get to just shrug their shoulders and move on.

The real remedies – the remedies that matter to politicians; the remedies spoken in a language they understand; the remedies that really cause them to care about the law – are the remedies from outside the courtroom.

4. Judging the Judges

On 1 December 2020, the Divisional Court handed down its decision in Keira Bell's case.[1] Keira had been given puberty blockers as a 16-year-old by the Tavistock and Portman NHS Foundation Trust, had later taken male hormones, and then as an adult had begun surgery. She regretted embarking upon that pathway and had asked the Court to declare that it was unlawful to prescribe puberty blockers without an order of the Court.

Puberty blockers have been used for many decades. They are prescribed, largely without controversy, to children who experience 'precocious' (i.e. very early) puberty. The desired effect from their prescription is to suspend that puberty. If you stop taking them your puberty returns. If you were assigned the sex of female at birth, puberty blockers stop you having periods, developing breasts and your hips broadening. If you were assigned the sex of male at birth, they stop your voice deepening, the development of facial hair and an Adam's apple.

For kids with precocious puberty their prescription is, as I have said, largely uncontroversial. For young trans people, especially in the UK, it could hardly be more controversial, despite the fact that the Endocrine Society – the international medical organisation of endocrinologists, the body of professionals who prescribe hormones – describe their effect as 'fully reversible'.[2]

For young people who don't identify as their sex assigned at birth, puberty blockers are a critical part of what the medical profession refers to as a treatment protocol. The thinking expressed in long-standing documents revised over time by two separate international bodies of health-care professionals – the Endocrine Society (which deals with all uses of endocrinology) and WPATH (the World Professional Association for Transgender Health) – is that puberty isn't a great time in one's life to be making decisions about the long-term. So even if you are trans, there is much to be said for holding fire before making decisions which are irreversible when you are still young.

What those treatment protocols say is that, until you are 16, you shouldn't take the hormones of the gender with which you now identify. You don't take testosterone if you were assigned female at birth or oestrogen and progestin if you were assigned male at birth. You don't take these so-called 'cross-sex' hormones because their effects can't entirely be reversed. Instead, you take puberty blockers, which pause the changes that would otherwise occur and which are irreversible. The idea is that you buy yourself time to think.

You'll remember it too – how self-conscious you were as a teenager. I remember being so self-conscious about how I walked that I struggled to make it across the playground at school. And worrying about having had puffy nipples. (It wasn't until I typed this paragraph that I thought to wonder whether this is actually a thing. Turns out it is. It's called gynaecomastia and like so much else at puberty it 'usually clears up as boys get older and their hormone levels become more stable', to quote the NHS website.)

Even now for me those memories are painful and humiliating. You probably have similar ones. Now, try and project yourself into the mind of a teenager who is trans. That is, of course, if you're cis – the antonym of trans, meaning 'on this side of' as opposed to 'the other side of' – because if you're trans you won't need to. Having 'girl's' nipples despite being a boy gave me some modest insight. But of course, it is but a thimble from a deep well of pain you would experience were you a pubescent trans girl obliged to do nothing as her voice deepened, and her Adam's apple developed and she had erections as she woke in the morning. The distress she will experience I cannot begin to contemplate.

But even this is as nothing compared to the knowledge that many of the changes she is experiencing will never be able to be reversed. They will make it impossible for her to 'pass', should she want to, and will mark her out to broader society as being trans. And she will be well aware of what, in a society disfigured by increasing transphobia, that means. So much of this, she will know, will be avoided if only she can access puberty blockers.

The issue at the heart of the *Bell* case was whether those under 18 could consent to having puberty blockers. Because of how important the case was I followed the noise from the outset – although I had little choice given how much sport the media has in reporting on trans people. But, although I am a King's Counsel and I took a very active interest in the case, and I was given the key documents, its progress was hard to understand. Because of how important the case was to the trans community I instructed very experienced public-law lawyers, the best there were. But its progress seemed to defy legal gravity.

The judges making decisions about management of the case made a series of decisions that were – both to me and the lawyers I had instructed – inexplicable.

The law around whether children could consent to medical treatment was settled in a case called *Gillick*.[3] 'The main question in this appeal,' Lord Fraser had said, 'is whether a doctor can lawfully prescribe contraception for a girl under 16 years of age, without the consent of her parents.' Mrs Gillick objected to advice being given unless there was parental consent.

So the issue was about who had the right to choose whether a young person should receive contraception. Mother or daughter?

What the most senior court in the land held, when the case reached it, was that parental rights existed only to safeguard the best interests of a child. The question of whether a child could consent to treatment, against the wishes of their parent, depended on a doctor's assessment of whether the child had 'sufficient understanding and intelligence to understand fully what is proposed'. Were they of a level of intellectual immaturity to need their interests to be safeguarded by their parent? Were they, as it came to be known, '*Gillick*-competent'?

The question in the *Bell* case was much simpler.

The issue was not a contest between parents and child as to whether a child should have puberty blockers. The issue was one that arose even where both the parents and the child wanted the child to have puberty blockers – and where the specialist doctor agreed the child should.

The issue was whether, even in those circumstances where everyone agreed, puberty blockers could be prescribed.

What happened as the case progressed towards a hearing seemed to me remarkable – and alarming. Despite the assessment of the senior public lawyers I instructed that the case was hopeless, the Court gave Ms Bell 'permission' to bring her judicial review, a hurdle that involves the Court assessing that the case had some sensible prospect of succeeding.

It then refused permission for Mermaids, a charity that represents young transgender people, and Stonewall, the country's leading LGBT+ charity, to intervene in the case. And, having initially allowed it, the Court then changed its mind and rejected an intervention from a trans child. But it did allow an intervention from an anti-trans pressure group, Transgender Trend, which was not affected by the case and which had no recognised professional expertise in treatment protocols for trans children.

One of the guiding principles of the conduct of justice is that you should hear from those who are affected. But the decisions made by the Court meant that it was left without any advocacy from or representation of the community (or individuals) most closely affected by its decision. This was a shocking breach of basic justice even if you ignore the difference in the treatment of Transgender Trend.

What the Court went on to do in its judgment, advancing observations which went far beyond the narrow legal question of consent before it, made those earlier decisions even more remarkable.

Ignoring the usual procedural safeguards, the Court admitted evidence from witnesses without pertinent (or any) medical expertise in the field. Their witness statements did not even pretend to be in the form usually required by a court for expert evidence. And they were submitted so late in the day that the defendants, the Tavistock, did not have a proper opportunity to respond. Moreover, in a decision that sits uncomfortably with normal principles of open justice, and despite the importance of the issue they were deciding, the

Court ordered that the evidence given by those witnesses should not be published.

Some of these decisions were explicable in isolation. Viewed together they were profoundly alarming – frames from a slow-motion miscarriage of justice.

The decision of the Court, released some weeks after the hearing, confirmed my fears.

The Court decided, on the basis of the evidence it did hear, that the 'quite possibly, unique' nature of the treatment before it meant that there is 'no age-appropriate way to explain' what taking puberty blockers would mean. And, despite the fact that the *Gillick* assessment is one for doctors to make, the Court gave guidance that 'it is highly unlikely' a child aged 13 or under would ever be *Gillick*-competent, and it was very doubtful a child of 14 or 15 could understand the decision. And that clinicians treating someone of 16 or 17 'may well consider that it is not appropriate to move to treatment . . . without the involvement of the court'.

Taken as a whole, the decision, to which each of the judges agreed, was an extraordinary piece of judicial overreach.

The case had ceased to be about consent. It was a full-throated attack on orthodox prescribing practice. The judges decided, on the basis of one-sided and highly partial evidence, that they, in effect, knew more about the uses of puberty blockers than the medical establishment.

The aftermath of the decision was predictable – and alarming. Those parts of our media that are ignorant – or motivated by hostility – on trans issues reported the decision in a tone of triumph. As it became clear that it would mean an end to puberty blockers on the NHS for the foreseeable future, there were a number of suicide attempts by young transgender people.

And there were profound cultural consequences too, which I discussed in an interview for publication with the US academic, Grace Lavery, who was an Associate Professor of English at the University of California at Berkeley and general editor of *Transgender Studies Quarterly* at Duke University Press.[4] Speaking to her, I said:

> What we will be left with, I fear – I hope, you know, I desperately hope I'm wrong – but what we will be left with, I fear, is that transphobia will have been institutionalised by that decision. Transphobic views will now find support from not a place of marginalisation but from a centre of power and notionally a centre of independence, and that is the, I think, long-lasting and profoundly damaging consequence of the *Bell* decision. I think reversing that is a generation's work.

The deterioration in the mainstream political discourse around trans people that has followed that decision bears out that fear. In that interview, I was also asked why the Court might have decided the matter as it did. And to that question I said:

> I mean it's pretty clear that the Divisional Court brought to that decision and indeed to the trial process a series of preconceptions about gender incongruence and about ways to treat gender incongruence. And that those preconceptions were articulated in the procedural decisions the court made and in the substantive decisions that eventually the court arrived at. If you're a lawyer, it's heresy to say something like that. To say it as nakedly as I have. But it's also completely orthodox. Because we as lawyers talk all the time about the importance of having a diverse judiciary. We do that because we recognise, at some level, that the law is a human

instrument. Once you recognise that diversity is important because the law is a human instrument, you necessarily logically have also to recognise that judges bring their own biases to decision-making. I can't think of a worse example of that happening in English law in recent times.

The formulation I used ('brought a series of preconceptions') is one which encompasses both conscious and unconscious bias.

Professor Lavery then asked whether external factors – beyond the courtroom – might help explain the decision.

To that I pointed out that the solicitor representing Ms Bell had a long-standing association with the religious right and had acted in a number of cases involving attacks on abortion rights, and on gay rights, raising similar arguments about consent in those cases to the arguments Ms Bell raised here.

As to the judge I understood to have written the judgment, I offered a candid explanation. I said she was:

> simultaneously a hero amongst the Good Law Project's overwhelmingly female staff team for the work that she's done as a judge protecting the right to an abortion. And now, a sort of fallen hero for what we all regard as the work that she's done to roll back trans rights, to empower transphobia and transphobes in domestic public discourse. She comes from a very particular place, and I don't know whether this is mirrored around the world, but in England there is a very, very dominant strand of feminism. Not dominant numerically but dominant because it's a feminism of privilege, that is deeply opposed to trans rights. And that demographic is the demographic that she fits perfectly in. I am not saying she is a transphobe. I am just saying that she is in that demographic.

This response to a question about what might have motivated the decision caused very considerable discontent within my profession. Not for the first time, I was subject to vigorous and widespread criticism on social media for breaching what was said to be a professional omerta on criticising judges who, it is claimed, 'can't defend themselves'. And for undermining public confidence in the rule of law.

In an especially egregious abuse of institutional power, a BBC journalist, using his BBC email account, sent to my professional regulator, the Bar Standards Board, what the BSB described as 'a report about my professional conduct'. And, 'following a preliminary assessment of the report', it opened an investigation. Responding to my regulator cost about £10,000 in professional fees.

In the background, friendly lawyers communicated to me how deeply unhappy these comments had made a number of judges. Within my own executive team, there were distinctly mixed feelings about my comments and the publication of the interview was roughly coincident with the start of a period of froideur, which has not yet reversed, on the part of many in the judiciary towards Good Law Project.

It was an expensive interview.

Away from the world of trans rights, judges are routinely criticised. By newspapers. By ministers. By those with far greater institutional power than I have.

And those criticisms – very often – go unremarked upon and their critics are not punished in the Courts. Indeed, sometimes, the most common example being when judges point the finger of blame at women or children who have been raped, those criticisms are applauded. I couldn't help but think that the line I had really crossed was to speak about an injustice done to a community that – this was the real, the embedded, criticism – seemingly didn't deserve justice.

Some months after my interview, the Divisional Court's decision was overturned in the Court of Appeal.[5] That decision repeated many of the criticisms of the Divisional Court that I had advanced. Paul Conrathe, the lawyer who acted for Ms Bell, issued a statement suggesting he intended to ask the Supreme Court to overrule the Gillick test, which protects the right of young people to seek an abortion even where their parents disagree. But the Supreme Court rejected his request. There, at least so far as the law is concerned, is where the matter stands. But of course the cultural consequences linger – the Divisional Court decision continues to have effects that suggest it *is* the law rather than, as it was revealed to be, a travesty of the law. At the time of writing Good Law Project is working in various ways with four families of transgender kids who have taken their own lives. But we are barely scratching the surface.

I was cleared by the Bar Standards Board, which said:

> The Panel bore in mind the provisions of Article 10 of the European Convention on Human Rights and Fundamental Freedoms, as incorporated into the law of England and Wales by the provisions of the Human Rights Act 1998, and the importance of people to be able to express views on controversial topics, including reasoned criticisms of public judgments, without fear of punishment. The Panel decided that the comments, whatever the merits of the reasoning or the conclusion, represented your sincerely

held view and did not amount to gratuitous abuse. For these reasons, the Panel was satisfied that you were entitled to make those comments and therefore the conduct alleged and admitted did not amount to a breach of Core Duty 5 [the duty not to behave in such a way as diminishes the trust and confidence which people place in me or the profession].

I wouldn't claim that the fact that the Court of Appeal overturned the decision makes my criticisms right (just like I wouldn't have accepted that my criticisms were wrong had the Court of Appeal upheld the decision). And the fact my professional regulator cleared me of wrongdoing doesn't have the consequence that my interview was sensible, or ethical, or fair to the judge, or wise. It's tempting to treat a fact-sensitive and context-specific answer given to one question as somehow carrying meaning for a different question, especially if the answer is one that vindicates you. It's tempting, but it's wrong.

I don't often feel pride in what I say or do. I am always keenly aware of how I could have spoken with greater precision, how I could have done better or more. I take little pleasure from my successes.

But when I re-read that interview, what emerges on the page is what I wanted to say. I think it was fair and careful and nuanced – and brave. It's incredibly important to protect the spaces that there are for those without power, like the trans community, perhaps particularly for those without power, to speak without fear to those who have power, and in particular those who wield it.

That's all those communities have.

I have talked about this in Chapter Two, but marginal-ised voices are rarely given space, let alone fair space, in the national press.

I am aware of only one trans judge. Indeed, I am only aware of a very small number of trans barristers. And I know of only one trans MP – of 650 – and he has not socially transi-tioned. It is bad enough that the doors to the places where decisions are made about the lives of trans people are closed to them. They – and those who would speak in their support – should not be punished for saying clearly that this is wrong.

When I became a 'silk' I wrote that:

> What the silk system does is require advocates to demon-strate judgment, intelligence and sensitivity. It then liberates them – because the imprimatur cannot be removed – to exer-cise those qualities to provide that challenge. To be the buf-feting wind that encourages the law to grow stronger. I think that's a good thing.[6]

My voice is heard in places and by people that voices within the trans community are not. I take very seriously that moral responsibility to a community that thinks of itself, I believe reasonably, as voiceless. It feels to me right that I help shoul-der the burden of advocating for it. It is important to call our miscarriages of justice what they are, whatever the cost, and especially when no one else will. That is the second of a bar-rister's code duties – it requires us 'to promote fearlessly and by all proper and lawful means the lay client's best interests and to do so without regard to their own interests'.

Judges can make mistakes. Judges can act out their biases. Judges have immense power. They must never be beyond account.

The Need for Scrutiny

It's a truism that people go to court because they don't know who'll win. Of course there are instances where one side has a bad case of hubris – or greedy lawyers. But in most cases, certainly in most involving serious litigation, neither knows.

It's also why we have the type of system of justice we do. Ours is an 'adversarial' system. That's not a description of how the lawyers behave towards one another in court, although it can also describe that. The idea is that the process of the putting of arguments by one side and the testing of them by the other side stands the best chance of causing the truth to emerge.

There are two things that are supposed to emerge from that process.

The first is the 'true' facts – i.e. whose of the competing accounts of what happened is right. In testing the evidence, including the accounts of witnesses, which you test by asking them questions, you help the decision-maker, sometimes a judge and sometimes a jury, answer the question of whose account is more plausible.

The other thing that is supposed to emerge is the best view of the law. It was a sufficiently striking moment for me thirty years ago, attending my first ever law lecture, that I still remember being told that people go to court because they don't know what the law is. How can you have all these clever people paid, in some areas, hundreds or even thousands of pounds an hour and them still not know what the law is?

But they don't. They go to court and they argue about it and a judge decides.

These are the two elements – the facts and the law – involved in a decision. You decide what the facts are and then you apply what you understand to be the law to those facts. That's how you work out who has won.

Sitting back and watching, deciding the victor, is the judge. The judge always decides whose view of the law is right. And often – sometimes they share this function with a jury – the judge also decides whose facts are true.

The story we tell ourselves is that this is fine because judges get scrutinised incredibly closely. And sometimes they do.

In January 2022, I argued a case in the Supreme Court about the relationship between best accounting practice and tax liability.[7] The Supreme Court agreed with me that, even if an employer didn't make a cash payment to employees because it paid employees in options, nevertheless, those services were still relevant in calculating the – stay awake at the back! – amount on which the employer had to pay tax.

I had won the case when I argued it before the specialist tax tribunal. HMRC were adamant the decision was wrong – and so they argued it again before the specialist appeal tribunal. They lost again. And then they argued it again before the general appeal court, the Court of Appeal. And they lost again. Then they argued it before the Supreme Court.

When they started the case, they were represented by a Queen's Counsel and a junior barrister. By the time they got to the Supreme Court, the junior had himself become a Queen's Counsel and so they instructed another junior, meaning they were represented by two QCs and a junior. Each of those two QCs, and the junior, and a large team of lawyers instructed by HMRC, had worked on identifying errors that, they believed, the specialist tax tribunal had made.

They had three rounds of very detailed scrutiny of the decision of the specialist tax tribunal. Moreover, each of those four decisions was reported in the law reports so a (theoretically) interested public could see what the judges were doing and whether they were doing it right.

Each of those decisions – of the specialist tax tribunal, specialist appeal tribunal, the general appeal court and the Supreme Court – which was published in the endless series of law reports was pored over by other professionals who wrote articles about the decisions. And, as always, there was lots of money involved, and so large firms of accountants poured resources into analysing the decisions too and lobbying me to make their pet points. After all of that, it turned out that the decision of the specialist tax tribunal was right.

So, you might say, there is lots of scrutiny of the enormous power that judges hold: how could there be more? But it is only in a very narrow range of cases that there is scrutiny and even then it is only of a very narrow type. When I worked as a tax lawyer, I used to quip that I knew a great deal about very little. That's also the scrutiny that appeals deliver: a great deal about very little.

With few exceptions, only cases involving legal principles can be appealed. And, again with few exceptions, it is only cases involving legal principles that are published.

What a judge decides about the facts cannot generally be appealed. So questions of who a judge chooses to believe, and why, are not scrutinised.

Then there are the decisions judges make about how a case should be 'managed', like those I mentioned in the *Bell* case earlier. They include matters like whether a particular witness can give evidence; whether a party can submit written evidence; how long each side gets to put their arguments; who has to pay the costs of different bits of the trial and how much; what punishment (if any) should be attached to technical breaches of the rules.

Like a referee without VAR in an untelevised match played behind closed doors (because lots of case-management decisions are made without a hearing), those decisions can have a profound impact on the shape and outcome of a result. They can be decisive.

So even when it comes to decisions of appellate judges deciding important points of law – the *ne plus ultra* of judicial scrutiny – the opportunities for scrutiny are limited. They exclude what the judge has done with the facts and they exclude how the judge has managed the case.

Appeals are therefore generally a process whereby a senior judge scrutinises whether a junior judge misunderstood the law in making their decision. But a mistake in understanding or applying the law is only one of the ways in which the question 'who a judge is' can creep into the judicial process.

The Sorts of People Who Become Judges

I'm absolutely not saying our judges are 'good' or 'bad' people. I'm saying they are people, made of the same crooked timber as you and me. Almost all of them were lawyers before they became judges, and all of them were human beings before they became lawyers. But they are no better than you or I. They are skilled in the practice of law and they are skilled in judging. But there is nothing in the judicial appointments ceremony that transports participants to a higher moral plane. There's no baptism to wash away their prejudices or their shortcomings, so we should be interested, profoundly interested, in who they are.

Other countries have a professional judiciary, but in the UK judges come from the legal professions – solicitors and barristers – and overwhelmingly from the ranks of the latter. If you are a lawyer in practice and you think you want to be a judge you keep your eye on the vacancies advertised by the Judicial Appointments Commission – and then you apply.

There are lots of different reasons why lawyers choose to become judges. Some want a different type of intellectual challenge after many years of practice. For barristers it was for a long time a great way to build up a pension. And some lawyers see a chance to write themselves into the legal history books as makers of the common law.

What's certainly true is those lawyers who become judges – and certainly those who become senior judges – are likely to be more establishment-minded and small-c conservative. The legal establishment has – for perfectly understandable reasons to do with protecting the idea it thinks the public has of the law as neutral – an institutional dislike of controversy.

This institutional bias towards the conservative has effects on who rises within the profession. I don't invite you, patient reader, to believe I now pretend to shy away from controversy. But until I became a Queen's Counsel I was conservative, perhaps relatively conservative would be a better way of putting it, in what I was prepared to say publicly. That was very much because I saw my ability to become a Queen's Counsel – the only imprimatur of professional success that is available to barristers – as contingent upon whether I was approved of by judges and colleagues.

That wasn't some clever insight. It was obvious. To become a KC, you have to nominate dozens of referees from amongst your clients, fellow barristers and judges. That was true for me – and it is true of the profession. Collectively we understand, and we understand clearly, that kicking against powerful colleagues is antithetical to success.

What is true for lawyers as a class is even more clearly true of those who think they might like to become judges. You can't be a judge on issues where you have taken a public position – and it's not even desirable to be understood privately within the profession to have a 'view' on particular issues. So those who had a tongue to start with – already a subset – and mean to get on, learn to bite it. And, over time, what began as a sensible piece of careerist positioning becomes innate.

Add to the mix that the profession from which judges are drawn is disproportionately 'establishment' – in the sense of being drawn from the pools of the privately educated, upper middle classes, white and so on – and you begin to see some stark compounding effects. Judges are the conformist portion of the senior ranks of a profession which rewards conformism and whose membership is drawn disproportionately from establishment sections of society.

I love them, of course, but radical they are not.

Judicial Diversity Matters

What the data reveals about who our judges are does not inspire confidence.

There are a vanishingly small number of Black judges. There are none at senior levels of the judiciary. Women remain very under-represented at senior levels.[8] It is fair to say there has been some improvement, but the fact that the present Supreme Court has three times as many Davids as women tells its own story. Judges are overwhelmingly privately educated. 'Elitist Britain', a 2019 study by the Sutton Trust and Social Mobility Commission, showed that although only 7 per cent of the population went to private schools, 65 per cent of all senior judges did.[9] And 71 per cent went to Oxbridge, compared with only 1 per cent of the population. No profession in Britain is less socially diverse.

When it comes to measuring how many judges we have from working-class backgrounds, how many are gay or trans, how many are Muslim, how many disabled, let alone those who sit at intersections of disadvantage, we just don't know. We collect data on applicants for judicial posts but we don't know about the composition of the judiciary, or at different levels of the judiciary.

Fairness looks different to those who have grown up in communities where the pathways to highly paid professional positions are clearly mapped and well-trodden compared to how it looks for those whose peers could not see a way out and amongst whom criminality is a commonplace.

The judiciary knows it must do better and it has a five-year strategy.[10] This strategy is led by a judge, Ingrid Simler, who is committed to, and understands, why diversity and inclusion matter. But hers is the latest of many similar efforts and it is hard to feel optimistic.

What's more, the discussion is couched in the language of whether a judiciary that looks old and white and male reflects the composition of broader society and so fosters public confidence in it. But this, how the profession *looks*, is the wrong way of framing the problem.

Who are these notional members of the public who study the published statistics on judicial diversity to form a view about whether the make-up of the judiciary is reflective of the composition of society? Even if they do exist, and in sufficient numbers to render relevant their assessment of whether the scale of under-representation is a problem, what are they to make of the fact that from the vague official statistics they can see so little of who our judiciary is?

The truth, I would say, is that this presentation of the issue is a delicate dance around the real problem.

Litigants are interested in what the judge before them does, communities are interested in how they are treated by the Courts, and the public at large is interested in the judgments put before them to consume. No one, save for policymakers, is interested in how the judiciary taken as a whole looks.

Standing back, our impression of the legitimacy of the rule of law and the judiciary who administer it is outcome-driven, not form-driven. What we say is that the lack of judicial diversity matters because it gives a false impression of what our judiciary does. But the truth is that the lack of judicial diversity matters because the homogeneity of our judiciary gives a true impression of what our judiciary does. The judiciary is homogenous and the 'justice' it hands down reflects its homogeneity.

Judges overwhelmingly drawn from narrow strata of social experience – and who mix in judicial circles with others like them – will reflect that experience in their judging.

Every now and again the issue bubbles up on social media and some lawyers get sufficiently angry – they fear the cost of speaking out against power – to overcome their professional reticence. And you will read the experiences of lawyers, typically those who work in the less well-paid parts of the profession where barristers who don't conform to the archetype are over-represented, where the archetype judge confronts the non-conforming lawyer.

It's troubling reading.

White lawyers who are conscious of their privilege will talk of being embarrassed by the warm welcome they receive when they make points that drew hostility when made by their Black or Brown colleagues. They talk about the open class-signalling of judges – references to public schools or the opera – to privilege advocates like them. And Black lawyers will talk of less enlightened white colleagues exploiting, for their client's advantage, the inherent racism of some judges. The Court of Appeal judge Geoffrey Vos made many of these points recently.[11]

If we see or experience racism in the police force and we learn that the justice system has not sanctioned those responsible for it our trust in policing declines. If our concern is for public confidence in the law, we should ask people of colour what they think and if we learn that they don't rate it as highly as white people, we should make sure their reality is also represented on the judicial benches. And we should do that not because we think it will look better to people who lack confidence in the system. We should do it because we know it will give different outcomes – because judges who have been whacked by this stuff will deliver something closer to justice.

But doing this would require us explicitly to acknowledge that the law administered by a judiciary disproportionately composed of the sons and daughters of upper-middle-class white families will have a quality that, quite understandably, reflects their lived experiences. And so, to some degree, lacks legitimacy. You'd need to acknowledge that the problem is not just one of perception – but also of actuality. The law is unfair because of the people who deliver it.

To try and test this thinking, Good Law Project asked people what they thought. It commissioned polling from YouGov which showed that, indeed, people of colour do have lower levels of trust in judges. Asked 'How much, if at all, do you trust judges?' 65 per cent of the general population (including people of colour) said: 'a lot' or 'a fair amount'. That figure fell to 61 per cent for 'Black, Asian and Minority Ethnic' adults but only 47 per cent or 50 per cent for Pakistani and Bangladeshi people respectively (albeit from a small cohort). The only group that had less confidence in the judiciary was trans people at 46 per cent (40 per cent of all trans people said their confidence in the judiciary had fallen).[12]

I may have missed it but I'm not aware of previous detailed polling on trust in the judiciary across minoritised strands. And that is striking given the importance the legal profession attaches – or says it attaches – to upholding public confidence in the law. It raises the question whether public confidence is really the concern.

If it was, wouldn't you want to know who had confidence in the judicial system?

The YouGov data shows that the closer you are to the archetypal judge the greater the degree of confidence you have in judges and the rule of law: those from higher social classes have more confidence than lower; older people have more confidence than younger; white people have more confidence than people of colour; straight people have more confidence than gay; able-bodied people have more confidence than disabled; and cis people have more confidence than trans.

Of course, many of these relative levels of confidence also exist in relation to other institutions too. My point is not that they are unique to the law; my point is that lawyers' attitudes to them (that they shall not be acknowledged or spoken of) is unique and unhelpful. There is much to unpack in the data and unpacking it is a job for a social scientist rather than for me. But the differences are striking.

What is really being contended by those who say, 'You must not criticise judges, you must not undermine public confidence in them'? If the concern really was to protect confidence in judges, would they not be asking why it is that society's 'winners' have the most confidence? Perhaps the true concern revealed by this selective silence and silencing is that things are working well for them and they do not want things to change.

Another question: why is public confidence in the rule of law given an elevated importance? For sure, it has value, but is it more important than the law working properly and fairly? And if a thing is broken, or damaged, is it right to encourage people to have confidence in it?

How is it that you really ensure confidence in judges and the law? Do you do it by protecting them from criticism? Or do you do it through interrogation? Most lawyers, if asked to comment on any other feature of society, would say that the best way to keep things honest, and functioning properly, is through scrutiny, to interrogate whether things are actually working.

If that is right of everything else, why should it not also be true of justice and judges? There is a powerful professional omerta against speaking of these things in the name of 'preserving public confidence in the judiciary' – but whose outcome is corrosive of public confidence in the judiciary as discussion of its failings is silenced.

Perhaps Hilary Mantel was right when she wrote that 'the law is not an instrument to find out truth. It is there to create a fiction that will help us move past atrocious acts and face our future.' But for it to do even that job requires that we constantly press against and interrogate who is within that 'us'.

Political Context Matters Too

Of course, the biases judges acquire in their lives aren't the only way their humanity seeps into the process of judging. The political context matters hugely too.

I wrote in Chapter Two about how the tide of judicial attitudes towards tax avoidance turned in the aftermath of the financial crisis in 2008. In Chapters Six and Seven, I write about how, in choosing to litigate Brexit cases in Scotland, whose institutions and population were pro-Remain, I was able, despite very slender legal resources, to win cases that better-funded legal teams lost in pro-Brexit England.

But no one gets to change the judicial temperature like the Government.

In the years since Brexit, the Conservative Party, and the media to which it is increasingly the political wing, have kept up a constant string of attacks on the judiciary. In his leadership campaign, Rishi Sunak, now prime minister, described judges finding against the Government as 'recidivist' and in doing so was trying to bully them into deciding more cases in his favour. This was a formulation whose poison has been matched in recent times only by the *Daily Mail*'s channelling of Nazi tropes in describing the Divisional Court as 'Enemies of the People' after it ruled, rather modestly, that Parliament's consent was needed before a prime minister who had not been chosen in a general election could choose to start the process which would end with our departure from the European Union.[13]

Alongside the media drumbeat is the constant threat of legislation to remove from judges, or further limit, such powers as they have to secure the Government's compliance with the law. Both the intention, and effect, of these threats is to cause judges to change their attitudes towards lawbreaking by the Government; to tilt the playing field in the Government's favour. It's a strategy that Government uses with other institutions that threaten to perform their democratic function in a way Government finds inconvenient. The most obvious comparison is the retaliatory threats the BBC faces on those occasions when it remembers that its editorial guidelines define the public interest as including the holding to account of power.

And it works, for Government.

You can see this in the data. It shows a collapse in the frequency with which claimants succeed in legal challenges to the lawfulness of Government conduct: at the time of writing these had halved in 2021, from previous years, to a bit over 2 per cent. The disregard, widely acknowledged across broader civil society, that Government has for the rule of law might cause one to expect a rise in the success rate of challenges – but so successful has it been in changing the judicial temperature that what the data shows is the calamitous opposite.

In private, judges worry about this. As I mentioned in Chapter Two, a prominent sitting Court of Appeal judge has said explicitly that claimants are going to lose a lot of cases in the coming years because the judiciary is worried about what he described as another 'prorogation-type' event. He didn't have in mind, as I understood his words, that the prime minister would once again threaten to cancel Parliament if it, again, became inconvenient. It was more that he was worried about a legislative measure that placed the Government above the rule of law.

Put plainly, he thought judges, rather than applying the law as they understood it, should ignore lawbreaking and conserve their power in case Government did something very bad indeed.

Of course, the judiciary is not some Borg Monolith. It does not think and speak and act with a single mind. And this also throws up some rather awkward issues.

We all know it, us lawyers, and we talk about it behind closed doors, although never in public, but who your judge is makes an enormous difference. Typically, you don't find out who you've got until a day or two beforehand. But when you do, you'll have a pre-match huddle of legal team and client to discuss what it means: will your judge have a stance on you, your case, or the underlying issues? Are they, to use the language, 'a good draw'?

In a now forgotten Brexit case about whether the Government could introduce so-called 'serious shortage protocols', which enabled a pharmacist to swap the drug your doctor had prescribed you for another one in the event of post 'No Deal' shortage, I was refused permission 'on the papers' by one judge who had a reputation for being Government-minded.[14]

We asked for an 'oral renewal', and when we learned who our judge was going to be our very grand barrister quipped that there was a 17.4 million to one chance of us getting both of those judges to decide on whether we should have 'permission'. (17.4 million, for those who have mercifully forgotten, was the number of people who voted to leave the EU.) He was telling me, gently, that he did not think we would get permission from that judge either, and we did not.

I tweeted this information. The case had been crowdfunded – by thousands of people – and I wanted to tell them that I didn't expect us to get permission.

My colleagues were very cross.

But I feel about it now as I felt about it then. How was it right for my lawyers – as lawyers do, whoever their client is – to give me a strong steer on whether a particular judge being allocated to my case was good or not but wrong for me to share that information with those who were funding the case? Are we really in a world in which some information is too sensitive for Joe Public to know? How does that walk the talk of justice being seen to be done?

Public Trust in Justice

There is an important, related, issue.

Given that the predispositions of particular judges on certain issues are well known by insiders; given that the system leaves enormous space for those predispositions to play out in terms of the outcome in ways that are neither transparent nor remediable on appeal; you might ask yourself, 'well, where it is that "justice" actually happens?'

That would be a question that many senior public lawyers pose too, albeit only in private.

Shortly after Good Law Project lost in the Court of Appeal a case I had been very much expecting us to win, I got an email from a sitting High Court judge suggesting that we had deliberately been allocated '3 Tories'. Another, again in writing, echoed the 'prominent sitting Court of Appeal judge' I mention above in expressing the view that it had been 'self/career preservation' rather than politics that had delivered that outcome.

Of course, I can't know whether this is true. All I can say is that it is widely perceived within the profession to be true.

Whenever I raise these issues in gatherings of lawyers there's a sharp intake of breath and people start looking at their feet. But that response, at least to my mind, is a cultural aversion rather than an analytical reaction to the question. And I think the cultural aversion is driven by a perception that once you start asking these questions things get very messy very quickly.

What would it really mean for us to take seriously the (self-evidently true) notion that judges have biases? The fear must be that public confidence in the system of justice would suffer. But, as I've argued above, it is wrong to prioritise public confidence in the system of justice above doing our damnedest to ensure that the system we have is just. A decline in public confidence in justice would be better than a system where the thing we call justice could be done (or not done) not in the courtroom but in the process of allocating judges.

How close an interest do we actually take in levels of public confidence in our system of justice? And in whether those levels of public confidence in our system of justice are distributed equally throughout society? Or is it only 'us', the successful and culturally powerful lawyers for whom by definition the system has worked well, who need to have confidence in justice?

Is that, I cannot but wonder, the real reason why lawyers don't tend to ask these questions? Lawyers are disproportionately white, older, born into privilege, wealthy and (if senior) men. And judges, having once been lawyers themselves, are just like that (only more so). So, of course, we lawyers tend to think the system of justice is working well. For people like us, it *does* work well, because the biases of the judges we appear in front of mirror our own. They are people who see the world in the same ways we do.

The society that operates the law and constructs the common law is the society of lawyers and judges and not of us all. And I don't think we are curious enough about the ways in which the law embeds and privileges the culture biases of that society.

These are serious charges I make. All of these things that impact how the law really works are things the law is supposed to be blind to. The supposed impartiality of the law is the wellspring of its authority. And because they are serious they merit further examination – I have tried to say as plainly as I can the basis upon which I advance them. But that basis is narrow and there is much more work to be done.

This stuff matters, profoundly. Justice isn't a science – and it is foolish to pretend that it is. What we should want from our judges is humanity, a readiness to hear constructive challenge and a willingness to be thoughtful about what it means that they are made of the same crooked timber of humanity as the people they judge. It's that combination of qualities that is most likely to site them in the desired quartile of a grid whose vague axes are 'rules-based' and 'fair'. Most judges, I think, have these muscles, but they atrophy unless they are exercised in the fresh air of public debate.

Unless we talk about how the system really works – where it operates as it should and where it fails – we have no chance of making it better.

We need to take an interest in outcomes.

The power exercised by the judiciary is such that – even if it was your heartfelt belief that they were, taken as a whole body, uniquely blessed with kindliness, wisdom and equanimity – you might still think it wise systematically to monitor their actions just, you know . . . just to be sure.

The law requires large employers to produce and then publish their gender pay gap. It does this, in part, to pose questions to employers about why their figures look like they do. Perhaps there are good and satisfactory answers – but without the production of the data it may well be that they would never think to ask them. And the publication of the data serves another purpose – it forces them to care.

There is no reason why we should not produce equivalent data for judges. Sometimes the data will only serve the purpose of asking questions about outlier judges. If the data shows that a particular judge is more likely to arrive at a particular outcome than their judicial colleagues, shouldn't they know? Might it help them gain awareness of the possibility of biases in their conduct? Might that data form part of the interrogation of whether they should be promoted up the judicial ladder?

Kick their tyres, and well-worn aphorisms about the law often reveal themselves to be expressions of what Antonio Gramsci would have called the cultural hegemony. They are part of the way in which those with power hold it to themselves and to their benefit. They amply justify Judith Shklar's acid observation that the 'rule of law' has:

> become just another one of those self-congratulatory rhetorical devices that grace the public utterances of Anglo-American politicians. No intellectual effort need therefore be wasted on this bit of ruling-class chatter.[15]

Those who would like to fend off that powerful criticism (I count myself amongst them) do so best by muscular engagement with what the law and judges do, and how and why, rather than an intellectually demeaning mixture of Victorian paternalism and thoughtless indignation. If the conduct of the law is to remain more than empty performance of our own sense of virtue these questions cannot be dodged.

I would also say this. There is a surprising pessimism embedded in the idea that the sky will fall in if lawyers take the same muscular approach to scrutiny of justice as is done in other institutions.

By and large, I think the legal profession is a good one. I am very proud to be a barrister. I am very proud to be a King's Counsel. I know how diligently most of us work to address disadvantage in the ways in which we recruit. I don't think we're incapable of solving the problem.

But we need to start by acknowledging that we have one.

PART TWO
Fighting Back

5. Setting Up Good Law Project

I arrived in England in 1989, aged 17, having grown up in Fiji and New Zealand. I had been brought up in a house in which my adoptive father had taught beekeeping and organic gardening at the local polytech, and my mother was an occasional supply teacher but had mostly relinquished her career to bring up me and my three younger siblings.

I arrived knowing literally no one and moved into an abandoned, not literally because people lived in it, but abandoned all the same, former pit village called Highfield, not too far from Tyneside. 'Aunty' Betty and her husband, and sons, made generous space for me in their home and in the Rowlands Gill Working Men's Club where, unforgettably, I first drank Newcastle Brown Ale. And Betty got me a job at Fenwick's in Newcastle – as a boy I worked in the stereo department, she was in linens – for which I was paid £77 a week, just over £3 an hour gross, which also happened to be about my return daily bus fare.

Several months later, I met my biological father – ex-Eton, ex-Balliol – then working as readings editor at the BBC. I stayed a number of times in the large detached house where he lived with his wife and children in Teddington. I remember sitting in the kitchen, before anyone else had risen, and listening to Radio 4 broadcasting to a nation that was not the one where I lived in Highfield.

Shuttling backwards and forwards on the National Express bus between Teddington and Highfield, I learned that there were two Englands, each of which had as much in common with New Zealand, 12,000 miles away, as with one another. The England of my father in 1989 had no interest in the England of Highfield and, given you can still buy a house in Highfield for under £100k, I doubt the story today is any different. Britain is a poor country with some very rich people, as John Burn-Murdoch observed in the *Financial Times*.[1]

I remember my first experience with the English education system – visiting Hatfield College at Durham University for an interview and attending a late term 'formal' in academic gowns and suit. I couldn't tie a tie but my peers who could, the first students I had met since moving to England, threw food at one another and fell asleep, drunk, at the dinner table.

During that period, my first years in England, I saw, without being invested in them, how things worked, and didn't work, and why. I saw them with the clarity of youth and the distance of an outsider. And what I saw was a class of people who had no contact with, or interest in, the lives lived in that other England. They might, occasionally, perform acts of concern, penances, in faint discharge of perceived obligation. But the imperative was to scratch a moral itch rather than to improve anyone's life.

As I studied, and graduated, and became a barrister and then a silk, the immediacy faded. As my income grew my ability to transport myself into the lives of the people I had met in the Working Men's Club in Rowlands Gill shrank. It became harder and harder and I was the lesser for it and I knew it.

When, briefly, I contemplated trying to be an MP I was a rarity: I was that person who wanted a seat *outside* of London. I knew I had forgotten too much and that I needed to remember.

I am reduced now to the fumes of anger at that division – but I try to hold them in my lungs to power the work that Good Law Project does and the choices it makes.

Perhaps the most important decision we made was not to become a charity.

Charitable status is hugely advantageous. There are a number of foundations whose raison d'être is the sustaining of the gently progressive think-tank sector but who by and large will only fund charities. Charitable status protects you from tax burdens – such as VAT and business rates – that non charities must bear. And, perhaps most importantly of all, it's much cheaper to give money to a charity. It costs an additional-rate taxpayer 55p to put a pound in the pocket of a charity. But it would cost him – they're usually hims – a pound to put a pound in ours. So being a charity increases your income from foundations, increases your income from taxpayers, and decreases your own tax burden.

It also, quite understandably, connotes respectability. It never feels dangerous – donating to a charity from company funds, or platforming a charity on the BBC, or working with a charity if you want to give your time. These factors drive many new organisations to seek charitable status. The status is, looking in from the outside, a warm hearth and a welcoming smile.

But it wasn't right for us.

I believe in regulation. Regulation causes you to become more thoughtful about the actions you take. And it challenges you to act in the public interest.

That's not an empty assertion – you can see it from our actions. When we set up our own law firm, Good Law Practice, we could have taken advantage of the statutory loophole that enables not-for-profits to have in-house law firms without those law firms being regulated. But we didn't because we thought the firm would benefit from initial, and indeed ongoing, regulation.

When Dominic Cummings tried to crowdsource a referral of my conduct to my professional regulator, the Bar Standards Board, I tweeted out his call and encouraged anyone who thought I had breached my professional standards to contribute to his efforts.

But regulatory lines are not always clear. They require that you engage thoughtfully with the principles those lines protect. And that you do so trusting your regulator to do the same.

In my many years as a campaigner, and as a regulated barrister, I have been investigated twice: once in relation to the interview I gave to Professor Lavery (see Chapter Four) and once after the prorogation case (Chapter Seven) when I talked about having been given inside information about Boris Johnson's plans to prorogue Parliament. Both investigations led to no action being taken. I also referred myself to the BSB after tweeting about killing a fox (see Chapter One), but it decided to stand behind the RSPCA investigation. During this time, I have been subject to hundreds, likely thousands, of complaints but I have always felt able to trust my regulator.

But regulation involves having a regulator. And the Charity Commission is not or is not principally a regulator.

It's a matter of public record that the Runnymede Trust, whose charitable objects include understanding and educating people about racism, was investigated by the Charity Commission after, alongside us, it successfully challenged the Government's failure to have regard for the under-representation of Black and disabled people in the senior ranks of the civil service.[2] So too was Mermaids, who also worked with us to challenge the charitable status of an organisation granted charitable status for its activities attacking trans people. Other charities that have worked with us privately report similar experiences. They are being warned off.

I have also worked privately with impactful charities assisting refugees who the Charity Commission seems to have set out to destroy for what seem to me to be trivial and formalistic transgressions.

Meanwhile, it ignores the toxicity spread in the name of 'education' by ideological allies of the Government, like the Policy Exchange, and the Big Oil advocacy done by the global warmers at the Global Warming Policy Foundation.

It is no longer just a watchdog of the public interest, it is also a guard dog of the Government's. And when these roles conflict it is the latter that seems to win out.

We also wanted Good Law Project to be impactful – we wanted to change what Government did.

And here I return to the Good Chap, first discussed in Chapter Two.

So much of civil society in the UK is constructed around the notion that Government endorses some conception of the public interest. We have endless think tanks writing papers and holding conferences about what will make the world better. They are an output that traditional funders like to fund – projects with low political risk and that only require funders to commit themselves to short-time horizons.

But what if that notion is bunk? What if the Good Chap is not ascendant? What if he is now the school swot who sits, ignored, in the corner? What if the public interest has been cuckooed by a government of self-interest, whose purpose is to perpetuate its own power? Its choices of what to do, its narratives and policies and resource allocation, its whole mode of being, day-to-day and long-term, driven by how it is perceived by actual or potential voters. It would be, to borrow Sidney Blumenthal's phrase, a government in permanent campaign mode whose policy choices are driven by regular polling.

How would you cause that government to act or be different? For a government like that, appeals to or descriptions of the public interest won't do the job. They are like trying to coax your printer back to life by reading it poetry.

There is only one language a government in campaigning mode speaks – the language of political pain. Less carrot, more stick. We thought our best chance of influencing how Government acted, of having an impact, was to threaten the popularity of its actions, to try and shift how parts of the public think about an issue.

To do this we needed to be able to speak our diagnosis clearly and plainly. If you want to reach those outside the British establishment you cannot use its politely coded language. You need to campaign in a way that resonates with the electorate rather than policy-makers.

We also wanted to do things differently. To be free to follow the political agenda. And these were never things the Charity Commission was going to be comfortable with. We have a long way to go before we can pretend to have executed our strategy. But we have made a start.

During the Brexit years – from when I established the Good Law Project website in early 2017 with the help of some interns, until the end of 2019 – the institutional infrastructure of Good Law Project was modest. We had no employees, although I briefly had the benefit of a brilliant researcher, Jenna Corderoy, now a reporter at openDemocracy. You can read about the work I did during those years in Chapters Six and Seven.

In mid-2019, struggling with the triple burden of maintaining the vestiges of my practice as a tax lawyer, running the Brexit litigation, and trying to develop Good Law Project into something that was more than a name and a Twitter account, I eventually allowed my board to persuade me that I really did need to find a chief operating officer.

Some act of the gods caused our advertisement to catch the eye of a Palestinian refugee who had come to the UK by way of Lebanon and Cyprus, Siham Bortcosh. Her reward for joining us was, in addition to a modest day rate, being handed the keys to the Good Law Project's organisational superstructure, which consisted of a bank account – whose debit and credit entries represented the entirety of our financial record-keeping – a website and whatever I could fish out from my busy email accounts.

She successfully negotiated the competing needs for us to begin to professionalise the organisation whilst minimising the additional burden on me and she enabled us to embark on the financial planning that would help the organisation to employ staff and grow.

I also hired one of the foremost talents to emerge from the training ground for digital campaigning that is 38 Degrees, Trish Murray. The money to employ her and Siham had come from the income generated by the almost 2,000 direct debits I had managed to build up in the three years since starting

Good Law Project in 2017. We had, when she joined us, something like £100,000 in our bank account and an income of £180,000 per annum – not nearly enough to support the organisation I planned for us to be.

We employed Trish on a year's contract at a fair salary that we wouldn't be able to afford for ever: 'Spend like we'll succeed,' I told her, 'and if we do we'll be able to make your contract permanent.' She made a further hire in her team, Andreea Atudorei, and I hired a legal director, Gemma Abbott, whose legal nous and campaigning instincts I had spotted from her campaigning initiatives for free period products in schools.

We had, to borrow Jim Collins' evocative phrase, got the right people on the bus, but we needed to work out where we were going.

At the start of 2020, I was dealing with the aftermath of my fox tweet. This involved liaising with my professional regulator – the tweet and the resultant media coverage had sparked what I was later told was a record number of complaints to the long-suffering staff of the Bar Standards Board – and a lengthy and dispiriting process with the RSPCA, whose exuberant social media team had created a demand that its prosecutorial team was struggling, despite multiple detailed forensic reports on the body of the unfortunate fox, to meet.

Meanwhile Good Law Project was having to remake itself in the aftermath of Brexit. The series of cases we had brought to try and enhance parliamentary control of Brexit – working alongside the brave Gina Miller to win a vote for Parliament on whether to trigger the Article 50 process, winning the right for Parliament to revoke the Article 50 notice if it wanted, reinforcing that the prime minister was subject to the will of Parliament by forcing him to send the request for an extension required by the so-called Benn Act, and joining forces with Ms Miller once again to thwart the prime minister's unlawful suspension of Parliament – had come to an abrupt end with the huge majority won by Boris Johnson in the 2019 general election.

We decided to try and use the model we had learned in the environmental space. With some two-year funding from Dale Vince, the noted environmental entrepreneur, we hired an 'Ecotricity Fellow' who became our first employee: Gabriella de Souza Crook.

One of the jobs we asked Gabriella to do was survey the field to identify some environmental litigation we might bring. She introduced me to a barrister specialising in environmental law, Alex Goodman, who floated the prospect that we might challenge some planning guidance that tilted the playing field in favour of carbon-emitting energy infrastructure projects and against renewable energy infrastructure: the very opposite of what a government that wanted to tackle climate change would have produced.

I was able to persuade the environmental campaigners George Monbiot and Dale Vince to be co-claimants with Good Law Project in a judicial review of the policy, and we were away.

But this was an action rather than a programme. And we were still trying to find our way when the pandemic hit in spring 2020.

One of the first steps Government took was to close schools.

It very quickly became clear that their doors would remain shut well into – if not for the duration of – the summer term.

The Government's plan was that lessons would shift online. But the problem was that Gavin Williamson, then Education Secretary, had made no arrangements for the million or so children, almost exclusively from lower-income families, who would be left behind because they were sharing a tablet or laptop with siblings or parents who also found themselves working from home, or who didn't have a device or home internet access at all.

It was unthinkable to us that students from those families, already the most educationally disadvantaged, should fall further behind. If teaching online was to replace that in classrooms, all children should have access to it, both devices and home internet, whether their parents were wealthy or not. We identified an obligation in the Education Act on local authorities to provide a suitable education for children, whether inside or outside school. And it also occurred to us that, given Gavin Williamson had directed that schools be closed, imposing a fresh burden on local authorities, he should at least consider whether to share that burden.

We instructed lawyers, Caoilfhionn Gallagher QC, Adam Wagner and Dan Rosenberg, and on 9 April 2020 wrote to the minister threatening to bring proceedings. After several rounds of correspondence, he committed to investing around £85 million, and providing 200,000 laptops, to try and ensure that the most disadvantaged children didn't fall behind in their education whilst schools were closed. This was the first of a number of successful legal interventions around children and schools during the pandemic.

Generous and largely successful though the Government's package for furloughed workers was, it still left a number of families struggling to make ends meet. The qualification rules excluded large numbers. Its structure created some risks – without financial rewards – for those who engaged casual labour. And it was less generous to the self-employed.

The Office for National Statistics reported that 2.6 million households were struggling to cover expenses such as energy and food. And we knew from other research that hundreds of thousands of children were having to skip meals because their families could not afford food.[3]

The Government recognised the scale of the problem when it introduced a food voucher scheme so that children in England who had been eligible for free lunches at school could continue to get one at home. It meant children could receive at least one decent meal a day when schools closed during the COVID-19 lockdown. But the Government ruled out continuing the food voucher scheme over the summer holidays.

Again, we instructed lawyers, and again we took the first formal step in legal proceedings against Government and, again, Government folded, this time after the charismatic England footballer Marcus Rashford intervened in the public debate.

Our third intervention in relation to Covid and schools was in relation to the A levels fiasco.

Following the cancellation of exams in 2020 because of the pandemic, Gavin Williamson chose to issue A level results based not on how well a teacher thought a student would do but instead on the basis of an algorithm. This wasn't a problem per se – the problem was the assumptions made by the algorithm.

It assumed that a school's A level results in 2020 would match those achieved by the school in previous years. The result was that a brilliant pupil in an underperforming school – very often an underperforming state school – would be punished for the school's past poor performance. And a weak student in an over-performing school – very often a private school – would be pulled up by the school's success in previous years.

In summary, it tended to punish outstanding kids from poorer families and reward mediocre students from richer ones. This was an appalling outcome in a country with one of the lowest levels of social mobility in the developed world.[4]

The stories of how the algorithm was misfunctioning started to emerge on the Thursday after results came out. We were staying with my in-laws in France between lockdowns and on the Friday we drove the seven hours back to the Channel Tunnel to get into the UK before the borders closed again.

I swapped driving shifts with Claire as we went so that I could take calls with the lawyers on speakerphone. I arrived home that evening just in time to brief the *Sunday Times* and *Observer*. The following morning we put up our crowdfunding page, attaching our letter before action, and began a media blitz – speaking to more or less every major news outlet and broadcaster in the country. The Sunday papers were packed with heart-breaking stories of students who had worked incredibly hard against the odds and been downgraded by the algorithm from high predicted grades to incompletes or fails.

On Monday Gavin Williamson folded, again.

This work, and the work I describe in Chapter Nine tackling sleazy pandemic procurement, persuaded the public that there was life for Good Law Project after Brexit.

On 1 January 2020, we had zero employees. By spring 2023 we will have more than forty, including those employed by the independent law firm, Good Law Practice, which we set up in summer 2022.

We also exercise an important public function in trying to cause, inasmuch as our constitution enables it, a government with little respect for the rule of law to act within it nevertheless.

The standing threat of litigation undoubtedly improves governance. Problems we have highlighted have been taken up by the National Audit Office and internal government reviews. And the Government lawyers, troubled by the ethical decay around them, who apply to join us tell us that the fact of our existence means ministers who would once have acted without regard for the law are now forced to reflect on how their conduct would be viewed by the Courts.

We also publish our impact.

On our website is a list of all the cases we have ever brought together with their outcomes, legal and campaigning.[5] At the time of writing, our transparent assessment (we show our workings) of legal outcomes is that 45 per cent are wins, 20 per cent are mixed, and 35 per cent are losses. Our assessment of campaigning outcomes is that 45 per cent are wins and 20 per cent have delivered some real campaigning advantages. Of 47 cases where we think we can specify a legal or campaigning outcome, 68 per cent (32 cases) are successes and only 9 per cent (4 cases) are losses.

There are no direct comparables. But, as a baseline, Government statistics show that the proportion of judicial review claimants over the last six years who had judgments in their favour in Court was at its highest 5.2 per cent (2019), and at its lowest 2.2 per cent (2021).

It's far from perfect as a measure of success. We could easily change it in our favour by choosing easier cases to fight. But that would mean relinquishing impact for the appearance of success. That's not what we're about. Nevertheless, however you assess it our success rate does well against that baseline.

But the better metric is the frequency and aggression of the attacks directed against us by Government ministers. Of the present holders of the so-called four great offices of State, I have been targeted by three: the Home Secretary, the Foreign Secretary and the prime minister. During his run for the Conservative leadership, Rishi Sunak sent out a furious press release naming me ten times.

If we were failing, they wouldn't direct their fire at us.

Key to our success is our funding. Our funding comes overwhelmingly from tens of thousands of small donations. More than 60,000 people made a donation to us in our last financial year and we have around 30,000 regular givers who make a donation to us every month. This funding model is enormously powerful. If we were a political party, our 'subscription' income would be the second biggest in the country behind only the Labour Party.

It means we can plan over the long-term. We can invest in infrastructure which is important but might take many years to bear fruit. We can chase political impact over time horizons that are longer than a general election cycle. We can hire staff without having to worry about whether there will be money to employ them when a 'grant' runs out.

Very little of our funding is what accountants call 'restricted' income. Most larger slugs of income – the type that small- and medium-sized charities tend to rely on – come with strings attached. The donor gives the charity money to deliver a programme of work that it has specified and would like to fund. The work is within your purposes, but it may not be right at the heart of how you think you can bring about change.

But the regular giving numbers also represent a more subtle kind of power. The fact of larger donors making up such a small proportion – a single-digit percentage – of our income means that we can speak clearly and without fear. There is no single donor on which we have any meaningful financial dependence and who we need to be wary of offending. That diverse pool of funders gives us freedom of speech. We are able to speak in ways that resonate clearly with audiences whose ears have become accustomed to the muffled sound of triangulating politicians, or think tanks who need to retain the ear of Government, or charities mindful of whether their funders might find objectionable a full-throated diagnosis.

Support in this form both funds the organisation but also creates the conditions in which we can thrive. I am proud that we are people-powered, because it feels like a vindication of the choices that we are making. It feels to me to be symbiotic: the freedom we have to speak and the support we attract by using that freedom.

But it also brings complexity.

Because we are not a charity with narrowly defined objectives, we have to ask ourselves constantly what we are for. We also don't have the simple logic of businesses that exist to maximise their profits. We have to make decisions about how we allocate resources and about whether we are getting value for the people who donate to us. And we have to do all of this in a world in which Government is putting huge pressure on the Courts to stop us.

We try and meet these challenges by fostering a relationship of respect and trust with people who fund us. And by listening to our other stakeholders – including our staff team, the communities we try to help, and the rest of the campaigning ecology.

We recognise an obligation to be transparent about why we do what we do. We value the accountability that comes with transparency: we believe it sharpens our thinking and it makes us better. We also recognise that the act of articulating what we are for – and the transparency and accountability it promotes – is a way that we can distribute power that might otherwise too readily accumulate in my hands.

But we're not going to please everyone and we don't aspire to. There are plenty of organisations around doing the job of gentle persuasion. There is space for that model – although if my thesis of permanent campaigning is right too much of civil society is clustered in a world that no longer exists – but a healthy campaigning ecology also has space for others. We're set up to do something different – to speak, plainly and without fear, the truth of what we see.

I get criticism from unsurprising places. The fact that the newspapers of Murdoch and Rothermere and the Barclay Brothers attack us is a sign of our success.

But we get a lot of criticism from liberal voices too.

If your work is very consciously about challenging structures of power which you think are failing you will make people inside those structures, or who serve them, or who they benefit, uncomfortable. They will feel threatened and, initially at least, angry. And the fact of who they are means they have voices which they will raise against you.

I haven't used 'liberal voices' as a synonym for 'those who voted Liberal Democrat in 2019', but it is genuinely extraordinary that the YouGov polling we commissioned on trust in judges shows Lib Dem voters as having (of any segment polled) the highest trust in judges, teachers, civil servants, doctors, lawyers and police officers. Every single profession we asked about, in a huge sample of 4,687 adults, Lib Dem voters trusted more than any other segment in society.[6]

Those people are going to find it especially challenging to hear that things aren't working well.

Of course, I get stuff wrong. But even criticism from moderate voices can be a feature rather than a bug.

In 2018, I wrote an article for the *New Statesman* about the epidemic of sexual violence against women and the failures of the criminal justice system effectively to deter it:

> A full fifth of women have been sexually assaulted since turning 16. Well over a million have been raped or 'assaulted by penetration' (including attempts).
>
> And the tragedy that is rape does not end when the crime is done. The physical act merely fires the starting gun. Two thirds of women who are raped suffer mental or emotional problems as a result. Half have difficulty trusting people or in relationships. One in ten attempt suicide. But these, although large, are only numbers. And each of those numbers is a woman.[7]

And I argued that a system constructed around the (unexamined) assertion that it was 'better for ten guilty men to escape than one innocent man to suffer' was one that could and should be interrogated:

> It is better, of course, for the guilty men. But it is worse for the women whose lives are destroyed by rapes that only happen because of a system that convicts in one in 56 [cases] or fewer. We must weigh on the scales both the tragedy endured by a tiny number of men wrongly convicted of rape, but also the tragedy of the huge numbers of women whose rapes would be prevented if our system more effectively deterred rape. We must engage with that balance.

I also took my own profession to task:

> We lobby against changes to the status quo. We assert a unique expertise that excludes other voices. But we do not use that expertise to design positive change.

The piece attracted a lot of attention – partly in consequence of it being tweeted out by Michael Gove, who was Environment Secretary at the time and a former Lord Chancellor. But a heavy proportion of the attention, much from within my profession, was enormously hostile. And not just or even principally hostile to the arguments – it was very, very personal.

The attacks weren't sourced from a belief that the outcomes the criminal justice system as a whole delivered were right. Indeed, many of my colleagues who attacked me were clear that they were not. It was more that people were hostile to the idea that the system they worked in might not be a good one.

The dynamic felt very familiar, as I remembered how the tax profession had reacted when Margaret Hodge MP, as Chair of the Public Accounts Committee, and Richard

Murphy and others, including me, walking in their footsteps, had challenged its large-scale facilitation of tax avoidance.

But you have to believe that change does come if there are organisations with platforms, like Good Law Project, who are willing to ask fundamental questions and take the flack.

6. Taking On the Brexit Goliath

Time has not diminished my astonishment at the scale of democratic failure around the Brexit vote.

Parliament legislated to hold a referendum, without any constitutional safeguards, because it was advisory. It was not meant to be binding. This is what MPs were told in a briefing note prepared for them by the House of Commons library:

> This Bill requires a referendum to be held on the question of the UK's continued membership of the European Union (EU) before the end of 2017. It does not contain any requirement for the UK Government to implement the results of the referendum, nor set a time limit by which a vote to leave the EU should be implemented. Instead, this is a type of referendum known as pre-legislative or consultative, which enables the electorate to voice an opinion which then influences the Government in its policy decisions.[1]

Note those words – 'influences the Government in its policy decisions'.

The same point was also made by the Conservative Party's David Lidington during debates on the legislation that enacted the referendum. Rejecting the need for an amendment that would redefine a leave vote as being one with a majority in each of England, Wales, Scotland and Northern Ireland, he said it:

does not make sense in the context of the Bill. The legislation is about holding a vote; it makes no provision for what follows. The referendum is advisory, as was the case for both the 1975 referendum on Europe and the Scottish independence vote last year. In neither of those cases was there a threshold for the interpretation of the result.[2]

Lidington was the Europe minister at the time.

Referendums in Australia, for example, have a 'double lock' on changes to the constitution. They must achieve a majority of voters as a whole, and a majority in a majority of states. Closer to home, the referendums on devolution in Scotland and Wales in 1979 had a requirement that 40 per cent of *all* electors should vote in favour of change.

This is what grown-up governments do before they make profound constitutional change: they ask for a stronger mandate than a simple majority.

Super-majorities or double locks are just an example of the types of safeguard legislation enacting a binding referendum would contain. You'd also expect to find provisions discouraging cheating – lying or overspending. Speaking about cheating in a mayoral election, our own Elections Court has said:

> In elections, as in sport, those who win by cheating have not properly won and are disqualified. Nor is it of any avail . . . to say 'I would have won anyway' because cheating leads to disqualification whether it was necessary for the victory or not.[3]

The purpose of these provisions – which tend to be tightly drawn – isn't to provide a losers' charter. It is to improve the quality of the campaign around the vote. They safeguard elections for a local councillor – but they were stripped out of the legislation enacting the EU referendum in 2016.

If you overspend in a general election campaign that's an 'illegal practice' (see section 76 of the Representation of the People Act 1983). If illegal practices 'may be reasonably supposed to have affected the result' the election is void (see section 164 of that same Act). The European Union Referendum Act 2015 made provision for regulations. And those regulations made provision for some of the protections in the 1983 Act to be carried over into the referendum. But they made no provision to carry over section 164.

Forgive me, I know this is geeky, but it's also important. The summary is, there were greater legal protections in place to ensure the process for electing your local councillor is fair than there were for leaving the European Union.

And this didn't just create the conditions for electoral misconduct. It actively encouraged it.

Both the official Vote Leave campaign and the unofficial Leave.EU campaigns committed serious breaches of the rules around referendum spending. (Such was the political climate that the so-called elections watchdog, the Electoral Commission, refused to investigate the breaches by Vote Leave. It took a judicial review I brought wearing my Good Law Project hat before it agreed to investigate Vote Leave.[4] It duly found serious breaches – but because the safeguards had been stripped out all it could do was levy a fine.[5])

The Venice Convention on Good Practice on Referendums (to which the United Kingdom was a signatory) states that: 'In the event of a failure to abide by the statutory requirements, for instance if the cap on spending is exceeded by a significant margin, the vote may be annulled.'[6]

But in UK law there was no such sanction – because this was not a referendum that was intended to bind Parliament.

These absences are very likely to have shaped the very close outcome. Certainly Leave campaigners took full advantage of them. In a leaked email, Steve Baker MP wrote to his colleagues at Vote Leave that:

> The designated campaign will be permitted to spend £7m . . . It is open to the Vote Leave family to create separate legal entities each of which could spend £700k: Vote Leave will be able to spend as much money as is necessary to win the referendum.[7]

He had not found a loophole. This conduct was unlawful. But it was exactly what Vote Leave went on to do – unlawfully, as the Electoral Commission eventually found.

The absence of safeguards was not the only governance failure in the conduct of the referendum. The electorate was also invited to vote for a blank sheet of paper which bore only a brilliant, if empty, slogan ('Take Back Control').

The 1975 referendum on EU membership was held *after* the re-negotiated terms of the UK's membership had been agreed with the EU and the terms set out in a White Paper and agreed by Parliament. This made obvious sense. How could you ask the electorate to consent to major constitutional change without telling it what that change looked like?

How could you ask it to confront the hard choices that leaving involved – between ending free movement for others and ending it for ourselves, between enhancing sovereignty and the economic costs of doing so, between bringing power to Westminster but creating the conditions for the break-up of the United Kingdom?

Even leavers didn't know what Brexit meant. Vote Leave's director of strategy, Dominic Cummings, observed before the referendum that:

> Creating an exit plan that makes sense and which all reasonable people could unite around seems an almost insuperable task. Eurosceptic groups have been divided for years about many of the basic policy and political questions.[8]

The solution eventually adopted was to bake in contradictory promises about what Brexit meant because it was the only way to get 'consent' to leave over the line. But what did people consent to? No one knows.

None of this stuff is rocket science.

The need for clarity over the constitutional changes the electorate was being asked to vote on had been the position of the Conservative Party and leading campaigners for Brexit when confronted in the late 1990s with the legislation enacting the advisory referendums that led to the creation of the Scottish Parliament and the Welsh Assembly. William Hague (then leader of the opposition Conservative Party) argued in Parliament that:

> The central contention of the Opposition tonight is that referendums should be held, but they should be held when the electorate are in the best possible position to judge. They should be held when people can view all the pros and cons.[9]

He also noted that: 'It is one thing to use a referendum to give added legitimacy and final approval to a major change fully debated by Parliament, and quite another to use it to distort the parliamentary process and to bully those who object to it.' Voting with him, following those stirring words, were leading Brexiters David Davis, Liam Fox, John Redwood and Bill Cash. Another notable who voted with William Hague was Theresa May, whose best remembered contribution to delineating what the public had voted for in 2016 was 'Brexit means Brexit'.

You might also contrast what happened in the Brexit referendum with the decision made by the pro-independence side in the 2014 Scottish independence referendum to produce and publish a detailed strategy paper called 'Scotland's Future'.

The solution to the lack of any description of what people were voting on in 2016, or at least the solution which it was convenient to many Leave campaigners to advance during the referendum campaign, was that there should be a second referendum on the final deal. Over to Dominic Cummings again:

> As a matter of fact a NO vote does not mean we would immediately leave and it seems likely that the parties will be forced by public opinion to offer a second vote, and therefore this could be turned to the advantage of NO.[10]

He made the same point again in an interview with the *Economist*. Asked whether, in the event of an 'out' vote, the Government would seek to hold another referendum on the terms of Brexit, Cummings said:

> I think that is a distinct possibility, yes. It's obviously not something that we can force. We're a campaign group. But I think it is perfectly possible that leadership candidates to replace David Cameron will say that they think there are good grounds for a new government team to offer the

public a voice on what the deal looks like. And we obviously wouldn't oppose that, if that's what senior politicians want to offer. I think there's a strong democratic case for it.[11]

This was also Boris Johnson's position, as briefed to *The Times*: 'Johnson has told friends that a "no" vote is desirable because it would prompt Brussels to offer a much better deal, which the public could then support in a second referendum.'[12]

But all of this was quietly swept under the carpet in the aftermath of the result.

Lidington, who had said there was no need for safeguards because the referendum was advisory, changed his position: 'We all told the people in 2016 you're having the final say . . . I do worry about the harm that would be done to fragile public confidence in our democratic institutions.'[13]

The second referendum that Johnson and Cummings had used to tempt wavering voters before the vote was repackaged after the vote into a full-blooded democratic outrage. And the fact of Parliament having failed to adopt an amendment tabled by two backbench Conservative MPs to outlaw a second referendum was quickly forgotten.

It is, of course, perfectly legitimate to point by way of response to the promise contained in the leaflet distributed by the Government during the referendum campaign: 'The Government will implement what you decide.'

A lawyer would say that a promise made by an anonymous civil servant in a campaign leaflet is not binding on Parliament. It cannot create a legal obligation. In reality, how the campaign leaflet read was very likely to have been approved by Cameron or his team. But it is only one of the things, alongside the quality of the campaign, the nature of the deal and public support for it, that MPs ought to have taken into account in deciding what to do with the referendum outcome.

What Parliament really ought to have done was follow the Cummings/Johnson Plan One (strike a provisional deal and put it back to the people in a Deal or Remain vote) rather than the Cummings/Johnson Plan Two (having baited wavering voters with the offer of a second referendum, switch to smearing as anti-democratic voters who asked for the promise to be made good).

But although that Plan One, in the years following the referendum result, gathered huge support amongst the people, it was almost friendless amongst those with influence.

Theresa May, then PM, was clear that 'Brexit means Brexit'. Jeremy Corbyn, Leader of (on many things) the Opposition, urged 'Article 50 has to be invoked now' within hours of the result being declared.[14] Nick Robinson, former president of the Oxford University Conservative Association and presenter of the BBC's flagship news programme *Today*, said that 'The duty we broadcasters had to "broadly balance" the views of the two sides is at an end.'[15] And the other Fleet Street big hitters didn't even have to pretend to hide their enthusiasm for the Brexit project.

What to do?

The political force of the result – despite the profound failures in governance – was considerable. Writing on 24 June 2016, the day after the referendum, every bit as shell-shocked as Michael Gove and Boris Johnson looked in their now notorious broadcast interview, I said that:

The referendum result creates a *democratic* imperative for the UK to depart but . . . it doesn't create a *legal* one. The legal one follows not from the referendum result but from our decision to trigger the exit procedure in Article 50 . . . Some have mooted that our Parliament could simply ignore the referendum result. Although that may be right in legal theory I don't, myself, consider it a practical likelihood. But, what democracy has commanded shall be done it can also command to be undone. Or, to put the matter less grandly, a second vote, this time for Remain, would undo the democratic imperative of the first.[16]

And I slowly began to see the outline of a mirror strategy to that adopted by Leavers. They had used legal failures in the European Union Referendum Act 2015 to shape the politics of the vote to leave; perhaps legal successes might re-shape the politics after the result and deliver a vote to remain?

This was no easy thing to contemplate.

There had been a referendum and Leave had won. That was a political decision which judges could not overrule.

What's more, judges hate having to get involved in areas of political controversy – even where you can identify what are properly legal questions. They understand that their decisions will be misrepresented as political and that it can diminish public trust in judges.

Finally, although lawyers are great believers in process – 'good processes deliver good outcomes' is probably the core belief of public lawyers – the law is not set up to retrofit these after the event. Typically, judges confronted with a flawed process ask for it to be re-run, only better, but the machinery that might have enabled a re-run of the referendum was stripped out of the 2015 Act. So the decision of what to do with the outcome of the referendum was one Parliament had plainly intended to be for MPs and not for judges.

Over the course of the next six months, I developed a plan that involved working with the grain of the 2015 Act and using the law to try and create political room for MPs to do what they thought, over time, was in the national interest.

On the 27 June 2016, three of the country's leading constitutional scholars – Nick Barber, Tom Hickman and Jeff King – published what is undoubtedly the most influential legal blog in the nation's (short) history of legal blogs. It was called: 'Pulling the Article 50 "Trigger": Parliament's Indispensable Role'.[17]

Article 50 was the legal mechanism in the Lisbon Treaty by which a member state of the European Union could cease to be a member state. The process started, unsurprisingly enough, by notifying the EU of your intention to leave. In their blog, the three scholars argued that once you notified the EU that you wanted to leave it was pretty clear that there was no way back. Triggering Article 50 was like firing a bullet from a gun – there was no way to return the bullet to the chamber. It followed that the act of notifying would bring about changes to the United Kingdom, and the rights of its citizens, so radical as to require an Act of Parliament.

The EU rights we enjoyed in the UK we enjoyed by virtue of an Act of Parliament: the European Communities Act 1972. The fact of triggering Article 50 would, ran the argument, empty the Act of content. It would render it, by commencing a process that was bound to conclude with our withdrawal from the European Union, an empty vessel, a dead parrot. And the idea that the prime minister, by her or his action, might be able to empty an Act of Parliament of content suggested we were less democracy and more autocracy.

The point was brought into sharper focus still when you considered the context. David Cameron had already resigned as prime minister. The choice as to what to do would thus be made by someone chosen by members of the Conservative Party – not MPs – who had never asked the voters for consent. This added fuel to a blazing fire.

I didn't wait around.

On 28 June 2016, the day after the blog was published, I took legal advice on whether a case might be brought along the lines outlined in the blog. I instructed John Halford, a leading solicitor at Bindmans specialising in public law, and put up a crowdfunding page, my first ever, seeking to raise £10,000 for initial advice with individual donations capped at a maximum of £100.

Journalists were sceptical – but within a few hours we had raised the full amount.

On 8 July 2016, we wrote to the Government asking it to state whether it accepted that (1) notice under Article 50, once triggered, could not be reversed save with the agreement of the other member states; and (2) Article 50 could only be triggered by an Act of Parliament. And we set out our reasoning.

In the face of opposition from some within my legal team I published our letter to the Government. And I wrote to the 406 people who had contributed to the crowdfunder to explain why. The concern the legal team had expressed was that other possible litigants in an Article 50 case would be able to purloin the results of the legal research that the crowd-funders had paid for. What I said was:

> Wherever I can – and it won't always be possible but wher-ever I can – I will ensure that this all happens in the public domain. This is a really important moment in the life of our country and it's right that everyone gets to see what the law-yers are doing.

This level of transparency was unusual then and remains rela-tively unusual even today, partly for the reasons my team were concerned about but also because, culturally, lawyers shy away from publicity.

You can't always see around corners and there are bound to be instances where it will turn out that you would have been better off had you kept your cards close to your chest. But if you plan to be around for a while you also need to bake into your thinking that you will inevitably drop an egg from time to time. My experience is that people tend to be quite forgiv-ing of mistakes – if they can see your behaviour generally expresses values that align with theirs.

Transparency is one of the ways in which you can signal your values; there are others too, like quickly putting your hand up and apologising when you get stuff wrong. It hap-pens so infrequently these days that people find it rather dis-arming and you can sometimes emerge from an error in net credit.

But there was an even better reason, actually, to have adopted this stance. It's best expressed by the old line that 'It's amazing what you can accomplish if you do not care who gets the credit.' Would it really matter if other would-be claimants in the case we wanted to bring about Article 50 took the results of the work we had done and used it to make their case better?

It's not an easy motto to live by – getting credit for stuff is one of the ways in which we pay the bills – but in a world in which the problems are ever larger and feel more and more intractable there is a need for civil society to pull together.

In correspondence, Government refused to deal with the arguments we had raised – but ours was only one of a number of similar claims that had started in the meantime. And the Divisional Court – which would hear the cases first – had arranged a 'directions' hearing to sort everything out.

When I instructed John Halford I had asked him who we should use as our barrister. He was very clear that it should be Lord David Pannick QC. He called up David's clerk at Blackstone Chambers and was told: 'David has a piece in *The Times* on Thursday in which he expresses a view on the argument. Once you've read it, give me a call. Lord Pannick has had several approaches and he wants people to read his piece first.' At 7am on Thursday morning, John called David's clerk and was told he was already acting for Gina Miller.

At the directions hearing, it was clear that the Court wanted David to be the lead advocate and, hence, Ms Miller's became the lead case. She may not have known – certainly I didn't – quite how poisonous things would become. But she's a brave and formidable campaigner – and I don't think anyone could have handled what happened better than she did.

John was very clear that our case should continue – I had asked the question whether there was a point to us continuing given that the arguments were going to be put anyway, by

Gina Miller, through Lord Pannick. He was equally clear that I shouldn't be the claimant. So I busied myself finding, and introducing to him, a number of students who might be the claimants instead. Together they brought the case that became styled as the People's Challenge.

I was very new to this, and I hadn't worked out that, in agreeing to his request that I not be the claimant, I was relinquishing any control over the shape the litigation would take.

There were some big calls to make on how the litigation was handled and John, and the barrister he instructed – Helen Mountfield QC – had very clear views on what those should be. I tried to lobby the students directly on the politics, but it was very difficult for them to ignore the advice they were getting from John and Helen.

Politically, the picture was complicated.

Winning the case would give Parliament the power to do two things. The first was to decide whether or not to trigger Article 50. But given the mood of Parliament it was clear, or clear to me at any rate, that even if Gina Miller won Parliament would trigger Article 50.

So if your concern was to stop Brexit the case didn't really matter – even if it succeeded in court the case would make no difference. For my own part I thought – and said as much in media interviews – that if I had been an MP, I would have voted to trigger Article 50.

But the second thing the case represented was an opportunity for Parliament to tell the Government what sort of Brexit it should go for.

As I've explained, the official Leave campaign in the referendum had chosen not to do this, thinking that the best way to build a majority was not to confront people with the inevitable trade-offs. Nor had Parliament ever spoken on the subject, not in the EU Referendum Act or otherwise.

My thinking was that the question 'What does Brexit actually mean?' was one, really, that Parliament needed to grasp.

The binary formulation put to the electorate – 'Should the United Kingdom remain a member of the European Union or leave the European Union?' – skated over many branching futures offered up during the campaign: lower and not lower immigration, inside and not inside the single market, money spent and not spent on the NHS, retained and not retained regional investment and agricultural subsidies, and so on.

These, and the trade-offs between them, were profoundly important questions. But they were not put in the referendum; they figured in no election manifesto; no politician could claim a democratic mandate to answer them. And nor could a prime minister chosen by the private rules of the Conservative Party (David Cameron having resigned) claim any democratic mandate to decide them.

It felt to me like setting down some ground rules about the deal we should negotiate was something Parliament should – and just might be persuaded to – do, if the opportunity was given to it. There was certainly a lot of appetite amongst the public to have a say. An Ipsos MORI poll in late June 2016 asked whether 'There should be another General Election before negotiations start so that people can vote on political parties' plans for Britain's future relationship with the European Union.' Of those polled, 48 per cent agreed and only 23 per cent disagreed.

But there was another choice, too, in the litigation.

The weak link in the Barber/Hickman/King argument was the contention that triggering Article 50 was irreversible. If notifying the EU of our intention to leave started a chain reaction that made our departure inevitable then Ms Miller, and the various other claimants, were on strong ground. But if they were wrong and the notice of our intention to leave was reversible then the only legal effect of triggering Article 50 was to start a negotiation – at the end of which we could leave or remain.

Which view was right was a question of European law: ultimately it could only be answered by the European Court of Justice in Luxembourg (ECJ). There was provision for a UK court to 'refer' the question to Luxembourg and get an answer.

I began to think this was the best way forward.

If the answer was 'irreversible' we would probably win our case and it would be very clear to Parliament what it was authorising. If the answer was 'reversible' we would probably lose but, importantly, it would keep open into the future the question whether we would really leave. And MPs would have a chance to think and reflect.

Government faced much the same dilemma. If the Government argued in court that Article 50 could be reversed it was likely to win the Miller case and keep power in the hands of the prime minister. But if it lost, certainly if it lost because Article 50 was reversible, it would breathe new life into the Remain campaign by leaving the door ajar to our continued membership of the European Union for what might very well prove to be a lengthy period of time. (And as it turned out, it was not until 2020, three and a half years and two general elections after the referendum, that the issue was finally settled.)

Government served its written argument on 2 September. It seemed from their argument that the Government had come to the same conclusion: breathing new life into the Remain campaign would be worse for it than losing the case. And so it did not contend that Article 50 could be reversed.

I tried very hard to persuade people – John Halford, Lord Pannick, and those bringing other parallel claims – to ask the Divisional Court to refer the question to Europe. The fact Government wanted to close the door on the possibility of Parliament later changing its mind and deciding to remain made it even clearer to me that it was the best thing for those who, like me, were troubled by the way the referendum had been run. But I was blocked at every turn by people who were very focused on winning the case in front of them. I again tried to lobby the students who I had introduced to John Halford, but again was told how difficult it was for them to ignore the advice they were getting from John and Helen.

During the hearing, it became clear that the Court was also troubled by whether the notice under Article 50 was reversible.

At the time, it was perfectly possible to imagine a world in which the Court assumed Article 50 was irreversible, gave a decision that empowered Parliament to (for example) tell the prime minister that Brexit meant remaining in the single market, and the Government duly negotiated that outcome. If it later transpired that the notice could be reversed, the Court would, I would say illegitimately, have reshaped the course of history. Brexiters who didn't want membership of the single market would have been furious, and rightly so.

The problem for the Court was not a legal one – they were all top-drawer lawyers and could see everything that I could see and more besides. It was that they were not making this decision in a political vacuum. They were, no doubt, extremely worried about what it would mean to refer the question of whether the decision to leave the EU was reversible to Luxembourg.

The rule of law as it lives between the covers of books is an abstraction, oblivious to influence and power, indomitable. But in the world it is a living thing, and its gardeners are judges, who tend and conserve it in times of stress, lest it weaken or fail.

The Court's decision followed a couple of weeks later, in early November. The question of the reversibility of Article 50 was addressed in only a single line: 'Important matters in respect of Article 50 were common ground between the parties . . . a notice under Article 50(2) cannot be withdrawn, once it is given . . .'[18]

The eagle-eyed reader will note the judges themselves expressed no view on the key question, but on the substance the Court decided that:

> the Crown cannot through the exercise of its prerogative powers alter the domestic law of the United Kingdom and modify rights acquired in domestic law under the ECA 1972 or the other legal effects of that Act. We agree with the claimants that, on this further basis, the Crown cannot give notice under Article 50(2).

Ms Miller had won. What the judges had done, all they had done, was to choose who – a Parliament elected by the people or a prime minister elected under the private rules of the Conservative Party – should have the power to shape Brexit. Parliament would be given the opportunity to address the trade-offs that the Leave campaign had left unresolved.

But for the right-wing press this was an outrage.

'Who do EU think you are?' asked the *Sun*, whose proprietor's parties Conservative prime ministers attend. 'The Judges versus the People', roared the *Daily Telegraph*, then owned by two brothers who lived in a castle on their own private offshore tax haven. And, most notorious of all, the judges were 'Enemies of the People', warned Lord Rothermere's *Daily Mail*, echoing the language of the Third Reich in a manner it is hard to believe was accidental.[19] The man who wrote that *Daily Mail* article was James Slack, and he was soon appointed Theresa May's official spokesperson.

It took a full month for the Lord Chancellor, who had sworn an oath to defend the independence of the judiciary, to respond. What she, Liz Truss, said was this:

> The independence of the judiciary is the foundation upon which our rule of law is built and our judiciary is rightly respected the world over for its independence and impartiality. In relation to the case heard in the high court, the government has made it clear it will appeal to the supreme court. Legal process must be followed[.][20]

She did not condemn the attacks. Indeed, she did not even acknowledge that they had occurred. And she did not offer support to the judiciary – her statement suggested they had got their decision wrong.

All of this can hardly have calmed fears amongst judges that the media attempts to intimidate them had been tolerated – if not encouraged – by the Government. And what we later learned from appearances before a parliamentary select committee was that senior judges had, for the first time, been obliged to seek police protection.[21]

The Supreme Court heard the Government's appeal in December and on 24 January dismissed it by an eight to three majority.[22] It agreed with the decision that notifying under Article 50 required an Act. And it also found that the consent of the Assemblies or Parliaments of Wales, Scotland and Northern Ireland, which the Government had not sought, it did not need. The majority went further, describing, wrongly as it later transpired, the act of giving notice as irrevocable.

Three days later, the Government placed before Parliament the European Union (Notification of Withdrawal) Bill. Earlier that month, on 17 January 2017, Theresa May had given a speech at Lancaster House setting out, in a form that did not bind the Government, its negotiating position.[23]

She offered Parliament a vote on the deal the Government negotiated. This, it turned out, was enough. The various amendments tabled by the opposition parties in the Commons, including to protect the economic benefits of membership of the EU, to maintain EU standards on tackling tax avoidance and evasion, to have regard to the Good Friday Agreement and to protect the rights of EU citizens, all failed.

As it happened, winning the case turned out to be somewhat unhelpful to those who wanted to remain within the EU. Later, much later, the wheels began to fall off Theresa May's government and then Boris Johnson's first government, and a second referendum or revocation began to feel politically possible. But Leavers were able to point to the fact that Parliament, believing Article 50 could not be revoked, had nevertheless voted to 'pull the trigger' on our departure from the EU. Had Theresa May triggered Article 50 herself, the inevitable consequence of the Miller case losing, Remainers would have instead been able to say that the source of supreme power in our constitution, Parliament, had never authorised us to leave.

The victory in the Supreme Court compelled Parliament, at a moment when the referendum result was still fresh, before the sunlit uplands with no conceivable downside of Brexit were exposed as a mirage, to translate the political mandate of a flawed advisory referendum into a legal mandate.

It forced a decision at the very worst time.

It's impossible to know, when you start a case, how the world will change around it. Neither the prime minister who resisted the argument that Parliament should decide, nor the newspapers that attacked judges for their finding, expected that the result would come to be cited as adding constitutional credibility to the decision to Leave. Although it had become clear to me that Parliament would vote to Leave, hence my attempt to pivot to the question of whether a decision to Leave was irrevocable, I too had not foreseen any longer-term consequences of winning the right for Parliament to vote. If there are broader lessons to be drawn from this they will have to be drawn by others. I cannot see beyond the chess adage that it is wise, when ahead, to simplify, and when behind, to complicate.

But still, I wanted to leave the door ajar for Parliament to change its mind.

Article 50 allowed for up to two years of negotiations after being triggered.

Two years is a long time in politics. Any number of things might happen to cause voters, or Parliament, to reassess whether leaving the EU really was in the national interest. There might be another democratic event to undo the first, a general election or a further referendum. Perhaps Theresa May would find it impossible to negotiate a good deal with the EU. The politics might change in any number of ways. Would it serve the national interest if MPs were legally obliged to go ahead no matter what?

Why make a decision now – if you can make it later, when you have more information? I wanted to create a clearly marked off-ramp, for all to see.

After an early abortive attempt in the Courts in Dublin, I found the right legal team in Scotland.

It was led by Aidan O'Neill QC, a great grumpy bear of a man, but a brave and tenacious lawyer, and a Queen's Counsel in the legal systems of both England and Wales and Scotland. He was a man who delighted in taking on the establishment. At Aidan's suggestion, I instructed as solicitor Elaine Motion, the chair of Balfour + Manson, and one of Edinburgh's great legal operators.

The petitioners were me and three members of the Scottish Parliament – Andy Wightman, Ross Greer and Catherine Stihler; two members of the European Parliament – Alyn Smyth and David Martin; and the Westminster MP Joanna Cherry. In November 2017, we wrote to David Davis MP, then the Secretary of State for Exiting the European Union.

The EU had already signalled it would be possible for the UK to reverse its decision to leave if it wanted to – but that it would require the consent of all of the other member states. The consensus view amongst the great and the good of the

Remain campaign was that matters should be left there: it was always possible to find a political consensus with the EU and there was a risk of making our position worse: perhaps the ECJ would follow the view expressed by our Supreme Court – that you couldn't revoke under any circumstances – and close a door that was just about ajar.

But I saw things very clearly.

It's the chess adage, again: simplify when you're ahead and complicate when you're behind. Remain was very much behind – and I didn't see how a conservative, low-risk approach was going to turn things around. I thought it would just guarantee failure.

I was also very focused on what the world would look like if the politics changed such that revoking the notice and remaining became a political possibility. If that world did not eventuate then nothing I could do would matter. But if it did come to pass, and Brexiters were compelled to talk about the possibility that we might Remain, it seemed highly likely that they would try and poison the well of public opinion by asserting that, even if we went cap in hand to the EU, consent would come with strings attached: we would have to give up our opt-outs or rebate, if we remained we'd have 'an even worse deal'. On the other hand, if we had the right to revoke our Article 50 notice – if we could revoke without needing permission – we could avoid those attack lines.

The other point was more abstract but also, I thought, even more important.

For revocation to become a political possibility there had to be a change in the way the country looked at Brexit. Instead of barrelling down a corridor with only one exit, we needed to understand that there were alternatives. We needed to start to think that, at the end of everything, we would face a T-junction and we could choose either course. We could accept whatever deal was on the table or we could reject it and remain.

Either way, we needed collectively to understand and understand clearly that remaining in the EU was possible.

Revocation would only be a possibility if the politics changed – but the knowledge that revocation was possible might help change those politics. And when it came to changing the politics there was, I thought, a huge difference between *maybe* being able to revoke and *certainly* being able to revoke.

But I still needed to find a way to position the case.

There was real scepticism amongst the remain-supporting public that the case would ever matter. Despite the weakening of Theresa May's position in the 2017 general election, most people at the time thought that Brexit was a done deal. What I eventually settled upon was the idea of putting power into Parliament's hands. When the time came for Parliament to assess the deal, in the meaningful vote Theresa May had promised in her Lancaster House speech, MPs needed to have all options on the table, not to be constrained in their assessment of where the national interest lay.

Why would MPs not want this?

The legal argument in the case – what we would say to the court in Luxembourg about why the Lisbon Treaty gave to the UK the right to change its mind – was not straightforward. And the fear that we might lose and the ECJ declare that it was not possible to remain – even with the permission of the other member states – was what had turned many other

Remain campaigners against the idea. But I thought we had the better argument.

Article 50 did not deal explicitly with a member state who gave notice of their intention to leave and then changed its mind. All it said was that: 'Any Member State may decide to withdraw from the Union in accordance with its own constitutional requirements.' You just had to notify the Union of your intention to do so. And if you did:

> The Treaties shall cease to apply to the State in question from the date of entry into force of the withdrawal agreement or, failing that, two years after the notification . . . unless the European Council, in agreement with the Member State concerned, unanimously decides to extend this period.

The argument against us, a point that had been briefed out to the media by the governments of Italy, the Netherlands, Germany and elsewhere, was that if the United Kingdom could unilaterally revoke, that would shift the balance of power to the UK in the negotiations. It would mean the UK could extend the two-year time frame stipulated in the treaty by revoking at one year and eleven months and then re-notifying.

Superficially, this was attractive. Superficially, it found support in the language of Article 50. But my argument was that the law could not be understood as some abstract concept, isolated from reality. It operated in the real world. And in the real world the concern was not a valid one.

A decision to leave (or, indeed, a decision to reverse your decision to leave) would always be a real decision made in a real-world context. It would be clear from the facts that you had made a real decision to leave. In our case, we'd had a referendum and then Parliament had voted to implement the result. That decision to leave was a real decision.

Some possible future decision to revoke would also be made in the real world. It would be a real decision to revoke. It would be abundantly clear from the factual context of the decision to revoke – likely to be the result of a further referendum or a general election with revocation as a campaigning platform – whether the decision was some tricksy ruse to extend our negotiating period (which the EU would rightly ignore) or a real reversal of our previously stated intention to leave (which it would accept).

All of this made sense, or at least it made sense to me. I thought we had the better of the arguments, and was strongly of the view that it was right to try.

In the meantime, the legal team was focused on a much more prosaic difficulty: how to get a national court to refer the question to Luxembourg. The only body able to rule on the interpretation of provisions of the EU treaties was the ECJ. But you couldn't just rock up to the ECJ with any question you like. The question had to have been referred by a national court, and be a question arising out of some litigation in that national law case.

And this was why I had gone to Scotland.

The Scottish courts had a reputation for being legally conservative, even more so than the courts in London. And this was a novel case: the petitioners were saying to the national court, 'You need to refer the question to Luxembourg so that we know how to exercise our functions as elected members. We need to know whether the UK can revoke so that we can decide how to vote.' So, from that perspective, the Court of Session in Edinburgh was a strange choice of destination.

On the other hand, the London courts were still reeling from the attacks by the London press during and after Gina Miller's case, attacks which certainly felt as though they had been tacitly endorsed by ministers. One, Sajid Javid, then Secretary of State for Housing, Communities and Local Government, had gone so far as to say that the *Miller* case was 'an attempt to frustrate the will of the British people, and it is unacceptable.'[24]

I thought that we could only get a reference if we were before judges who were a long way from Westminster – and from Fleet Street.

That assessment was right – just.

Judicial review in Scotland works, in some senses at least, like judicial review in England (see Chapter Two). You need to have permission to bring a judicial review case.

On 2 February 2018, we had a hearing before the Outer House of the Court of Session, who refused us permission four days later on 6 February. On 9 February we announced we were appealing the judge's decision in Scotland's highest court, the Inner House of the Court of Session. On 20 March we got their decision, allowing our appeal and giving us permission to bring a judicial review.

We had crossed the first hurdle – we could bring our case – but now we needed to start over again, in the Outer House. On 8 June we got its decision, dismissing our claim. And again we appealed to the Inner House.

I thought fondly, during this judicial ping-pong, of what Jean Monnet, one of the architects of the European Community, had said: 'I am not optimistic. I am not pessimistic. I am determined.'

I don't think the UK Government took any of this terribly seriously. Not, at least, until 21 September, when, after the summer adjournment, the Inner House handed down its decision.

It began by setting out the factual context:

> At the expiry of the two-year period, there may or may not be an agreement. If there is an agreement, Parliament will have to decide whether to approve it. If it is not approved, and nothing further occurs, the treaties will cease to apply to the UK on 29 March 2019. The stark choice is either to approve the agreement or to leave the EU with no agreement. The petitioners seek a ruling on whether there is a valid third choice; that is to revoke the notification with the consequence, on one view, that the UK would remain in the EU. If that choice were available, the petitioners argue, members of the UK Parliament could decide which of three options was preferable. They could not only elect to reject the agreement because it was, in their view, a worse deal than having no agreement at all, but also because both the agreement or the absence of an agreement were worse than remaining in the EU; a situation which could be achieved by revoking the notification. If such revocation were not a legally valid option, the stark choice would be all that was left. The petitioners wish to have a definitive ruling, to enable them to make informed choices based on the options legally available.[25]

Asking the ECJ whether Article 50 could be revoked would clarify the options open to MPs in the lead-up to the vote. And the Court of Session agreed to make that request, coupled with a request that the question be answered quickly. Moving with unusual speed, the ECJ scheduled an emergency hearing for 27 November.

There then followed a period of silence, on the part of the Government at least.

And to be fair, the reference to the ECJ presented the UK Government with some serious dilemmas.

How would it affect the prospects of getting Prime Minister Theresa May's deal over the line? A meaningful vote before Parliament for that deal had been scheduled, but its prospects of passing looked slim. Might losing the case in the ECJ elevate the threat of remaining in the minds of MPs and cause them to think her deal was better than no Brexit?

And what would the Government say to the ECJ if it heard our case? That the Article 50 notice, properly understood, could not be reversed, that European law took an option off the table for our Parliament? It would be strange for the UK Government to argue that its MPs should have fewer options; less control. Wasn't Brexit supposed to be about more control for our Parliament? But it also seemed unlikely that Number 10 would instruct its lawyers to say that Brexit could be reversed. That would give Parliament another option – but it would also infuriate many in May's own party.

For almost a month, the Government's legal team pondered before concluding that, really, this was all much too difficult.

What followed was a series of frantic attempts to stop the question reaching the ECJ. The Government asked the Inner House to withdraw the reference. Unsuccessful. It asked the Court of Session for permission to appeal to the Supreme Court the Court of Session's decision to refer. Unsuccessful.

And finally, it engaged no fewer than five QCs to try and persuade the Supreme Court that it should have permission to appeal against the Inner House's decision.

It felt extraordinary to me that Government would spend these huge sums of public money in service of no better aim than keeping Parliament in the dark. But regardless, they were spent to no avail – on 20 November, only seven days prior to the scheduled hearing in Luxembourg, the Supreme Court agreed with us that the rules of procedure simply didn't permit an appeal.

Our task before the ECJ was a formidable one. Both the EU Council and the EU Commission were against us. Both contended that, although the United Kingdom might revoke with the permission of all of the other member states, it couldn't do so unilaterally. To bolster our legal team we brought in two EU law specialists – the academic Piet Eeckhout and the public international law specialist Maya Lester QC – alongside Aidan O'Neill QC and our solicitor, Elaine Motion.

On 26 November we all flew out to Luxembourg. Rupert Evans, whose £10,000 donation in early 2017 had led to me setting up Good Law Project, came too. We had dinner amongst the well-fed burghers of the tiny Principality of Luxembourg and, like them, went early to bed. Well, except for Aidan, who stayed up a while practising his speech before a patient Elaine.

Hearings in Luxembourg are not like hearings in London.

The Continent's legal tradition relies mostly on written argument, and speeches are expected to be short, measured in minutes not hours. But still, it was an extraordinary occasion. The ECJ had sat as a full court on only a handful of previous occasions, and it was quite a thing to see 28 judges, one from each of the member states, file into the grand court-room, one after the other, along with an advocate general, who writes a preliminary, advisory opinion, to take their seats around the long semi-circular bench at the front.

It was also very moving for me at a personal level.

I had not been to the Court since taking a few weeks out of my studies in Leuven to work as an intern in the cabinet of Walter van Gerven, the Belgian Advocate General and one of my professors. Twenty-five years on, he was no longer at the Court, nor amongst us at all, but the President of the Court was Koen Lenaerts, who had been another of Leuven's pro-fessors (I couldn't quite confess to my legal team that I had only attended one of his lectures). I walked up the aisle and sat a row or two behind Lord Keen, the Westminster Gov-ernment's legal representative in Edinburgh who would be arguing the case for the UK Government, so that he could hear my gentle sledging. A row of the public seating had been reserved for Leuven students, including some on the Erasmus exchange programme.

It was all over very quickly.

Poor Lord Keen had been given instructions by the Gov-ernment to decline to answer the question of whether Arti-cle 50 could be revoked or not as a matter of law. 'It's not our plan to,' was all he could say, which might well have been true but was also irrelevant. The six weeks subsequent had brought the Government no nearer to resolving what they had been unable to answer in the month following the decision of Scot-land's highest court to send the question to Luxembourg.

What seemed of particular interest to the ECJ was which view of Article 50 better respected national sovereignty. If a member state had the right to choose to leave, asked the Court, if it didn't need the permission of the other members to take that course, why should it need their permission to stay?

By lunch the hearing was over and, although we did not have a decision, I knew in my heart we had won. I gathered the other petitioners around me in the lobby of the Court and told them we may that day have made history.

Barely a week later, on 4 December, we got the decision of the advocate general expressing the opinion that Article 50 was unilaterally revocable.[26] That decision was only advisory but it was a good sign of what the ECJ was likely to do.

Claire had booked a week's cookery course at Leith's and our middle child was to have her tonsils removed on 10 December, the day the Court would hand down its final decision. I could not bear for Claire not to go, she had carried the family for so long, so I spent the morning the judgment came out doing two jobs badly. I was an inattentive father to my middle child and gave distracted interviews to exasperated broadcasters over the hubbub of the hospital lobby.

But it didn't really matter: we had won.[27]

What the ECJ decided was that, because a member state could not be forced to join the European Union against its will, neither could it be forced to leave the European Union against its will. It followed that it needed to have the right to revoke any earlier decision it had made to leave. It dismissed the argument that had so engaged commentators that a right to unilateral revocation would thwart the right of the other member states to reject a request for an extension of the two-year negotiating period.

And we, just me and a couple of Parliamentarians using the law, came so very close to rewriting history.

As Theresa May lost a series of votes in the House of Commons the possibility of remaining began to creep back up the political agenda. Michael Gove had already begun to talk to the newspapers, as I had anticipated, about the rubbish deal we would have to suck up if we decided to remain. But the Luxembourg judgment cut that line off at the knees. A petition on the Government's petitions website to revoke Article 50 notched up over six million signatures, which also helped.

Eventually, in March 2019, in despair, Theresa May asked Parliament to tell her what it wanted in a series of indicative votes. A motion to revoke if the alternative was no deal was tabled by a cross-party group of MPs on 26 March, but failed by 184 votes to 293.[28] The Labour leadership recommended to the 250 Labour MPs that they abstain or oppose the motion. Only 111 Labour MPs voted in support and 22 voted against.[29]

I drafted a revised version of the motion which provided that if the choices were no deal or revoke there would be a revocation, and then a concrete plan for Brexit would be constructed and put to the country in a further referendum. This was what Dominic Cummings had said would be the right thing to do before the 2016 referendum – and I thought he had got it then.

At the end of that month, on 31 March 2019, a poll carried out for the *Mail on Sunday* showed a small majority in the country to revoke Article 50. And on 1 April, this second version of the motion was put to a vote. It got closer but, again, could not command a majority, 191 to 292, after Labour again refused to back it.[30]

Using the law, crowdfunded with no big financial backers, we took on the right-wing press, the BBC, the Westminster Government, the Westminster Opposition, the EU Council and the EU Commission. We came so very close to righting the governance wrongs of the Brexit referendum. We failed – but we tried.

7. When the Chips Are Down

Some things turn out just how you expect.

On the morning of 24 September 2019, Joanna Cherry MP and I walked out to face the press camped outside the Supreme Court. The challenge Good Law Project had orchestrated to the prime minister's suspension of Parliament had succeeded.[1] But I wasn't surprised. I had never been able to imagine it any other way.

Boris Johnson's decision to suspend Parliament – why dignify his assault on democracy with the politer 'prorogation' left over from fourteenth-century Middle English – was a democratic outrage. A man chosen as prime minister by 92,000 members of the Conservative Party had abused one of the residual powers of the monarch to cancel a Parliament elected by 46 million voters.

And he had done it because Parliament, supposedly the supreme source of power under our constitution, was interfering with what he wanted.

If his suspension of Parliament was lawful, what was left of democracy?

The wishes of those millions of voters – transmitted to Parliament through the 650 members of Parliament they elected – could be thwarted. The prime minister could, if his lawyers were right, suspend Parliament the day after a general election and do so for the full term of a Parliament. Other than military coups it is difficult to find other examples in democracies of elected legislative bodies being 'taken out' without, indeed contrary to, their consent. But the United Kingdom Parliament that Boris Johnson was claiming an entitlement to suspend had not been asked to consent – indeed, the fact it wouldn't do his bidding was why he chose to suspend it.

Almost 8,000 people contributed to a crowdfunding campaign – and about seventy MPs and peers joined a legal action we started in late July – more than a month before Parliament was suspended. The judges in the highest courts of both Scotland and the United Kingdom – in both courts unanimously – had showed they would respond when the chips were down.

This was the moment our work cut through. We proved that our model of litigation funded by the people could deliver change.

In Chapter Four, I have written about so many of the things our judges are not.

They are not constitutionally insulated against, and they do not act free from, political pressure. Our legal tradition, of which they are the gatekeepers, does not, I think, engage in a manner honest enough about what parliamentary suprem- acy really means (see Chapter Two). And they do not wrestle enough with what it means for judges to have biases.

Judges are not a monolith – like the rest of us they think and do different things. And that is an important caution against all generalisations about the judiciary, including mine. But the prorogation case showed what they will do when all the chips are down.

In this chapter I talk about two moments of real constitu- tional crisis. The prorogation case, when the prime minister suspended Parliament, and the Nobile Officium case, when he explicitly and knowingly promised to break the law.

Both arose from the battle between Government and Parliament during the period before the 2019 general election, when the Government, first Theresa May's and then Boris Johnson's, had no workable majority in Parliament.

The roots of the prorogation case can be found in the decision made by the official leave campaign, Vote Leave, not to specify what leaving the EU would mean. This decision – apparently consciously made – made the referendum much easier to win. Writing in 2015, Dominic Cummings talked of bringing together 'a coalition between a) those who think we should just leave (about a third) and b) those who dislike the EU but are worried about leaving (about a third)' by offering a confirmatory referendum on whatever deal resulted.[2]

I discuss this decision more in Chapter Six, but it is possible or even likely that it was this decision that nudged the Leave vote over the line in the referendum.

It became much harder for the Remain side to point to the costs of Brexit, because these depended on what shape Brexit took. And it became easier for the Leave side to assert the benefits of Brexit – because depending on the model you were looking at you could have all of them: you could end free movement for other EU citizens, continue to enjoy free movement yourself, all whilst our exporters continued to enjoy frictionless access to the EU and we reasserted the primacy in all legislative matters of our domestic Parliament.

The decision had huge advantages, if you didn't care what followed the vote, but left enormous problems in its wake.

There was no majority in Parliament for any single model of life outside the EU, which surprisingly enough involved costs as well as benefits. (The decline in support amongst voters for Brexit as the trade-offs have become clearer suggests that there was never any majority in the electorate either – but that's a different story.)

When the result rolled in the fact that no one knew what Brexit meant was immediately apparent. It took Theresa May an age to decide whether the United Kingdom would remain within or leave the single market – leaving the EU was consistent with either possibility – and she only eventually announced in January 2017, seven months after the vote, that we would leave it.

Ultimately, those unresolved contradictions ended her premiership – and delivered the constitutional crisis that was the prorogation.

The Prorogation Case

Very broadly, EU law gives a country that wants to leave the EU two years to prepare to do so. Within that time, the country has to negotiate a withdrawal agreement, ask for an extension to the two years, or leave without any deal at all.

Two years might seem like quite a long time to negotiate an agreement, and it is. But only if you know what you want. And the problem with the way in which the referendum was conducted was that it left all of the really difficult questions unanswered. The referendum didn't ask the public about any of the trade-offs – and MPs couldn't agree on them either.

Theresa May could not get Parliament to agree on any model of life outside the EU – or any other solution to the democratic mess created by the form of the referendum campaign. Eventually, in despair, she put them all before Parliament in a series of what were called indicative votes, including revoking and remaining, a second referendum, leaving without a deal, leaving with her deal, and remaining within the single market. But despite a number of extensions to our departure date – at the time it stood at 31 October 2019 – all her attempts to get Parliament to agree to something – for God's sake, anything! – had ended in failure.

But the thing was, under EU law we didn't need a deal to leave. And this was what Boris Johnson fastened upon as the fix.

We could leave automatically, by virtue of the passing of time, if no extension was sought to our departure date. But, although a sizeable minority in Parliament was happy to leave without a deal (at the time a sizeable minority could be found in Parliament for anything), the majority of MPs had made it clear that they were not prepared to leave without a deal and they kept blocking Johnson's path.

What to do? How to get MPs out of the way?

There is a parliamentary mechanism – known as a 'sittings motion' – for Parliament to agree to be suspended. But it requires Parliament to consent, and Parliament would not agree to any suspension that had as its intention the thwarting of its desire that we not leave without a deal.

But there was also another mechanism: a prorogation. Prorogations are used to suspend Parliament between 'sessions' and don't require the permission of MPs. A plan started to take shape within Boris Johnson's office. Johnson might force through our departure, against the wishes of MPs, by operation of EU law, using a prorogation to suspend Parliament for a time sufficiently long enough that they could not interfere with his plan.

You might think that an unelected prime minister using EU law to thwart the wishes of a majority of MPs in our national Parliament was a strange type of Taking Back Control. I certainly did. But we were living in very strange times. Political gravity had been suspended.

I first heard rumblings of a plan to suspend Parliament in early June 2019.

During the 2019 campaign to replace Theresa May as prime minister, Beth Rigby, Sky News' political editor, reported that Andrea Leadsom, who was then Leader of the House of Commons and in the hunt for the leadership, had taken advice on the possibility earlier that year.[3] Leadsom was not a fan – 'I'm passionate about parliament democracy,' she said – but a number of candidates refused to rule it out.

This felt absolutely extraordinary to me.

What kind of message would this send around the world about our values when so many have given so much for the rights of democratic freedom?

A policy on Brexit to prorogue Parliament would mean the end of the Conservative Party as a serious party of Government.

These were Matt Hancock's words on 6 June 2019, during his bid for leadership of the Conservative Party.[4] Eleven days later, having pulled out of the race, he backed Boris Johnson, who had refused to rule out proroguing Parliament.[5] By the end of August he was openly supporting prorogation.[6]

I agreed with Matt Hancock. Well, with his first thoughts on the subject, anyway

Suspending Parliament should have meant the end of the Conservative Party as a serious party of government. It was an outrageous attack on democracy. And, although notionally the power to prorogue belonged to the Queen, in reality, it was that of the prime minister. As it became clearer and clearer that Johnson would win, placing a suspension of parliamentary democracy firmly on the agenda, I decided to act.

On 22 July 2019, having persuaded a coalition of parliamentarians to join me – including Joanna Cherry MP, who I had worked with on the case about whether Article 50 could be revoked (known as *Wightman*; see Chapter Six), Jo Swinson, then leader of the Liberal Democrats, and a number of Labour, Green, independent and Plaid Cymru MPs – we wrote to the Government in Scotland saying that any decision to suspend Parliament would be unlawful.

Scotland and England do have separate legal systems, but that wasn't the reason we decided to take action in Scotland. It wasn't that I thought the law was better north of the border – indeed, the advice I had consistently been given in the *Wightman* case was that the Scottish legal system was more conservative than that in England and likely to be more hostile to constitutional challenges.

My reasoning proceeded from a very different premise. It's not the sort of thing you ever read in the law books, but I thought that English judges, burned by how they were treated by the press after the Gina Miller case I discuss earlier in this book and living and working in the middle of an increasingly toxic political climate, would be fearful of acting in a way that Scottish judges would not.

There were some other advantages too. The Court of Session, the court in Edinburgh in which the case would be heard, sat through August. And the precedent established in our *Wightman* case, which had also been heard in Scotland, that the Courts would in appropriate circumstances declare what the law was in advance of the question arising, might help us. At the time we launched our legal action, of course, Parliament had not yet been suspended.

We sent the formal letter that fired the starting gun on legal proceedings and, working once again with Balfour + Manson and Aidan O'Neill, began to assemble a coalition of MPs and peers as co-petitioners. Eventually we got to more than seventy.

Over the summer, I tried to take some time off to spend with my young family. It had been a long slog since the referendum. In addition to continuing my practice at the tax bar I had been running Good Law Project more or less single-handedly.

Organising the litigation was demanding enough, but that wasn't all I was doing. I was also putting up crowdfunding pages, trying to build a mailing list and writing emails for that list, and constantly briefing journalists about our plans. I had done all of this on my own for three years and, frankly, I was exhausted.

But it proved to be a very short break. On the evening of 25 August, I heard from a contact that the prorogation was 'on'. Three days later, on the 28th, Jacob Rees-Mogg made the journey to Balmoral to see the Queen and to let her know that the prime minister wished to suspend Parliament from a date in early September until 14 October, just 17 days before we were due to leave the EU.

For the rest of the week, the last of my notional holiday, I squeezed in a few media interviews in the evenings before travelling back to London on Monday 2 September. And I jumped on a train to my parents-in-law's apartment in Edinburgh for the hearing before Scotland's first instance Court, which was scheduled to take place on the Tuesday.

As the argument had developed, the central issue in the case was the purpose for which the Government had suspended Parliament. Was it, as the Government contended, nothing at all to do with Brexit? Was the fact of an unprecedentedly lengthy suspension of Parliament, outside the context of a general election campaign, without Parliament's consent, and at a moment convenient to those who wanted to leave without a deal, a complete coincidence?

Or was it an illegitimate abuse of the power to prorogue?

Waking up on the Tuesday morning was quite a shock.

Overnight, the Government had ambushed us with a huge amount of evidence. Much of it was redacted – or blacked-out, for non-lawyers – including a paper supposedly prepared for the Cabinet which recommended suspending Parliament for reasons which had, the paper said, nothing at all to do with Brexit. The purpose of the suspension was said to be to prepare for a new legislative programme, to be contained in HM the Queen's speech on 14 October, and to cover the period of the party conferences, during which time Parliament tends to be in recess. Also included were what appeared to be minutes of a Cabinet meeting and a handwritten note from the prime minister purporting to approve the prorogation.

None of these materials were supported by an affidavit – sworn evidence that they were what they pretended to be. And they didn't 'feel' right. Cabinet minutes are not usually published, and these were duly marked 'Official Sensitive', but they had every appearance of having been written for publication. They recorded the prime minister saying:

> It was important to emphasise that this decision to prorogue Parliament for a Queen's Speech was not driven by Brexit considerations: it was about pursuing an exciting and dynamic legislative programme to take forward the Government's agenda.

Litigation isn't supposed to work like this. You are supposed to have documents early enough to enable you to properly scrutinise them. But these had been given to us in a form which made it impossible to check with contacts whether they were what they looked like: 'These documents must be treated in the strictest confidence as between parties,' read the email serving them upon us at 10.55pm on the Monday night.

Had it been us serving documents so late in the day we would not have been given permission to rely on them. But the lived reality of every barrister who takes cases against the Government is that judges hold the Government to a much lower standard of conduct than those challenging them. They get to litigate on easy mode.

Things got worse when I arrived at Parliament House, where the Court sits. I was contacted by several parliamentarians who told me the papers served on us had been cooked up by the prime minister's political team. They did not, I was told, represent the real decision-making process but were, basically, a false trail which had been cooked up on unofficial messaging channels.

They also said that the reason we had been served with the papers so late was because the Government Legal

Department had prepared a witness statement which swore them to be true but then couldn't get anyone to sign it. They had, I was told, asked the prime minister's Director of Legislative Affairs, Nikki da Costa, and the Cabinet Secretary Mark Sedwill, but both had refused to sign.

Later, Dominic Grieve, the former Attorney General, attempted to get to the bottom of all of this with a parliamentary motion seeking to compel the production of all communications, including on WhatsApp, Telegram, Signal, Facebook Messenger, private email accounts both encrypted and unencrypted, text messaging and iMessage, relating to the prorogation of Parliament sent or received by a number of individuals, including a number of the prime minister's special advisers, and Dominic Cummings and Nikki da Costa.[7] The motion was carried – and should have been binding – but the Government all but ignored it.

What we later learned was that my suspicions had been right. In a podcast in 2022, Nikki da Costa said: 'It was intended as a mechanism for controlling a period of time to buy time to get to the EU Council on 16 October with the PM's hands unbound.'[8]

The Government Legal Department, I imagine acting unwittingly on the instructions of ministers, placed before the Court of Session documents that, according to the prime minister's then Director of Legislative Affairs, created a false impression of the reasons for the prorogation. No one has been held to account. We will shortly place this material before the Court of Session in Scotland to see whether it wants to take action against what might have been a deliberate attempt to place misleading evidence before the Court in perhaps the most important constitutional case of our generation.

But, at the time, all I could do was grump and listen to Aidan O'Neill QC, the Scottish silk we had instructed to act in the case, inviting the Court to draw inferences from the Government's failures:

> ... the refusal by the Prime Minister to explain the decision-making process and the reasoning underlying this decision to exercise the power of prorogation at this time and for the dates and in the manner in which it has been done means that this court can and should draw adverse inferences against the decision-maker. He doesn't get the benefit of any doubt. You look at the record, you try as best as you can to determine the credibility and reliability of what is said against the background of an individual whose personal, professional and political life has been characterised by incontinent mendacity: to make it plainer ...

(although I'm not sure it needed to be made plainer)

> ... an unwillingness or inability to acknowledge and speak the truth.

Readers outside the United Kingdom will not be aware how tongue-tied much of our media becomes in the presence of political power. To hear these words spoken publicly of Boris Johnson, and in a court room, was a powerful tonic.

The very next day, the Wednesday, Labour MP Jess Phillips asked Boris Johnson:

> Is it true that senior civil servants have refused to sign witness statements for ongoing legal proceedings relating to prorogation? Were the director of legislative affairs and the cabinet secretary asked to do so, and did they agree?[9]

He refused to answer.

I had expected us to lose at first instance – and had gently signalled as much to journalists. But I didn't mind because, as I said on Twitter, 'In law, unlike in politics, sentiment doesn't much matter' and I knew the case would go further. And the very next day, Wednesday, the Outer House of the Court of Session handed down its expected decision: the Courts could not get involved in a purely political decision.[10]

The recently retired Supreme Court judge turned legal commentator Lord Sumption had predicted this outcome – 'I don't think what the prime minister has said he is going to do is unlawful' – and his was very much an orthodox view.[11]

I issued a brief statement pointing out that:

The idea that if the PM suspends Parliament the Court can't get involved looses some ugly demons. If he can do it for 34 days, why not 34 weeks, or 34 months. Where does this political power end? It's the not the law as I understand it.

And we prepared for our appeal.

The Inner House had agreed to hear it the very next day. I hadn't planned for an extended stay in Edinburgh and knew I could purloin some of my father-in-law's wardrobe, but smalls seemed a bit much. So I popped into the Gap on my way back to their flat in the West End.

The hearing on Thursday before Scotland's highest court began with our application for unredacted copies of the documents served on us several days previously.

It occupied over an hour but I knew our application had failed as soon as David Johnston QC, the brilliant advocate the Government had instructed, stood up and said simply that he had read the unredacted documents and the words that were redacted were not relevant to the issues.

The judges believed him and I believed him too.

It's an extraordinary thing to be able to say this of such a high-stakes piece of litigation. That I can reflects the fact that we have, for the most part in the United Kingdom, an exceptional profession. Even where we are opponents, we often find it within ourselves to be guardians of values dearer to us than self-interest. That I immediately believed him made me very proud.

But it turned out not to matter.

Later that day, I heard from a source and was able to whisper into the ear of a visibly shocked Government lawyer that an unredacted version of the prime minister's memo had been leaked and would shortly be published. It came out on the Saturday and the missing words were 'girly swot Cameron' (as David Johnston had promised, not relevant to the issues). The prime minister's memo read:

(1) The whole September session is a rigmarole introduced by girly swot Cameron to show the public that MPs are earning their crust.

(2) So I don't see anything especially shocking about this prorogation.

(3) As Nikki notes, it is over the conference season so that the sitting days lost are actually very few.[12]

The hearing itself went much better than at first instance and I began briefing journalists that we expected the prorogation to be declared unlawful.

On 11 September, the Inner House refused to suspend disbelief. The key passage of Lord Carloway's decision was this:

The circumstances demonstrate that the true reason for the prorogation is to reduce the time available for Parliamentary scrutiny of Brexit at a time when such scrutiny would appear to be a matter of considerable importance, given the issues at stake. This is in the context of an anticipated no deal Brexit, in which case no further consideration of matters by Parliament is required. The Article 50 period, as extended, will have expired and withdrawal will occur automatically.[13]

Lord Drummond Young put the matter even more crisply. It was, he said, 'a tactic to frustrate Parliament'.

The previous day, a parallel legal action brought by Gina Miller in the Divisional Court in London had been dismissed amidst much press fanfare. The decision of Scotland's highest court made barely a ripple in the national press. The BBC made space for a single interview with me on its news channel, after a characteristic story about how, it said, immigrants were flooding in because our borders would be tighter after Brexit.

But I knew it was game on.

The Supreme Court moved swiftly to schedule a hearing of Ms Miller's appeal from the Divisional Court and the Government's appeal in our case from the Inner House. The three-day hearing began six days later, on 17 September.

It was quite grim, the atmosphere outside the Supreme Court during those three days. There was a large press contingent in an area cordoned off with metal barriers. And on each side of the entrance, separated by further metal barriers, were camped Leave and Remain supporters – Remain on the left and Leave on the right as you entered.

Recognised 'characters' in the legal drama attracted differing levels of affection or hostility as they passed through the crowd. This was somewhat muted for most of us – including me and Joanna Cherry – but the situation for Gina Miller was really frightening. There was a real sense of suppressed violence whenever she had to pass the throng, with her detail of bodyguards, to enter or leave the courtroom. It was visceral – Shami Chakrabarti, another woman of colour albeit much less well known than Gina Miller, was received with something similar when she entered the court – and it was not easy to avoid drawing the obvious conclusion.

This really wasn't an atmosphere conducive to the ability of the Supreme Court to make a decision on a fairly abstruse point of constitutional law around what lawyers call 'justiciability' – whether a question is one a court can even look at. The Supreme Court judges could, and did, try to issue reassuring statements that the case was not about Leave or Remain. And that was true – if you were wearing a wig. But no one in the courtroom – or outside it – was ignorant of the political implications of the case.

This atmosphere was also being whipped up by ministers. Bernard Jenkin MP wrote to a constituent saying that 'the Inner House of the Court of Session has given a ruling under Scottish law which may not apply in UK law.'[14] That was just not true – and as Chair of the Public Administration and Constitutional Affairs Committee he certainly should, and may well, have known better.

The whole thing felt rather sad as well. None of us can have enjoyed seeing the country so divided. But there was little I could do – beyond a gesture – to try and articulate this.

I did make a point, once or twice a day, of going and talking to the Leave supporters about the hearing and the issues it raised. An optimism about human nature is very much my default state. But I always sensed the substantial police presence begin to tense as I walked across the great divide.

The hearing itself went off much as someone who could not imagine any other outcome might have expected.

It was apparent to me throughout the hearing that the Supreme Court was onside. As I had said when we lost before the Outer House of the Court of Session, if the prime minister could suspend Parliament against its wishes, and that decision not be challengeable before the Courts, what would be left of parliamentary democracy? That was a result that was unimaginable to me, both as a lawyer and as a citizen. The point was perhaps best put by the Supreme Court judge Lord Wilson during oral argument: 'Is there any person better placed to defend the precious legal principle of parliamentary sovereignty than us here?'

Behind the scenes I was in frequent contact with a senior legal figure in Government who also held a political liaison role. I had decided voluntarily to brief them on how we thought the litigation was going to play out. This wasn't helpful to our prospects of winning the case. But I knew we – me and that individual – shared a profound concern for what the judgment would mean for the rule of law.

I understand that many of the Supreme Court judges shared that concern too. Although a neutral bystander would certainly have concluded from watching them during the hearing that most thought the prorogation was unlawful, several were clearly in two minds.

Within the legal team, we discussed how much time to spend on trying to bring the judges we thought were dissenters around. But the decision, when it came, was unanimous. The eleven judges spoke with one voice to declare the suspension unlawful. Some of the MPs who had joined the claim had come in to watch the decision being handed down and several were in tears.

I thought this unanimity was a very conscious decision, taken collectively, and born of a perception that there was a need to protect the authority of the law from the shitstorm to come. My statement read:

> The last few weeks has seen an extraordinary series of attacks on our democracy. A Parliament elected from 46 million was unlawfully suspended by a prime minister elected from 160,000. Judges have been threatened by a 'Number 10 source'. And those of us who have sought to protect the only institution with a UK-wide democratic mandate have been subjected to death threats and some of us have had our home addresses published.
>
> I am pleased that the Supreme Court today protected the foundational principle of any democracy – the right of MPs to do the job for which they were elected. But there is still much to be done.
>
> I am grateful for the support of our outstanding legal team. And to the almost 8,000 small donors who funded this litigation: this victory is yours.

That afternoon I went into Parliament, now unsuspended, for a drink to celebrate. We had taken on the Government, again, and defeated its attempt to snatch power from elected MPs.

The reaction was awful – and predictable.

Jacob Rees-Mogg, the leader of the Commons, accused the Supreme Court of a 'constitutional coup'.[15] Suella Braverman, then a backbencher, later said that judges had been 'pulled into the political sphere' and demanded reforms to the Supreme Court to restore what she called 'judicial deference'.[16] And Boris Johnson said: 'If judges are to pronounce on political questions in this way then there is at least an argument that there should be some form of accountability.'[17]

These criticisms were dangerous – and entirely wrong.

The fact that a legal decision has political consequences – which would have been true whatever the outcome – doesn't mean that judges are overstepping. All exercises of judicial review have political consequences.

Politicians get to choose how close to the legal line they sail. They can adopt a conservative position – being careful not to act unlawfully – or they can throw the dice and take their chances. Judges don't have that choice.

These very public attacks were intended to bully judges into compliance. The statistics since the prorogation case suggest those, and other bad faith attacks on judges, succeeded. Success rates in judicial review proceedings have declined sharply just as Government has become openly more hostile to judges, lawyers and the law, and it would be remarkable if this was mere coincidence.[18]

That battleground, of how judges negotiate serious law-breaking by leading politicians, was the subject of our other major constitutional challenge of 2019, the so-called Nobile Officium case.

The Nobile Officium Case

As I explain in Chapter Two, under our constitution Parliament is 'supreme'. It has this place in our constitutional set-up because of the tens of millions who vote and elect MPs in a general election.

In 2019, Boris Johnson was prime minister – not because voters had chosen him but because some tens of thousands of members of the Conservative Party had. Under EU law we would leave, with or without a deal, on 31 October 2019. And this was fine with him – but not with Parliament, which was not prepared to contemplate our departure from the EU unless we had a withdrawal agreement in place.

On 9 September, in the period between the prorogation hearing in the Inner House and its decision declaring the suspension of Parliament unlawful, Parliament passed the so-called Benn Act. That Act, formally known as the European Union (Withdrawal) (No. 2) Act 2019, sought to prevent a no-deal Brexit on 31 October 2019 by requiring the prime minister to send a letter to the EU asking for an extension of the date upon which we would leave the EU. That obligation would fall away if the House of Commons had approved a withdrawal agreement with the EU by 19 October 2019 – but no one thought that might happen.

So far so good.

The problem was that, both before and after the passing of the Benn Act, the prime minister was adamant he would defy Parliament and he would not seek an extension. At one point, I started keeping a list of all the times he had said so – and my list got up to 19 times, but it was only part of the total. In a letter to Conservative Party members, Boris Johnson wrote: 'They just passed a law that would force me to beg Brussels for an extension to the Brexit deadline. This is something I will never do'.[19]

He also said he would 'rather be dead in a ditch' than ask for a further delay.[20] And that 'we will leave by 31 October in all circumstances. There will be no further pointless delay.'[21]

It is hard to imagine a more direct challenge to the rule of law – and it came not from an idealistic student or a hardened anti-vaxxer but from the prime minister.

This was pretty extraordinary stuff, constitutionally speaking. And what made it even worse was that, however 'supreme' Parliament was as a matter of United Kingdom constitutional law, it couldn't change EU law. If the 31 October 2019 deadline passed without a request for an extension, we'd be out.

UK law might knock at the door – but EU law wouldn't let us in.

None of the traditional mechanisms in English law for dealing with situations like this seemed quite to work. Typically, the Court would order the prospective lawbreaker to comply – a mandatory injunction – and if they didn't they would be in contempt of court and go to prison. But if Johnson martyred himself by holding out for a day – what then? By operation of EU law, Parliament would be defied in a way the Courts could not remedy – we'd have left without a deal.

Parliament, by passing the legislation ordering Boris Johnson to ask for an extension, had done everything it could. It was simultaneously legislatively supreme and practically impotent.

I was contacted by a lecturer in commercial law at the University of Edinburgh, a man called Scott Wortley. 'Do you know,' he said, 'there is this thing in Scots law called the Nobile Officium?'

I did not, but I began to read up.

Translated literally it means 'Noble Office'. But so obscure was it that no one even knew how to pronounce it. Very much entering into the spirit of things, the BBC helpfully explained that: 'classical scholars argue about the pronunciation of the term, but there is widespread agreement the syllables should be of equal length with a hard "c".'[22]

What I learned was that the Nobile Officium was a sort of all-purpose remedy for righting wrongs where no other exists. What we thought it could do was enable the Court of Session to sign the request for an extension, as if it were Boris Johnson. It could 'pp' the letter – sign it on his behalf.

We couldn't find any use of the Nobile Officium that was quite like this – but then the law books weren't exactly overflowing with chapters headed 'What to do when the prime minister says he'll break the law'. And it seemed well worth a try.

On 10 September, whilst waiting for the Inner House, Scotland's Highest Court, to hand down its decision in the prorogation case, the three petitioners, being me, Joanna Cherry MP and the ecologist Dale Vince who also generously agreed to underwrite the costs, wrote asking Boris Johnson to undertake to comply with his obligations under the Benn Act, and to repudiate all suggestions to the contrary, and giving him until 4pm on the 12th.

When our deadline passed, and only a day after the Inner House handed down its judgment ruling the prorogation unlawful, we received a letter from rather weary Government lawyers telling us they would respond properly later.

That wasn't going to be good enough – the very purpose of the case was to try and stop the prime minister dragging his heels until it was too late – and so we issued proceedings in the Court of Session to try and force him to comply with the will of Parliament without 'delay, evasion or obfuscation' (as our case put it).

In the meantime, the prime minister's team had been briefing journalists that they had found a cunning ruse to sidestep the Benn Act that was (according to a rather breathless *Daily Mail* column) 'so sensitive that even members of Mr Johnson's inner circle have not been briefed on it'.[23]

This was all very exciting. The loophole, the *Mail* continued:

> . . . has only been seen by Boris Johnson and three key advisers, it was claimed last night. The identities of the three key advisers are unknown, but it is thought they could include Mr Johnson's right-hand man Dominic Cummings, Brexit Secretary Steve Barclay and the Attorney General Geoffrey Cox.

It's not a very public-spirited tax-lawyer skill set, the sniffing out of loopholes, but it has its uses and I had been wondering about this too.

On 15 September, I published on my Waiting for Tax blog details of a loophole I had identified in the Act.[24] I spent much of the afternoon fielding slightly panicked conversations with members of the coalition of MPs who had drafted the Benn Act but, fortunately, having been forewarned, MPs were able to sidestep the danger.

Meanwhile, the Outer House listed the hearing in the Nobile Officium case for 3 October – the Court's formal record listed it as a 'Petition to Nob Off', which I was much too grown up to find amusing although I understand others did – but the pressure began to mount up, on me and on the judges.

On Saturday 21 September I received a text message from Harry Cole, who then worked for the *Mail on Sunday*, telling me he had identified that an article published in *Country Life* about the renovation of a house in the South Downs National Park was about our family home.

He asked me why I hadn't been named in the piece, suggesting it was because I wanted to keep out of the public domain that we were well-off, and that they planned to carry a piece naming me. We had agreed to the piece at the request of the architects to promote their practice and, of course, the reason I had wanted to keep details of where I lived out of the public domain was because I routinely received death threats.

The location of the property was easy to identify online and I expressed amazement that he planned to publish details of my home address in a week where my safety was particularly at risk.

I promptly instructed lawyers and – to try and dissuade them – published on Twitter the *Mail on Sunday*'s threat.

Later that evening, we received an email from its managing editor, John Wellington, in which he said my connection with the address was in the public domain and asked me to take down my tweets. He was right that I had given an interview to a local paper, before I was a public figure, about my plans to restore a local landmark. But he was not a stupid man and I could not believe he was unaware of the whole new set of risks that would be posed to me and my young family should his newspaper tell its readers 'this is where that person we encourage you to hate lives'.

Fortunately, he concluded by saying that: 'In fact, the item about your client has not made the final draft of Mr Cole's column in any case.'

But, of course, I was a marked man. The following day, 22 September, the *Sunday Times* carried a briefing from Number 10 which stated:

> Remainers will also launch a case in the Scottish courts tomorrow that could lead to the judges themselves sending a letter to Brussels requesting an extension if the Prime Minister refuses to do so.
>
> A No. 10 source said: 'Remainiac lawyers now demand that Scottish judges take over the role of elected politicians and cancel Brexit. Hopefully judges will reflect deeply on the profound consequences for the judiciary if they are seen by the public to side with those trying to cancel the biggest democratic vote in our history.'[25]

This, of course, was a flat lie. The Nobile Officium case did not 'demand that Scottish judges take over the role of elected politicians' or 'cancel Brexit'. It asked the prime minister to comply with what elected politicians had enacted in Parliament – the Benn Act – and request an extension. At most, it would delay Brexit.

I had been called several days previously by Tim Shipman at the *Sunday Times*, who told me Dominic Cummings had suggested he speak to me. And, later that day, Julia Hartley Brewer went where (having been threatened by lawyers) the *Mail on Sunday* would not and published details of where I lived.[26]

I began to get calls – more than usual – from friendly MPs warning me I really ought to take care. The police put me on their 'rapid response' list for people who faced particular security risks and, on the advice of a senior police officer who talked about 'lone-wolf' threats, I bought a stab-proof vest and organised close security for future trips I would have to make to attend court in Edinburgh.[27]

Meanwhile, my chambers had been taking its own advice and introduced additional security measures. It was gently suggested to me that I might work from home. These risks were not over-stated – a number of men had turned up at the Inns of Court asking whether I worked there. I think this was the moment when I felt most physically vulnerable and I made plans to leave the country if I was named publicly by Number 10 as the 'Remainiac lawyer' in question.

Two days later, on 24 September, the Supreme Court handed down its decision in the prorogation case. It was nice to have Parliament back – but I was also quite keen that the prime minister be reminded that he was not some kind of World King but subject, like the rest of us, to the laws that it made.

A week later, on 3 October, we secured a major concession in the Nobile Officium case when Boris Johnson, through his lawyers, conceded to the Court that he had to, and would, comply with the law.[28] If the Act required it, he would 'send a letter in the form set out in the schedule by no later than 19 October 2019'. He also conceded that 'he cannot frustrate its purpose or the purpose of its provisions. Thus he cannot act so as to prevent the letter requesting the specified extension in the Act from being sent.'

The first hearing was the next day. And, with the fresh words of Number 10 ringing in his ears, the judge in the Outer House, Lord Pentland, faced a difficult task.

It's all well and good for lawyers to write this stuff down on paper, but what happens in real life? This was, at various times and in various forms, the question that had been put to me by journalists. 'What happens if the prime minister doesn't send the letter? Will he be arrested and put in prison, and how will that happen?' and 'Who will actually sign the letter if the prime minister won't and the Court has to exercise its Nobile Officium jurisdiction?'

These were easy questions to answer in the abstract: 'Of course, he would go to prison' and 'One of the judges will step into the prime minister's shoes and sign the letter', but I found them difficult to say. Even though I knew them to be right as a matter of legal form, there was still an air of unreality to my answers and I felt vaguely absurd giving them.

The Court faced exactly the same dilemma.

The issue, as the debate between the parties had developed, was that, although the prime minister had said to the Court, through his lawyers, that he would comply with the law, he had also said to everyone else, unequivocally and in the strongest possible terms with his own mouth, that he would not. So, we said, we still anticipate he might not and we need the assistance of the court to ensure that he will. After all, if he does not, it might be too late for the courts to make it right later. But the lawyers for the prime minister argued that he had confirmed to the Court that he would comply with the law and that really ought to be enough.

This was all rather awkward, and Lord Pentland concluded:

The Prime Minister and the government having thus formulated and presented to the court their considered legal position, there is no proper basis on which the court could hold that they are nonetheless liable to fail to do what they have in effect undertaken to the court that they will do . . .

And that:

> . . . the extra-judicial statements on which the petitioners rely must be understood in the political context in which they were made; that is as expressions of the government's political policy. They were clearly not intended to be taken as conclusive statements of the government's understanding of its legal obligations.

This couldn't be reconciled with what the prime minister had said – he had been quite categorical – and we pointed to the fact that there was no signed statement from the prime minister. Might he just hang his lawyers out to dry? I imagine that this was a question that the lawyers were privately asking themselves.

But being a judge is a bit like being a parent – your word is law. Having found against us, Lord Pentland went on to issue this coded warning:

> I approach matters on the basis that it would be destructive of one of the core principles of constitutional propriety and of the mutual trust that is the bedrock of the relationship between the court and the Crown for the Prime Minister or the government to renege on what they have assured the court that the Prime Minister intends to do.

It was cold comfort to us.

That judgment was released on 7 October. We immediately appealed and our appeal was set down to be heard on the 8th before the Inner House, which faced the same unpalatable choice as the Outer House: could it disbelieve the clear statements given by highly respected lawyers for the prime minister?

The judges in the Inner House found a very elegant solution indeed.

Faced with an unpalatable choice between doubting what the prime minister's lawyers had told the court and ignoring what the prime minister had told the world, the Inner House played for time:

> The court will . . . continue consideration of the reclaiming motion and the petition to the nobile officium until Monday, 21 October, by which time the position ought to be significantly clearer. At that time the court will expect to be addressed on the facts as they then present themselves.[29]

That was the first working day after the deadline set in the Benn Act for the prime minister to ask for an extension.

'We could not possibly suggest,' the judges seemed to be saying, 'that the prime minister might hang his lawyers out to dry. We could never find that assurances given to us by highly respected members of the legal profession should not be taken at face value. But, just in case, let's adjourn the case until the first working day after the prime minister has to send the letter. And then we'll be able to see.'

Genius.

Several weeks later, the prime minister ate his words and sent the letter. In an act of characteristic petulance, he sent an unsigned photocopy of the letter mandated by the Benn Act and sent it accompanied by another, signed letter, making the case why the EU should ignore the wishes of Parliament and listen to him instead. They didn't – and promptly granted the extension.

Would he have sought an extension without our action? Given how he responded to the neat solution found by the Inner House it's perfectly reasonable to think he would not have.

Ultimately, the Courts depend on the Government for their functioning. And if you have a government that is hell-bent on ignoring the law there are limits to what the Court can do. They have the power to declare what the law is – and they have the power to say that a thing should happen, like the prime minister should send a letter – but they don't have the power to ensure it does.

That power rests with public servants. What would have happened if Boris hadn't blinked first, if he hadn't sent the letter? Would he have been arrested? Imprisoned?

Judges, certainly experienced constitutional judges, will be very keenly aware, just as parents are with recalcitrant teenagers, that it would be a disaster for the limits of their power to become evident. Courts only have such power to enforce their judgments as governments give to them. So, like parents, they husband their power, they subtly negotiate its limits with ministers, and they try to avoid situations where they might be found out.

And where they have absolutely no choice? They draw themselves up to their full, majestic height and speak with a single voice.

8. Wrestling with Uber

Now for a busman's holiday. For the novitiate constitutional law reader, a journey into tax law. And for the experienced tax lawyer, rather than defending dodgy tax structures in court, the respite of prising them apart in public. My first foray into tax campaigning and Good Law Project's first ever case – against Uber.

Management books tell inspiring stories of how clever and hard-working men, and even the odd woman, successfully mined the rich seams of capitalism on level playing fields overcoming everything fate threw in their path with inspiration and perspiration in just the right proportions.

Not Uber. In the UK, Uber employed a private militia of lawyers and accountants to sniff out and exploit weaknesses in the social compact. The rules they sought to undermine are the rules which sustain the foundations of our society. They are the rules that ensure a fair deal between those who work for a living and the businesses who need their labour. They protect our schools and roads and courts and hospitals and safety nets and police forces, the very infrastructure that businesses like Uber relies on, by ensuring the infrastructure can be funded and maintained. And they seek to moderate the logic, inherent in capitalism, that profits should, whenever possible, be held privately whilst costs are put on the public at large.

Uber's lawyers sniffed out weaknesses in employment law, tax law and in the regulatory environment for public transport and then exploited them. And it exploited them through constructing an elaborate suite of agreements between passengers and drivers and regulators that attracted those advantages.

The agreements meant Uber had no obligation to provide drivers with a safety net if they got sick, or pregnant, or when they retired. It shifted those burdens to drivers themselves – and to the social security system that the rest of us pay for. With the agreements, Uber could take advantage of the VAT regime designed to reduce the administrative burden on small businesses, so that they didn't have to charge VAT. And they meant Uber would not have to pay employment taxes on its workforce of drivers.

But the world those agreements described bore no relationship to the world that actually existed. It was one where Uber, one of the largest consumer brands in the world, was actually a supplier of services to drivers; where, despite using its brand to build a huge global taxi business, it was not in the transportation business; and where, even though you booked using the Uber app, booked because of Uber's brand, paid Uber, complained about the service to Uber and were issued with receipts by Uber, you were not actually its customer.

The disjunction between these worlds ought to be a serious matter of professional ethics. The agreements Uber drafted were designed to strip from workers rights Parliament had given to them and to denude the Treasury of taxes which should sit in the public purse. The documents which do this work, the documents drawn up by the lawyers, sought to achieve these effects by incorporating falsehoods.

If our law is to function properly lawyers should be forced by their regulators to interrogate whether the documents they prepare are lies. And (as I argue in Chapter One) they ought to be trained to do so.

For regulators to embrace these points would require a profound change in how we conceive of the relationship between lawyers and clients. One of the two main regulators – the Solicitors' Regulation Authority – is moving, slowly, in this direction. In the meantime, the Courts have devised a doctrine to ensure the law applies to the world as it actually is rather than the world that would be convenient to Uber – and so many other businesses and individuals like it.

The doctrine they invented requires judges 'to consider whether or not the words of the written contract represent the true intentions or expectations of the parties', as it was put by Lady Justice Smith in a case called *Autoclenz*.[1] And if the world the lawyers' documents describe isn't the real world, judges will apply the law to the real world and not to the documents.

Uber is, to repurpose Matt Taibbi's immortal phrase about Goldman Sachs, 'a great vampire squid wrapped around the face of humanity, relentlessly jamming its blood funnel into anything that smells like money.'[2] And its structure exemplifies how the desire to exploit these weaknesses in the social compact have contorted what would otherwise look like sensible business practice.

If you wanted to set up a huge taxi firm, you'd take advantage of your buying power to buy fleets of cars and insurance and fuel. And to ensure security of supply and a high-quality customer experience, you'd employ drivers. These steps would meet an economist's definition of efficiency. But Uber took none of them.

What it did instead was driven by a desire not for business efficiency but to dodge its obligations under the social and legal compact between businesses and the societies that create the conditions in which those businesses can flourish.

And what we wanted to do was test whether Uber's plan worked.

On 28 October 2016, the Employment Tribunal published its decision in the case of Mr Aslam and Mr Farrar. The tribunal found that Uber's:

> general case and the written terms upon which they rely do not correspond with the practical reality. The notion that Uber in London is a mosaic of 30,000 small businesses linked by a common 'platform' is to our minds faintly ridiculous.[3]

The result was that drivers were workers, supplying their services not to passengers, with Uber somehow acting as agent of the drivers, but supplying their labour to Uber, so that they were its 'workers' entitled to benefit from statutory safeguards like minimum wage and holiday pay.

Over the next few years, increasingly desperate, and expensive, lawyers would try to dislodge this conclusion in the Employment Appeal Tribunal,[4] the Court of Appeal[5] and finally the Supreme Court.[6] On each occasion they failed. And in late 2021, Uber finally accepted that it had employment law obligations to drivers, like Mr Aslam and Mr Farrar, that it would have to meet.

But, as a campaigning tax lawyer, it was the tax consequences of the decision that I was most interested in.

What the Employment Tribunal had been asked to decide was whether the drivers were 'workers', a legal status that sits halfway between being an 'employee' (a closer relationship with the employer) and being self-employed (a more independent one). But what about if those drivers were employees? If you pay an employee you have to hand over to HMRC something like 25 per cent of what you pay them in employer's and employee's National Insurance contributions. Uber had been doing none of that.

What's more, if drivers were supplying their services to Uber, they couldn't be supplying them to passengers. But passengers were certainly getting transportation services, which meant someone was supplying them and if it wasn't drivers it had to be Uber. If Uber was supplying transportation services to passengers, then it could no longer pretend to be a small business, taking advantage of the exemption from VAT for small businesses. Going forward, I thought, it would have to allocate 20 per cent of whatever fare it charged to passengers to HMRC. And, looking back, it would owe HMRC 20 per cent of whatever fares it had collected over the last four years. These were sizeable sums. From evidence given by Uber executives to Parliament's Public Accounts Committee about Uber's market size, I estimated its liability to VAT and interest on it to be something like £1.1 billion.[7]

Just over a week after the decision of the Employment Tribunal, I had breakfast with a very senior official at Her Majesty's Commissioners of Revenue and Customs. We ate at the Delaunay Counter, several hundred yards west of the High Court and opposite the historic home of the Department of Inland Revenue, one of the predecessor agencies of HMRC.

I have written in Chapter One about how my Waiting for Tax blog had turned me into a real influencer on tax policy. The senior official and I would meet from time to time at industry events and trade (very English) blows. I remember asking him why so many tax authorities across Europe were taxing Facebook much more aggressively than HMRC was.

'Ah,' he said, 'because they are political.'

'But don't you suppose they think *you* are?' I replied.

But at breakfast it was Uber on my mind: was HMRC going to treat the Employment Tribunal decision as a spur to act on Uber? Not much time had passed and I didn't anticipate a concluded view. But I was pretty shocked at what I got – a shrug and a wrinkling of the nose. What to do?

Lord Hennessey's notion of the 'Good Chap' is not really a description of our system of government or our constitution. To think of it as such is to underplay its significance. It is the ground zero to all of institutional life in Britain. There is no need of rules or safeguards, checks or balances or a meaningful separation of powers because, dear boy, well . . . because this is Britain, where bad things do not happen.

You would think the public interest in the fair and proper collection of taxes is obvious.

The tax system is one of the two main junctures where vast sums of money move between private pockets and the public purse. The other – more on this in Chapter Nine – is public procurement. If as a judge you have absolute confidence that the country is run by Good Chaps you can sleep easy in your bed because it is inconceivable to you that in Britain sweetheart deals might be done for VIPs. There is no need for judicial scrutiny – why would there be?

And this is, broadly, what the law says. It says that there is no public interest in scrutiny of these junctures. The public should just accept the word of the power elites that run Britain that nothing bad ever happens behind those closed and bolted doors.

The law, let us remember, is made and administered by judges who move from private school to Oxbridge to the Bar and then the Bench. The Sutton Trust and Social Mobility Commission report 'Elitist Britain'[8] talks of a 'pipeline' from private schools through Oxbridge and into top jobs. Fifty-two per cent of senior judges move through that pipeline. And for the most senior ranks of civil servants, like the guy I met from HMRC, 59 per cent went to private schools and 56 per cent to Oxbridge.

They went to school with one another. They went to university with one another. They know each other – if not personally then each other's type – and they trust one another to do the right thing. Public scrutiny, knowing and seeing that the public interest is upheld: well, there is no need for any of that. They are Good Chaps who can bar the door to meddlers like me, and the tens of thousands who crowdfund us.

The absurd governance of VAT, that the Good Chaps at HMRC had ignored for years, did not just benefit Uber. One of its main competitors was the taxi company Addison Lee, which was owned by the huge private equity group Carlyle. Addison Lee operated two separate systems. If you were an 'account' customer – the type more likely to be a business which could claim VAT back – it would charge you VAT on your cab. But if you paid cash – so were more likely to be a private payer who could not recover VAT – it would not. Exactly the same service, but two different VAT treatments.

But I had a plan.

As a barrister supplying legal services I had to be registered for VAT. Every quarter, by law, I had to submit a VAT return. And on that VAT return I would declare my 'outputs' – the legal services I had supplied and the VAT I had charged on them. And I also had to declare my 'inputs' – the costs I had incurred in supplying those legal services and the VAT I had paid on them. The difference between the VAT I charged on my outputs and the VAT I collected on my inputs, the Tax on the Value I Added, I had to pay over to HMRC.

But the law also said that I had to have evidence of my inputs – the costs I had incurred in supplying my legal services – before I could set them against the tax I had charged. And that I had a right to get that evidence, in the form of a VAT invoice, from my suppliers.

So what if I took an Uber to visit a client?

I realised that if I could get the Courts to force Uber to give me a VAT receipt, it would mean that not just my Uber journey but everyone else's Uber journey would be subject to VAT. And Uber would have to pay all of the VAT – one sixth of its entire UK turnover, which was more than a billion pounds – over to HMRC. This would be an enormous addition, hundreds of millions every year, to public funds.

The value to me of my claim would be nothing – just the VAT on that journey. But in deciding whether I was entitled to a VAT invoice the Court would also decide whether everyone else who took an Uber would be entitled to a VAT invoice. It would be deciding what HMRC had refused to – that Uber was liable to charge VAT. I wouldn't need to try and persuade HMRC to collect tax from Uber.

It would be a row between me and Uber, over whether I had paid it VAT.

What's more, if Uber was liable for VAT, it wasn't just liable for future VAT. It was also liable for VAT that it should have paid to HMRC in the past.

The rules around unpaid tax allow HMRC, as you would expect, to collect tax that ought to have been paid in the past. But they also limit how far into the past HMRC can go. Unpaid tax from too long ago is lost for ever – the errant non-taxpayer profits from its own breach of the law. For VAT purposes, it seemed as though HMRC would be likely to be able to go back four years. And, as mentioned above, the amounts of past VAT Uber had failed to pay were significant – my calculations showed around a billion pounds during that four-year period.

The formal mechanism by which HMRC collects underpaid tax is an 'assessment'. And because of the time limits, when HMRC discovers a potential underpayment by a taxpayer going back into the past, its practice is to raise an assessment to protect its position. That way, if the *potential* underpayment does turn out to be an *actual* underpayment, the errant taxpayer doesn't profit from its own wrongdoing.

Raising a protective assessment doesn't impose any obligation on HMRC to collect the tax. Nor does it impose an obligation on the taxpayer to pay it. It's a protective or precautionary step – simple good practice – to look after the position of taxpayers generally: your position and my position.

The necessary logical consequence of the Employment Tribunal decision was that Uber was supplying transportation services. The European Court of Justice had said that Uber was supplying transportation services.[9] And every specialist tax barrister I spoke to considered that Uber was likely to be liable for VAT. But HMRC refused to raise a protective assessment. And every month that went by without one meant tens of millions in tax foregone: money that should have been in the public purse resting instead in the pockets of Uber's shareholders.

HMRC's conduct, as I saw it, was impossible to square with good administration. It was conspicuously wrong.

I had no illusions that taking on Uber would be easy. It was a global behemoth worth tens of billions and with considerable pulling power at the heart of Government. And I learned quite how much when I was sent a cache of emails from inside Transport for London dating back to 2013.

TfL's compliance team had spotted that Uber's business model breached legislation requiring 'private hire' bookings to be taken by the licensed operator (an Uber entity called Uber London Limited). But the Uber app, to maximise tax 'efficiency' (a polite word for 'dodging'), caused those bookings to be taken by a different Uber entity, based in the Netherlands. And a senior TfL executive – his name does not matter so let me call him G – decided to raise the issue with Uber.

You or I might have responded to G by paying a small additional amount of tax. Not Uber. It got its lobbyists to arrange a meeting with the senior team at Transport for London and to make a complaint to the British consulate in San Francisco: 'TfL has threatened to revoke our licence,' it said, before adding scornfully, 'if ever old law could be said to stand in the way of modern technology.'[10]

The British consulate wrote to their man in Downing Street, who at the time was working in the Policy Unit at Number 10, and asked for a name at Number 10 or the Department of Transport they might speak to. That contact instead wrote to Kit Malthouse, then working under Boris Johnson when he was London Mayor, and who went on to work under Boris Johnson when he was PM as a Home Office minister:

Could I ask you to take a look at a problem Uber seems to be facing with TfL. We are about to make a big pitch in Number 10 to make the UK a world leader in the 'sharing economy'. And it would be a real shame if we let incumbents in various markets, outdated rules or old-fashioned thinking block our effort to attract key firms to the UK and encourage home-grown companies . . . So I'd be really grateful if you could look into Uber's case and see what we might do.

Kit Malthouse forwarded that email to his colleague, the Deputy Mayor for London, Isabel Dedring, saying 'Plea from Number 10' and indicating they should sort it. She said that G, the TfL executive who had authorised the decision to raise the licensing concern with Uber in the first place, was 'probably best placed to explain where we have got to with Uber to date'. G got the message, in both senses, and replied quickly. He had met with Uber and:

their [private hire] licence is not in question! The meeting with them was very positive. The bigger problem we are going to have is with the [black cab trade] when we confirm we have no problem with the way Uber are operating. This is really all about competition within the industry – Uber are a big threat to all of them.

Fixed. And Uber appreciated it too: 'we interact with regulatory bodies the world over and TfL has always been among the more professional and forward-looking we've engaged with.'

It's not hard to understand their gratitude. In December 2021, the High Court finally got the chance to take a look at the question that had troubled G – at least until Number 10 told him not to be – and concluded that the position he had originally taken had been the right one.[11] And if you open the Uber app in London today, you will see that bookings are taken by Uber London Limited.

Politicians in their pocket, a bottomless pit of money to pay lawyers, and a billion pounds on the table. How could it possibly go wrong for me?

My assumption was that the reason HMRC would not assess Uber was because it was being leaned on by the most political part of our civil service, HM Treasury, then headed by Chancellor of the Exchequer George Osborne.

Earlier I had obtained from a small CD supplier, who was being undercut by VAT evasion effected via another tech giant, Amazon, a recording he'd taken of a conversation with a senior HMRC executive. The exchange went like this:

CD Supplier: *What worries me is that ministers have some kind of agenda to basically not annoy Amazon. If Amazon does something illegal, Amazon has to be punished, in my view. In America they tried things like 'that's it we are not building a warehouse in your state' and all this sort of stuff . . .*

HMRC Executive: *I've heard of that. I've heard from the Treasury; the Treasury didn't want us to be too hard on Amazon. But I think that was a brackets 'yet' close brackets.*[12]

There was a sense that the Conservative Party thought the UK's economic interests were best served by creating an accommodative fiscal environment for Big Tech. Or, as you and I would put it, letting the powerful off their taxes.

What I was banking on was that through a combination of the law and publicity I could generate enough legal and reputational risk for HMRC that it would rethink its decision not to assess. Its balance of risk – protecting the public purse versus staying on the right side of its political masters – already felt quite finely balanced. There was extraordinary jeopardy for HMRC in the possibility a judge might say it had wrongly failed to assess Uber to tax – that it had to be forced by a member of the public to protect the public purse and collect a billion of VAT.

In some senses, the ground was rather promising.

The target was an enormous US tech company which had generated breakneck growth by breaking the rules. In a 2014 email leaked to the *Guardian*, the then head of global communications at Uber had crisply summed up their relationship to regulators with 'sometimes we have problems because, well, we're just fucking illegal'.[13] And the sums of tax involved were vast – in a private briefing given by Uber CEO Dara Khosrowshahi to a leading tech journalist in early 2020, he said their historic VAT bill was a staggering $1.5 billion.[14] The case that it owed the tax was compelling – all but unanswerable, I believed. Our thesis – that special rules were being made for those with political connections – was one the public was ready to hear. And taking on this Goliath was a tiny not-for-profit, Good Law Project, with no employees or assets, acting entirely in the public interest.

For a court to conclude that HMRC had ignored the public interest by failing to assess Uber to tax would be a knock the complacent Good Chap might never recover from. This, I knew, would never be allowed to happen. But if we could keep the show on the road long enough, and generate enough publicity, we might just tilt the scales in favour of HMRC doing the right thing.

On 15 March 2017, I booked an Uber to take me from my chambers near the High Court to a meeting with clients, Simkins LLP, in Bloomsbury. The fare was £6.34 and the VAT, had they been charging any, would have been £1.06. I asked for, and was refused, a VAT invoice and five days later, with a letter threatening legal action for what I regarded as a breach, I squeezed into the back of an Uber, along with a camera crew from ITV, bound for its headquarters in the City.

I put up a crowdfunding page and, from almost 3,500 people, I managed to raise, after costs, £100,000. A taxi union gave us a further £20,000, which it had collected from its members. Two months later, on 23 May 2017, we issued proceedings to try and force Uber to give me an invoice.

But there were also some very real difficulties.

The way in which litigation works in the UK – with a few exceptions – is that the loser has to pay the winner's costs. The purpose of the rule is to deter bad claims. If you sue someone and your claim turns out to be a bad one, why should the winner have to bear the costs of defending it? Similarly, if you sue someone, and your claim turns out to be a good one, why should the value of your claim be reduced by the costs you incurred asserting your legal rights?

And this, it turned out, was our main problem.

My financial interest in the claim was pennies, a hundred and six of them, but Uber's was billions. It was likely to spend millions defending the claim and, if I lost, I would have to pay these or be bankrupted. As the judge went on to find: 'Uber's costs of these proceedings could reach £1 million at first instance, an estimate with which I did not understand Uber to take issue.'

To avoid the risk of costs stifling the bringing of litigation in the public interest, the rules of the court recognise a variety of different scenarios in which someone might be entitled to certainty regarding the costs they are liable to pay if they fight a case. And in those scenarios a 'cap' can be imposed on the amount they are liable for.

When we began the case against Uber, Good Law Project had already successfully obtained a number of 'cost capping' orders against the Government. The question, upon which we had taken advice and could see a tentative way forward, was whether we could get one from Uber.

The point was an important general one.

We had a powerful legal argument. It concerned hundreds of millions of pounds of public money. We had persuaded thousands of people that it was sufficiently important for them to stump up their own money to fund it. But without costs protection, none of this mattered. Uber would spend millions defending its position as the claim rose through the Courts. These were millions I would have to pay if my case turned out to be wrong and millions I didn't have.

And this question wasn't particular to me – or to this litigation against Uber. It is one faced by everyone who wants to bring, or to defend, litigation in England and Wales against private defendants.

The promises the law makes to us – of blindness to status and holding power to account – are attractive. But try and bank them against someone who is wealthy and powerful and you quickly wise up. Unless you can pool your resources with others who share the same goals, without funding from the many, you cannot use the law to take on the few. The law is shown up as lofty aspiration with no delivery.

Lawyers who write about access to justice tend to talk in terms of the rights that those without money cannot assert. But there is another side too.

The most glaring example is the law of defamation, where the rich and powerful use threats of libel to silence criticism. Even if the criticism is important, and in the public interest, indeed even if it is demonstrably true, the critic often feels forced to withdraw their comments. They are told that, if they lose, the consequences of having to pay their opponent's costs, which they cannot control, would be catastrophic. And they have no money to pay their own in the meantime.

I know of women who have been raped or sexually assaulted and, having failed to persuade the police to prosecute, have then named their rapist for a semblance of justice. They have then been sued for defamation and, unable to pay lawyers, have felt obliged to publicly resile from the truth and apologise to their rapist. Indeed, Good Law Project, which is financially stronger now than it was then, is currently providing financial backing to a woman who was sexually assaulted and is, at the time of writing, being sued by her abuser.

Once you appreciate that access to justice is about more than rights that everyday people cannot afford to assert, you begin to grasp how the law can become a wicked thing. What was once the subordination of the weak by physical force becomes instead the subordination of the poor by financial force. Our criminal law system punishes the former – and our civil law system encourages the latter.

When I started Good Law Project – and the case I brought against Uber was the first case it crowdfunded – our resources were modest indeed. We had no employees. We had no reserves. The witness statement I swore when we applied for a costs cap disclosed that we had £25,000 of income.

We now have something over forty employees, including those of our own law firm, Good Law Practice, headed by Jamie Potter, perhaps the leading public law solicitor in the country. And thanks to our regular contributors we have built up a cushion against future liabilities.

And we have begun to understand what it is possible to do with strategic litigation. How tens of thousands of regular folk with regular incomes, donating £2, £5, £10 or more a month, can together turn the power of the law back against the powerful. When we use the law, backed by the collective power of our tens of thousands of supporters, people take notice. The defamation threats against us, and against me personally, have become less frequent and what we get instead is a great compliment – lies and smears from Government ministers, and their emissaries in the newspapers. It is only by collectivising power that everyday people get to use the law.

But none of this was true of Good Law Project in 2017.

Nothing happens quickly in private litigation, and it was not until February 2019 that the court heard our application for a costs cap. We instructed a Queen's Counsel specialising in legal costs – Vikram Sachdeva – to represent us.

What the Court decided was that a claim brought against a private entity, Uber, by a private citizen, lacked a sufficient public interest to benefit from costs protection. The fact that I had a private interest of £1.06 meant that the case did not advance a public interest. The cost to the public purse – tens or hundreds of millions a year – did not matter.

The judgment revealed a profound constraint on what any one individual, or certainly an individual who lacked fantastic wealth, could do to take on power held in private hands.

But we learned.

We are currently working to bring litigation against another of the tech giants, Facebook (or Meta, as it now likes to be called), which also owns Instagram. The longer it keeps people watching the platform the more it can sell their eyeballs to advertisers. And to keep them watching it uses algorithms to feed them ever-more extreme versions of content – health becomes diet becomes anorexia – with appalling consequences for children.[15]

But this time round we hope to do it right. With some financial help to develop a case from a charitable foundation called Luminate, we were able to instruct a global law firm to scan Europe for the best jurisdictions in which to litigate.

Where litigation like this shows any sign of succeeding it is, usually, bought off by the defendant. But we want the issue resolved. So we have found a way, legally speaking, to tie our hands to the steering wheel and glue the accelerator to the floor. We don't know whether the case will win, but at least we should get to the finishing line. Meta will not be able to buy the litigation off. Children deserve better than to be sold to advertisers – or betrayed by the State.

The Uber story had a happy ending, too.

When it became clear that, in practice, it would be impossible for us to ask Uber directly to comply with the law, we changed tack.

The position of HMRC – when it had been asked about our claim by Parliament's public spending watchdog, the Public Accounts Committee – had always been it could not assess Uber to VAT until the Supreme Court had reached a decision on the case brought by the two Uber drivers, Mr Aslam and Mr Farrar. It could not raise what I have called above a 'protective' assessment to safeguard the public's position in the meantime.

We didn't think this was right. Every month that passed with HMRC sitting on its hands meant tens of millions of pounds more of unpaid VAT lost to the public purse forever. VAT that Uber would never have to pay – even if HMRC came to agree with us that Uber should charge VAT.

HMRC had made it clear to us in correspondence that they intended to continue to investigate and had not raised an assessment. But we thought, quite clearly, it needed to protect the public interest in the meantime. And in May 2019 we sued again – but this time HMRC.

The normal sequence of events would have been for HMRC to file a defence to our claim which we could publish. But, remarkably, HMRC applied to the Court to clarify whether they could even tell us what their defence was. They also wanted to keep it behind closed doors, stopping busybody journalists, too, from discovering and sharing the truth.

These were absolutely extraordinary applications for it to make. They represented profound departures from the principle that justice needed to be seen to be done. And they seemed to me to exemplify the very conduct on the part of HMRC that the case was designed to expose: sweetheart deals for the powerful.

In the meantime, after we filed our claim in the High Court, Uber disclosed in its accounts in the United States that HMRC was 'seeking to classify the Company as a transportation provider'. Remarkably, however, this did not prevent it from contending, at the hearing of HMRC's application to keep its defence under lock and key, that great secrecy attached to its VAT position.

But what was known to HMRC and Uber was also clear to us and to anyone watching: Uber had at last been assessed to VAT. And in March 2022, it bowed to the inevitable and agreed that it would show VAT on its invoices going forward.

In November 2022, more than five years after we started our litigation, it announced that it had paid the sum of £615 million in retrospective VAT to HMRC.[16] It seems likely – both from what appears to be well-informed inside information and from calculations done by lawyers Good Law Project instructed to look at this settlement – that HMRC has arrived at this number by extending to Uber the benefit of a special VAT regime that exists for tour operators. I have some questions about why HMRC settled at that number rather than having a fight for a sum measured in billions. But the advice I have had is that we cannot take the matter any further.

It took two pieces of litigation and five years of work. But Uber will now have to pay its taxes – taxes that fund the roads its vehicles drive on, the education system that trains the workers it uses and the hospitals that keep them healthy, along with the Government it so successfully lobbies – like everyone else.

Its huge private equity shareholders will have hundreds of millions of pounds less, but the public purse will be better funded to ensure children in our schools have food enough in their stomachs to learn.

9. Vampires and Sunlight: The PPE Cases

Orwell wrote of the 'subtle network of compromises by which the nation keeps itself in its familiar shape'.[1] A series of recent High Court and Court of Appeal judgments look likely to lock the door, once more, on public scrutiny of public money and leave the Good Chaps to get on with their thing.

But for a year, in 2021, helped by courageous civil servants who were so appalled by what they saw that they felt obliged to speak out; a judiciary that did 'right to all manner of people . . . without fear or favour'; and Geordie Greig, who ran in the *Daily Mail* a series of brave pieces by David Rose about pandemic corruption before getting sacked for speaking the difference between right and wrong, Good Law Project was able to use the law to expose the 'familiar shape' of things.

We read, agog, on social media about who was winning PPE contracts. A company with substantially no assets or experience supplying anything to the NHS won a series of PPE contracts worth £350 million. A hedge fund with links to Liz Truss won a contract for a cool quarter of a billion. But when it came to the 'why', the 'how', and the 'wtf', there was nothing. FOI requests were met with the straight-bat of 'commercial confidentiality' and ministerial press offices handed out platitudes and sometimes flat-out falsehoods.

A series of crowdfunded legal cases brought by Good Law Project, and the 'disclosure' that litigation brings, surfaced some of the essential detail. These cases were vastly expensive – Government lawyers ran up obscene costs bills which would have deterred even the wealthiest of individual litigants.

But the power of the crowd, tens of thousands of us, were able to use the law to approach the truth.

The story begins at start of the pandemic. On 25 March 2020, the day the Coronavirus Act became law, as we tried to build resilience for our families by overbuying food, backbench Conservative MP Alexander Stafford asked a question in Parliament about the 'disgusting scourge of black-market profiteering'. 'Yes, indeed,' said then prime minister Boris Johnson: 'The profiteering is something that we should be looking at from a legislative point of view in this House, as has happened before in this country.'[2]

What emerged was far worse than the private stockpiling of pasta and toilet roll. It was a looting of public resources on a grand scale. And not by families worrying about whether complicated supply chains would hold up, but by hedge-fund owners, secretive religious sects, publicans, and box-fresh special-purpose vehicles.

None of this was opportunism. The process involved ushering suppliers overwhelmingly handpicked by ministers through what was brazenly described as a VIP lane, with its own special processes and discrete team of handlers. But only suppliers lucky enough to enjoy political connections to the Conservative Party. Of the many referrals into the VIP lane from politicians, all were from Conservative MPs or peers.[3]

The asserted purpose of the VIP lane was to help civil servants identify promising suppliers of personal protective equipment – its predicate was the bizarre one that career politicians might have special insight into who could supply PPE – but the excuse does not survive first contact with the facts.

Rather than helping civil servants, it hindered them. On 14 April 2020, a despairing civil servant in the COVID-19 Emergency PPE Sourcing Team sent an email pushing back against the prioritisation of yet another VIP:

> . . . if he jumps to the front of the queue, it then has a knock-on effect to the remaining offers of help. We are currently drowning in VIP requests and 'High Priority' contacts that despite all of our work and best efforts do not either hold the correct certification or do not pass due diligence.[4]

At the height of the crisis, when they should have been occupied in getting PPE to the front line, civil servants found themselves occupied instead with managing the expectations of those with nothing to offer but friends in high places.

They were deeply concerned about what it would mean if they decided not to give a VIP a contract. When Andrew Mills, Liz Truss' adviser at the Department of International Trade (DIT), offered for sale a contract for facemasks for a quarter of a billion pounds, one senior civil servant wrote: 'Can we expedite this one please? It's a big opportunity . . . and we are close to losing it. Our contact has close ties to DIT so wouldn't be a good outcome.'[5] And 'Andrew comes through as highly backed as he sits on the Board for DIT – so I don't want things being escalated.'[6]

Others talked about it being 'career impeding' to stand up to ministers, a belief recognised in the coded language of a senior Government adviser, Nigel Boardman, who wrote in his official report of the need to:

> make sure that individuals . . . have . . . the . . . authority to challenge a suggested action if they feel it is necessary . . . it is essential for these senior officials . . . to create the conditions that enable robust and constructive challenge, even in the most difficult circumstances.[7]

Ayanda, the beneficiary of Andrew Mills' lobbying, was awarded its contract for face masks on extraordinary bespoke terms which excused it for late delivery. The profits (which Mr Mills took steps to disguise)[8] numbered in at least tens of millions of pounds and the contract involved the supply of over £150 million of face masks that the NHS was unable to use.[9]

Civil servants knew that if they didn't get what they wanted, these highly connected VIPs would kick off. The Conservative peer Baroness Mone referred a new company with which she was connected, PPE Medpro, to Lord Agnew, another Conservative peer. Later, a senior civil servant, Jacqui Rock, emailed colleagues saying:

> We do have an issue here. Baroness Mone is going to Michael Gove and Matt Hancock today as she is incandescent with rage on the way she believes Medpro have been treating [sic] in the matter.[10]

Michael Gove was, at the time, the minister running the Cabinet Office, the department which took charge of pandemic procurement, and Matt Hancock was the Secretary of State for Health. An investigation by David Conn at the *Guardian* revealed that PPE Medpro paid at least £65m in profits to Mone's husband just months after securing the contracts.[11] Some of those profits are likely to have come from a £122m contract for gowns that were rejected after a technical inspection carried out by officials, and have never been used in the NHS. And PPE Medpro is now under criminal investigation.[12]

For friends and associates of ministers who managed to elbow their way to the front of the queue, pandemic procurement was a feeding frenzy. For taxpayers, predictably, it was a catastrophe. We spent £12.5 billion on PPE, of which £10 billion was wasted.[13] Unfathomable fortunes were diverted to the well-connected. And a number of contracts remain under investigation by the National Crime Agency and the Serious Fraud Office.

No less odd was the volume of PPE we purchased.

A National Audit Office (NAO) report from November 2020 revealed that 32 billion items of PPE had been ordered by the end of July 2020.[14] But in the height of the first wave of the pandemic – between March and July – the volume of PPE distributed by the Department of Health to front-line organisations averaged just over 500 million items a month. Even if this heightened rate of consumption continued, the 32 billion items that had been ordered would last around five years (with obvious variations across the different types of PPE).

Indeed, we bought so much that we had to pay commercial waste disposal experts to dispose of it – much in incinerators – at a rate of 15,000 pallets a month. This after we spent, between April 2020 and August 2021, almost £700 million storing it.[15]

This was no after-the-event rationalisation – the NHS was producing (and publishing) weekly data showing the consumption of various types of PPE as they were buying it. To the best of my knowledge, there has still been no real attempt to explain the sheer scale of overbuying.

And not merely did we buy too much – we bought at an extraordinary price.

The same NAO report also revealed that due to the elevated levels of demand for PPE created by the pandemic, the £12.5 billion spent by the Department of Health on PPE involved buying at, on average, 500 per cent of normal prices. As the NAO put the matter: 'Had government been able to buy PPE between February and July 2020 at the same unit prices it paid in 2019, then overall expenditure on PPE would have been £2.5 billion.'

The disaster was summed up by Meg Hillier MP, chair of the Conservative majority Public Accounts Committee, who said:

> The story of PPE purchasing is perhaps the most shameful episode in the UK government response to the pandemic. At the start of the pandemic health service and social care staff were left to risk their own and their families' lives due to the lack of basic PPE. In a desperate bid to catch up the government splurged huge amounts of money, paying obscenely inflated prices and payments to middlemen in a chaotic rush during which they chucked out even the most cursory due diligence.[16]

Perhaps most shockingly of all, the process was institutionalised. This was not just a few bad apples. Quite brazenly, Government set up a special team of civil servants to gladhand the well-connected – not just with contracts but also through pricing. Leaked Government documents instructed civil servants only to ask questions about price if the proposal was to charge more than 25 per cent above the average paid to other suppliers.[17] Not merely could the well-connected receive vast contracts – but they could enjoy enormous margins on them.

Not one single minister resigned – or even apologised.

On 18 May 2020, the Government published details of a contract award to an entity it described as 'Crisp Websites t/a Pestfix' for £108.6 million. The contract had been awarded without any competition. And the lucky winner had recorded net assets at the time of £18,000, cash of less than £20,000 and creditors due within a year of £669,000. Several weeks earlier, it had set up a crowdfunding page in which it described itself, with charming candour, as: 'a small family run business that previously only supplied products needed for pest control and cleaning'.

This was all we knew, but it was enough. How did Government decide that it was an appropriate counterparty for what we were told was £108.6 million of public money? We had questions.

Several weeks later, on 24 June, Government published details of yet another startling beneficiary of £108 million of PPE contracts, again without any competitive process – this time an obscure Northern Irish company called Clandeboye Agencies Limited, whose business was the wholesale of confectionery.

And then, on 2 July 2020, a contract for £252 million to Ayanda Capital Limited.

We knew a little more about Ayanda – that it was a hedge fund owned through a particularly ugly tax haven with, like

Clandeboye, no experience supplying PPE. But Gemma Abbott, Good Law Project's astute legal director, dug up something more. He did not appear on Ayanda's website or the Companies House records, but one of its senior 'board advisers' was a man called Andrew Mills. And as it happened, he was also on the Board of Trade convened by Liz Truss, who was then the Secretary of State for International Trade and later, disastrously, prime minister. We found this out because he had boasted about it on his LinkedIn profile. When we published this connection, the Government removed from its website the names of its advisers on the Board of Trade.

This was all we had. But we smelled a rat. In fact, we smelled a plague.

I asked around to identify who might be the best lawyers. I had done a few bits and pieces with Alex Rook whilst he worked at the very established firm of Irwin Mitchell. He had set up a new law firm – Rook Irwin Sweeney – with a couple of friends, was keen to win new clients, and was super-responsive. And the consensus was that Jason Coppel QC was the leading procurement specialist at the Bar. We knew each other a little – he had acted for the Government (and against us) in the case about whether parliamentary consent was needed to trigger Article 50. As a barrister he was low-key and conservative in his advice – an Eeyore to my Tigger.

We spoke on the phone and he was as flummoxed as I was about the bare facts. And so I instructed him to take the first formal steps in judicial review proceedings by sending a formal 'pre-action protocol' letter to Matt Hancock to find out what on earth was going on. We also brought into our challenge a doctors' group, EveryDoctor, to represent the interests of the medical profession that had been so seriously affected by PPE shortages.

At that stage, all we had were some legal questions that we thought needed answers. In substance, what we had embarked on was a piece of exploratory journalism.

The law governing public procurement recognised that a so-called 'contract award notice' needed to be published within thirty days of the award of a contract and the Government's Transparency Principles also required publication of the contract.

The rationale was explained by the principles themselves:

> Transparency and accountability of public service delivery data and information builds public trust and confidence in public services. It enables citizens to see how taxpayers' money is being spent; and allows the performance of public services to be independently scrutinised. It also supports the functioning of competitive, innovative and open markets by providing all businesses with information about public sector purchasing and service providers' performance.

But the problem was that the law was being ignored and the principles undermined. Contract award notices were published many months late, were often inaccurate, initially failed to publish the contracts themselves, and when belatedly they were published were scrubbed of vital detail, such as pricing.

Good Law Project brought separate – successful – legal proceedings challenging those failures. What we learned was that the Government knew it was breaking the law. Indeed, even after the legal deadline for publishing contracts had passed, civil servants continued to be pushed for further delays by the prime minister's office so that contract publications could fit around other announcements in the so-called 'comms grid' – the PM's plan for press handling. They were, quite nakedly, ignoring the law for their own political convenience.

Of course, this is not a problem specific to pandemic procurement.

The revealed behaviour – that Government routinely tries to dodge accountability for the spending or misspending of public money – is a very familiar one to journalists. The important public interest in transparency found legislative form in the Freedom of Information Act 2000, one of the lasting legacies, along with the minimum wage, of Tony Blair's first term as prime minister. That Act tried to cure the disease of poor-quality and politically driven decision-making by exposing it to the disinfecting powers of sunlight.

But governments prefer to do their dirty business in the shadows. And the Conservative Party has systematically thwarted the Act by the very English mechanic of exhausting those who want disclosure. Make a politically salient FOI request and you will be met with lengthy delays in replying, demonstrably bad reasons for rejecting requests to trigger more delays via the appeals process, and ultimately giving patently inadequate disclosure which forces you to start the process all over again. Even when an increasingly agitated Information Commissioner, the official watchdog, gets involved, the response is often simply to ignore the demands.

And important work by openDemocracy has shown how Government ran a 'clearing house' with the apparent intention of blacklisting requests from certain journalists deemed unfriendly to Government.[18]

The effect of all of this is two-fold.

It reduces transparency by reducing the amount of information Government is ultimately forced to disclose – in the face of repeated refusals many requestors abandon their attempts. And even when information does come out, the delays erode the saliency of the information. The frantic pace of the news cycle means that all too often what emerges feels like yesterday's news.

This decline in transparency has been accelerated by the increasing tendency of ministers, their special advisers, and other MPs to use private email accounts, private and auto-deleting messaging services, and personal phones to conduct Government business.

The practice makes it difficult or impossible for civil servants to act as stewards of public money. It poses a profound risk to national security – private channels used by Number 10 have successfully been hacked. And it guts the clear public interest in good record-keeping.

Good Law Project has an ongoing legal challenge about this practice. Before the High Court, ministers, including the prime minister, contended that there was no legal duty on them to avoid that use. In a decision with profoundly troubling consequences for those with interests in transparency, national security and public record-keeping, the High Court agreed[19] and so did the Court of Appeal. At the time of writing, we are waiting to hear whether the Supreme Court will hear an appeal.

It's not easy, if you are a traditional journalist, to hold to account a government that is to transparency as a vampire is to sunlight.

Litigation, however, is a game with very different rules and a strong leaning towards transparency.

In judicial review proceedings, the forum for the determination of 'public' law challenges, where the issue is whether Government has acted in accordance with the law, ministers have a 'duty of candour'. And what's more, what is disclosed in the litigation, and referred to in court, can generally be published.

Judges, to try and protect public trust in the administration of justice, have established and protected what they call the principle of open justice – that justice needs to be seen to be done (as well, ideally at any rate, as being done). As the Supreme Court has recently put the matter,

> the argument and evidence is reduced into writing before the hearing takes place. Often, documents are not read out. It is difficult, if not impossible, in many cases, especially complicated civil cases, to know what is going on unless you have access to the written material.[20]

And so there is, or should be, public access to written materials placed before the Court.

Judges are also, to put it bluntly, less tolerant of bullshit.

The struggle journalists have to get a proper answer to a proper question from politicians is one courts are set up to address. Finding the facts, exposing who is making stuff up, is what courts do. The very purpose of litigation is to get to the truth of what happened – and then attach legal consequences to it. And so court rules embed all sorts of mechanics to enable these questions to be put and answers demanded. There is a threat of imprisonment. Before a court, the increasing knee-jerk tendency of ministers confronted with journalists – to deflect or lie – shouldn't wash.

Imagine what one of the great political journalists of our day – a Pippa Crerar or Emily Maitlis – might do in an interview with a politician who could face jail time if they gave a dishonest answer?

Of course, we don't get the opportunity in public law to grill politicians; evidence tends to be given by civil servants and in the form of witness statements upon which they cannot be cross-examined. But we can still look for and exploit the space between, on the one hand, the routine dissembling of ministers before journalists and, on the other, the rather different demands of the law. The litigation – discussed in Chapter Seven – which forced Boris Johnson to do what the law required exemplifies how we have done this.

This is the theory, of course. The reality, at least when you are suing the Government, is more complicated. Whatever their oaths say, the simple reality is that judges are more deferential to public bodies, and senior politicians, than they would be to normal litigants. And, in the face of persistent threats from ministers, they are becoming more so. Senior public lawyers never say so in public but, in private, you would struggle to find any who would dispute it. But still, the rhythms and dynamics of litigation retain some advantages over those of journalism. And these advantages, in this world of democratic backsliding, are still being worked out by the participants.

Let me be really clear. What I am describing is not how a healthy democracy functions. In such a society, litigation and journalism do different jobs. But through the act of closing one important door to the scrutiny that is necessary for a society to remain healthy – that of the Fourth Estate – the Government handed us an advantage. And we were able, time and time again, to be first to the story.

On 18 June we learned – from the response to our letter to Matt Hancock on Pestfix – that what the Government had said was a £108 million contract for gloves, masks and isolation suits was, in fact, a contract for isolation suits only and was for £32 million only. However, the response added ominously, 'a number of further contracts' had been concluded with Pestfix 'which will be published in the coming weeks'. On 10 August, Lord Bethell – then a minister working for Matt Hancock – told Parliament that in fact Pestfix had received eleven contracts. This, too, was false. The reality was that Pestfix received seven contracts worth a staggering £350 million. And the contracts were not published 'weeks' later, but in October.

We had also had some questions about how Pestfix had funded these huge contracts. If you are dealing with a tiny company – and net assets of £18,000 is barely a twentieth of 1 per cent of the initial £32 million contract – how can you know it will be in a position to deliver what you are buying from it? How can it cashflow those huge purchases of PPE in a sellers' market?

What we learned, again from documents disclosed in the litigation, was that civil servants acting for Health Secretary Matt Hancock had paid a deposit of £26 million upfront – despite the fact that Pestfix was entirely untested as a PPE supplier and was in no position to return that money if the PPE it supplied turned out not to be fit for purpose.[21]

And what of the reason given for buying isolation suits without a proper procurement process from a tiny and untested supplier? The rationale offered by Government – the need to move with extreme urgency – evaporated when we learned that, ten weeks later, some were sitting in a warehouse in Daventry, and the Department of Health had opted to delay delivery of the remainder. None, not a single one, had been released for use in the NHS. Indeed, the department had not even tested Pestfix's isolation suits to see whether they were what it had ordered.

Things had gone no better with Ayanda Capital Limited.

On 29 July, we received Matt Hancock's response to the letter we had sent about Ayanda. The original offer to supply face masks had come, not from the reasonably well-capitalised Ayanda, but from Liz Truss' adviser Andrew Mills and a box-fresh company with no meaningful assets he had set up called Prospermill (geddit?).

The contract was only later switched to Ayanda and at Mr Mills' request because – the Government asserted – 'Ayanda already had an established international banking infrastructure' that could be used to effect the necessary payments overseas, whereas Prospermill's own bank had indicated that it could take some time to set this up on its own account.[22] Perhaps this was true – but it didn't seem terribly plausible.

Disclosures leaked to *Private Eye* suggested one Ayanda director had made £11.6 million from the deal and that there had also been a substantial payment to another.[23] These were, to put it mildly, high fees for sharing the benefit of an 'established international banking infrastructure' to make payments.

It doesn't take a huge leap of the imagination to conjure alternative explanations for switching away a hugely lucrative no-bid public contract worth more than £250 million from a newly established company with, according to Companies House, a capital of £100 set up by an advisor to a Cabinet minister.

The contract, Government invited us to believe, had been awarded to Ayanda because Prospermill Limited had nevertheless 'secured exclusive rights to the full production capacity of a large factory in China'. This, in the middle of a pandemic with hot international competition to secure PPE supplies, beggared belief. Even Government seemed to find it a bit implausible, because in seeking to explain why it had concluded such an enormous contract with such alacrity it claimed that 'there was a real and imminent risk that the available manufacturing capacity would have been lost to a rival buyer.'[24] Hang on, I thought it had secured the exclusive rights?

And it got worse.

The contract had been for two types of face mask – IIR masks (the type you and I wear to protect other people from Covid we have) and FFP2 'respirator' masks worn by medical professionals to protect them from Covid that others have. The larger part – something over £150m – had been spent on FFP2 masks which (as Government put it) 'will not be used in the NHS' because of inadequate fixings.

Government also claimed that the pricing of the face masks was 'competitive' and that for IIR face masks 'prevailing market prices were . . . approximately 59p to 64p per unit'. In fact, on 29 April 2022, according to a confidential Government document leaked to us entitled 'PPE Buy Cell – Pricing Benchmarks', the average price being paid on the date of the Ayanda contract for IIR face masks was something like 43p per unit and the rolling 14-day weighted average price had never reached the heights of 64p. It transpired the price the taxpayer had paid was something like 65p per unit (plus transportation to the UK from China). Government, it seemed, had planned to overpay by something like £40m on the smaller element, the IIR face masks, alone. And had tried to cover up the fact.[25]

We never quite got to the bottom of exactly how much profit the VIPs made. When the Government (eventually) got around to publishing the PPE contracts it redacted all the prices it had paid to its associates to try and make it impossible to assess them for value for money. We now have a spreadsheet showing every price paid under every PPE contract – but we still don't know the prices at which VIPs bought the PPE they sold to us.

Except for one.

A company called Uniserve Limited was introduced to the VIP lane by the Tory peer Lord Agnew and shared the same address as Tory Health Minister Julia Lopez. It became involved in litigation when it got sued by the supplier to it of 80 million IIR face masks, Hitex Limited.

What we can see from the report of that litigation is that, in April 2020, Uniserve paid 22p per face mask to Hitex for a tranche of those 80 million face masks.[26] It also appears to have paid under an 'introduction and supply agreement' (which the Court describes as a 'commission contract') a further 24p a mask to a company called Caramel. It is not, in case you were wondering, usual to pay more in commission than is paid for the product itself, but even taking the 'commission' at face value, Uniserve appears to have paid 46p per face mask.

Just a week earlier, Uniserve had contracted with the Health Secretary Matt Hancock to sell to the NHS 80 million IIR face masks at 87p each. Subtract from the 87p the 46p paid and you get a per unit gross profit of 41p. Multiply that by 80 million, and you get Uniserve's gross profit of £32.8 million on a contract for £69.6 million.[27]

Uniserve, a VIP introduced by a Tory peer and sharing offices with a Tory MP, sold £79m of facemasks to the tax-payer at, it would appear, almost double what it paid.

Things really began to heat up in late October 2020.

Despite its duty of candour – to put 'all the cards face upwards on the table' – the Government had not disclosed to us in any of the correspondence about Pestfix, Clandeboye or Ayanda the existence of a VIP lane. The first we learned of it was when a contact leaked to me documents showing that the Cabinet Office – which under Michael Gove MP was the political centre of the vast pandemic procurement exercise – was feeding its contacts into the procurement process outside the normal channels.

When the three cases – Ayanda, Pestfix and Clandeboye – eventually came to court, it was in relation to the principle of equal treatment that Good Law Project succeeded. The VIP lane, ruled the High Court, was illegal because it breached the principle of equal treatment.[28]

The leaked documents also revealed the existence of a startling opportunity for price gouging by favoured suppliers. As mentioned above, it was only if prices were more than 25 per cent above the average paid to other suppliers that questions were to be asked about value for money.

I was being told by those suppliers in the market I was talking to that most were operating on a 10–20 per cent margin. The leaked documents reveal that the VIPs ministers were introducing were being handled by a special VIP team. If they were also being given help with pricing – if they were told Government would buy at prices 25 per cent higher than those paid to 'regular' suppliers – their margins could have been lifted into the stratosphere, on contracts sometimes worth hundreds of millions of pounds.

So extraordinary were these revelations that, when we published them, the media didn't know what to do. Social media channels were, quite rightly, outraged, but the traditional media channels by and large ignored them. It was not for another month, when the National Audit Office confirmed the existence of the VIP lane, and reported that being on it meant you were ten times more likely to win a PPE contract, that the media felt confident enough to begin to report the scandal.[29]

Meanwhile, the extraordinary stories kept coming.

Mr Saiger was a jeweller based in Miami who set up a business supplying PPE at the start of the pandemic. From that, you might think, unpromising beginning he nevertheless managed to win six contracts selling PPE to the Department of Health for something like £270 million. When asked by *GQ* magazine how he did it, he said: 'We went on Twitter. We contacted them. It is as simple as that.'[30]

Call me a cynic, but this does seem a highly plausible explanation for how someone wins contracts worth £270 million.

Nor was the Department of Health any more persuasive. The Foreign Office, Matt Hancock's team told us, had given Saiger an 'Amber rating', indicating his business posed a moderate financial risk:

> based in part due (sic.) to its lack of published financial information and lack of company headquarters, however Michael Saiger did appear to have a legitimate jewellery business and it was not inconceivable that the company would have the necessary manufacturing contacts in China to supply PPE and medical devices.[31]

Again, that it was 'not inconceivable' that he might be able to fulfil his obligations felt like a fairly flimsy basis for giving someone £270 million. And so we asked the leading international law firm, Hausfeld LLP, to do some investigating for us.

What Hausfeld uncovered was a breach of contract claim that Mr Saiger had filed in the Circuit Court of the 11th Judicial Circuit in Miami-Dade County, Florida, which was connected with Saiger's NHS contracts. Having won, as his filing disclosed, 'a number of lucrative contracts with the government of the United Kingdom', he began discussions with a Spanish resident called Gabriel González Andersson who he understood to be expert in contracts of that type.[32]

We know very little about Mr Andersson save for one snippet. In 2012, the Spanish newspaper *El País* had named him as an 'intermediary' in an official investigation into a Chinese businessman called Gao Ping accused of money laundering and tax evasion. Andersson's inclusion in the Spanish report doesn't suggest any wrongdoing on his part.[33]

Nevertheless, according to Mr Saiger's claim, he had discussed with Mr Andersson a role where he would be actively engaged in the procurement, logistics, due diligence, product sourcing and quality control of the PPE equipment – effectively acting as Saiger LLC's third-party chief operating officer on a project-by-project basis. So far so good. For Mr Andersson's assistance with the two completed NHS contracts, he had been paid more than $28 million (£21 million), and he was contracted to be paid a further $20 million under a further three agreements to supply the NHS with millions of gloves and surgical gowns.

I don't know about you, but these do seem to me like rather generous sums to be paid for acting as a chief operating officer on a project-by-project basis to a small Miami-based jeweller. Could he have been performing some other function?

And why, in late June 2020, having already purchased what NHS consumption data showed to be many years of supply, was Matt Hancock still making direct awards, without competition, to Florida jewellers at prices that enabled vast payments to be made to middlemen whilst still remaining 'lucrative' to Mr Saiger?

We gave what we had uncovered to the BBC – who covered the story on 17 November 2020 – and sat back and waited for Mr Andersson's response to Mr Saiger's claim in Miami-Dade County.[34] Sadly we were not to see it. Three days after the BBC covered the story, and before any further embarrassing revelations could emerge, the claim settled: 'an amicable resolution has been made', as Mr Saiger put the matter to *GQ*.

We don't know what happened to everything that Saiger supplied.

But we do know – again because Government was obliged to tell us in one of our claims – that one of the contracts, for over £70 million worth of sterile surgical gowns, went wrong because the NHS thought the gowns were not wrapped in a way that enabled their sterile quality to be preserved. And, according to information published by Government, under another contract we paid Saiger's company over £36 million for three different types of FFP2 face masks at per unit prices of $2.37, $2.57 and $2.93, at a point in time when we were paying others a rolling average price of about 60p per unit. All of these masks suffered from the same fixings issue that rendered the Ayanda masks unsuitable for use.

Stranger still were the Pharmaceuticals Direct Limited (PDL) transactions. Here we had a number of leaks from inside PDL and Government that, together with disclosure in the litigation, enabled us to build up a remarkable factual picture.

What the evidence suggested was that a Tory go-between called Samir Jassal, who was on first-name terms with one of the then prime ministers' key advisers, Munira Mirza, as well as then Home Secretary Priti Patel and then Health Secretary Matt Hancock, caused a face-mask contract worth £102.6 million to be given to PDL at a substantial over-value, as well as a further contract worth £28.8 million.

PDL, unlike many VIP winners of the taxpayer-funded bonanza, did at least start with a proper business – the wholesale of pharmaceutical goods – and meaningful assets.

Right at the start of the pandemic, it engaged a man called Surbjit Shergill on what it has told me was 'a wholly contingent, success basis . . . PDL's contractor would be paid nothing at all for all of its work on all unsuccessful tenders.' Mr Shergill, it added, 'used his own team of staff, which PDL believes included Mr Jassal'.

As it turned out, this arrangement was a rather lucrative one for Mr Shergill. I have seen invoices showing that, in the latter half of 2020, one of Mr Shergill's entities, Dymon Cap Limited, invoiced PDL almost £20 million (£16.37 million plus VAT). PDL denies only that it paid those sums for the £102.6 million contract and has not denied that it paid them. The net assets of another Shergill company, Brooklands Investment Group Limited, rose from £200 on 31 March 2020 to almost £10 million in February 2021. He then promptly wound it up and distributed the proceeds.

The *Daily Mail* has described Mr Shergill as a former brick-layer. There's nothing wrong with bricklaying, but it does not suggest an ability to help with PPE tenders. The real actor in the transaction was Samir Jassal, a different figure altogether.

Jassal has been photographed with Boris Johnson, Theresa May and David Cameron. A report by the Office of the Registrar of Consultant Lobbyists disclosed the work done by Mr Jassal for PDL via Shergill's Dymon Cap Limited, including contacting the Home Secretary Priti Patel, the Health Secretary Matt Hancock and the Minister for Pacific and the Environment Zac Goldsmith.[35] He was also copied in on communications notionally by Mr Shergill with Boris Johnson's controversial special adviser, Munira Mirza. I have seen many of those communications, which is how I know Jassal was on first-name terms with Hancock and Patel.

In March 2020, Mr Shergill wrote to 'Munira' (i.e. Mirza), copying in Mr Jassal, offering PPE and thanking her for speaking to him. We know she replied and the evidence suggests she caused civil servants to contact Mr Jassal about the supply of PPE.

Several months later, on 14 May 2020, Mr Shergill wrote to 'Priti' (i.e. Patel, then the Home Secretary), again copying in Mr Jassal, thanking her for her response and acknowledging that 'as a result of your intervention' PDL was in discussions to supply BYD Type IIR Fluid Resistant Surgical Masks and asking for her further assistance. Despite PPE not being her brief, and having no obvious constituency connection with him, she wrote back that very day saying she had drawn the attention of the Cabinet Office and the Secretary of State for Transport to his offer. A week later, PDL signed a contract for £28.8 million of BYD Type IIR face masks.

The price paid for those face masks was 48p each. This was higher than Government's internal benchmark price at the time of 42p. On 60 million face masks, that represents a cost of £3,600,000 more to the taxpayer.

We also hold a letter from lawyers for Matt Hancock in which he says that Mr Shergill emailed the Department of Health and Social Care (DHSC) with a quotation for Meixin 2016V FFP3 face masks on 26 June 2020, and 'Mr Jassal followed up with emails and phone calls.'

Only four days later, on 30 June 2016, a 'request for deal approval' was made to buy what we know to be 20 million of those same type of masks at what civil servants described as the 'outlier' price of £5.13 per mask.

A per-mask price of £5.13 was quite an 'outlier'. We hold documents that show civil servants discussing the transaction at the time and giving £2.69 as the average price per FFP3 mask then being paid. The cost difference between buying 20 million masks at £5.13 per mask and at £2.69 per mask is about £50 million.[36]

So what explanation was offered for paying that outlier price?

On 6 July 2020, the accounting officer, the senior civil servant asked to sign off on the deal, was told that 'FFP3 masks remain our key concern' and there was an 'acute shortfall of FFP3' and there was a risk of 'complete stock out of FFP3'.

But four days earlier, another supplier had been told that DHSC were 'no longer looking to purchase' such masks. And that 'DHSC now has sufficient supply arrangements in place to meet requirements over the coming months.'[37] I have also seen separate unpublished documents showing that there were a number of other potential suppliers of that very model, several offering materially lower prices.

It looks very much as though the accounting officer was misled in a manner which caused him to approve a contract with the highly politically connected PDL at what other civil servants thought was a vastly inflated price.

But that's not all. We are also aware that, connected to PDL, Mr Jassal has emailed Hancock – calling him simply 'Matt' – regarding antibody tests and acknowledging Hancock has been 'most helpful previously'. And Mr Hancock has also acknowledged replying to emails from Mr Jassal.[38]

Look at it as a bystander and it's a troubling picture. What you see is a toxic mix of weird and wonderful counterparties, contracts entered into on the back of falsehoods, well-connected go-betweens receiving huge sums of money, and senior ministers helping them out for reasons that are not easy to fathom.

Look at it from the perspective of PDL and it's even worse.

Here's the question to which there is simply no good answer: what politically blind procurement process causes PDL to think it is in its interests to pay a middleman sums of this size? What legitimate business, participating in what it understands to be a proper, non-corrupt, politically neutral procurement process, agrees to hand over tens of millions of pounds to a middleman connected to senior Government figures?

And what happened to the money that Mr Shergill's companies were paid?

I referred the Pharmaceuticals Direct Limited transactions to the Serious Fraud Office in summer 2021.

The challenge to the three transactions we started with – the £350 million contracts to Pestfix, the £108 million contracts to Clandeboye and the £252 million contract to Ayanda – was heard in May 2021, and judgment was handed down in January 2022.

The High Court ruled that the Government's operation of the VIP lane was unlawful: 'the Claimants have established that operation of the High Priority Lane was in breach of the obligation of equal treatment.'

The judge agreed the VIP lane conferred preferential treatment on bids: it sped up the process, which meant offers were considered sooner in a process where timing was critical, and VIPs' hands were held through the process. She said:

> . . . offers that were introduced through the Senior Referrers received earlier consideration at the outset of the process. The High Priority Lane Team was better resourced and able to respond to such offers on the same day that they arrived.

The Court also found the Government allocated offers to the VIP lane on a 'flawed basis' and did not properly prioritise bids: 'There is evidence that opportunities were treated as high priority even where there were no objectively justifiable grounds for expediting the offer.'

It was on the very point that the Government had – in breach of its duty of candour – failed to disclose in correspondence the existence of its sleazy VIP lane that we had won.

In truth, it was a disappointing decision, in particular to our legal team who had worked so hard on the case. We had wanted more. We thought the evidence showed failings far more serious than those the judge had been prepared to find. But those, as every public lawyer knows, are the realities of litigating against the Government.

But, at least from my perspective, it didn't really matter. What did matter was the finding that the VIP lane was illegal. The might of the crowd – we had received over 16,000 separate donations – helped us expose a series of transactions that stank of sleaze. Polling in November 2021 showed that 78 per cent of the public agreed that 'the system is rigged to serve the rich and influential.'[39]

I am one of those 78 per cent and I know the role the PPE litigation played in bringing this truth to light.

Like a seaside resort in October, public law in England is slowly packing itself up for the winter. How much of this is down to the legal philosophy of individual senior judges, how much to a fear that executive threats to punish 'recidivism' will lead to the legislating away of judicial power, and how much to an instinctive desire to conserve the status quo is up for grabs. Beyond sensible argument is that many judges – although the judiciary is not a monolith – are abandoning their posts. The question still open is whether there will be a spring again, when judges come out to resume guard against those vandalising the fragile public infrastructure of our constitution.

Meanwhile, ministers and their hangers-on – the think tanks, the lobbyists, the special advisers, the party donors – move without legal hindrance.

What drives decision-making, all too often, is political self-interest: how will this policy play with the voters they want to reach? By that metric, whether we spend one or ten billion pounds on PPE, whether we pay the right price or not, whether we buy from experienced suppliers or from rogues – all of these important questions if you are trying to do the right thing by the people, become secondary to the desire to respond to need with shock and awe.

And the need is not a public health need but a political need. Our Government treated the pandemic as a political problem, perhaps a political opportunity, not a public health issue to be solved. It opened the spending spigots – on PPE and vaccines and Test and Trace – and flushed the political problem away with vast sums of public money.

Only now is the cost – a real-world lessening of the ability of the State to tackle child poverty, or social care, or the catastrophe that is climate change – emerging. Only now, as we begin to test the tolerances of international bond markets for financial incontinence, does the real importance of these stories emerge. The law is not a parlour game for performing intellectuals. It must matter. We must make it matter.

Ministers care less and less about legal compliance: they attack judges, and they attack lawyers, and they deliberately set out to bring the law into disrepute. But the problem – that they view the world exclusively through the lens of politics – is also an opportunity for those who grasp the power of the law to help deliver political accountability.

In a world like this one, a world I would not choose but which we have no choice but to live in, and try to have an impact on, there is only one way we can demand that they 'must do better' that they will hear.

During the course of the two years we ran our PPE campaign we generated literally thousands of pieces of mainstream, national media coverage about the scandal, the cronyism, the sleaze, the corruption that was baked into how the Government responded to the pandemic. We spoke the language that they speak, the only language they speak – the language of political pain.

Against that background, the ultimate decision in the case was almost irrelevant. The best we could have hoped for was a declaration that the Government had broken the law. But we got one of those in the case I mentioned earlier in this chapter, about Matt Hancock's failure to publish Covid contracts on time, and he shrugged it off and said he believed he had got it right.

It might have been different, it might come to be different, if judges determining public law matters come to see (as I do) the jeopardy to the rule of law created when Cabinet ministers shrug it off as irrelevant. They might react with harder-edged remedies. But for the time being, with some types of case at least, the real court is that of public opinion.

This chapter will barely have scratched the surface of what really happened, of that I am sure. Each of the contracts we picked, without any inside information – Ayanda, Clandeboye and Pestfix – was revealed to have supplied PPE that for one reason or another was not able to be used in the NHS. And the public purse was lightened by the decisions to choose those suppliers.

It is not just the question of whether – after the cost of buying PPE, and salaries and dividends (and sums spent by key figures in Ayanda and Pestfix on threats to sue me for libel) – there will be any money left to pay to the taxpayer in damages for any duff PPE. It is also the toxic sense that what seems to be driving the conduct of ministers is the desire to prove in the court of political opinion that they were right to buy from these counterparties. And that they will abstain from suing because winning would demonstrate that they were wrong to award these contracts in the first place. Once again, it is the political interest that predominates.

What I still can't understand, an aspect the Court refused to look at, is why the Government bought so much. Why did it carry on buying long, long after it knew, from actual pandemic consumption figures, that it had enough? That's the question my mind circles around, again and again, and it always returns to the same place. It returns to a practice I saw when the cab-rank rule obliged me to argue film cases for tax avoiders.

For a while, in the nineties and noughties, investing in films was how wealthy individuals would, to use the polite form, 'shelter' their income from tax. Clever lawyers and accountants and financial advisers would construct tax shelters. And their promoters would negotiate deals with all the huge Hollywood film studios whereby wealthy individuals could 'invest' in their films for the tax breaks.

If you were the promoter, you got paid through a percentage commission on the investments made by those wealthy individuals. And although, if you were one of the investors, you had a notional preference for films that would perform well at the box office – 'notional' because all you were really interested in was the tax shelter – the promoters didn't. What the promoters wanted was big films, expensive films, films that could be said to merit enormous investments, because the bigger the investment the more they got to skim off in commission.

If you ran a loose ship, spending almost £50 billion on PPE and Test and Trace, the vast majority of it wasted, according to the Public Accounts Committee and National Audit Office, who would notice if some of those billions ended up where they shouldn't? We don't know what happened and all I can do is guess. But this is what seems to me to remain once you eliminate that which cannot be reconciled with the known facts.

10. Slingshots

In my mid-thirties I had some years – painful and often tedious but ultimately transformative – of psychotherapy. If you haven't had psychotherapy you might not know what happens. No couches were involved. And it's not the honing of a new skill, exercising a muscle, tennis lessons for the soul. There are no 'Open Sesames'.

I understand, of course, why you might think that.

It isn't a destination but about a process of telling, or retelling, your own story. The idea is that you no longer contort yourself around places of historic pain, and so strain or break in others, but are released to live with them, to incorporate them into who you are. And for it to become possible, by that process, to stretch and grow more naturally.

I don't recall much about it now but one thing I do remember informs so much of what I want Good Law Project to be and foster and do.

'It's such a waste, Jolyon, to be unhappy,' my psychotherapist, Paula Barnby, told me one morning.

Paula's words returned to me during the pandemic as I wondered why I, and so many of my colleagues at Good Law Project, had managed to remain well and happy during the successive lockdowns. She's right, Paula – to live an unhappy life is a tragedy. There is no Strava app for happiness, you can't deposit it in a bank, or measure it or gamify it. So living as we have come to, it is easy to afford happiness little weight in our personal dashboard of deliverables. But being happy is still, for each of us, the most important thing we can be.

It also seems to me to have a symbiotic relationship with the collective good. Happiness wants to reproduce, to spread and improve the lives of the bearer, to energise. Personal happiness can inure to the benefit of all of us – if the conditions are right. I began to wonder whether what kept us – and so many colleagues at Good Law Project – happy and useful was that we had found a way to respond to what was happening around us.

These themes returned in a different guise when Russia invaded Ukraine in February 2022. What did it mean to be living in Poland, on the borders of Ukraine, to find your day-to-day life engulfed by the refugee crisis, but also to have a way to respond? And how did it compare to living in the United Kingdom, where the invasion, and the slaughter, and the cruelty, happened mostly on our TV screens, or social-media feeds?

A week or so after the invasion of Ukraine, I had dinner with a Government minister. I asked them about the obstacles – perhaps uniquely difficult out of all the European nations – that the United Kingdom had placed in the path of Ukrainian refugees trying to enter the country. 'Of course,' the minister told me sadly, 'there is something of a security concern. But you might well think that those who want entry to pose a security risk will manage it somehow. Ultimately,' they continued, 'our assessment is that whatever people now say they want, in a couple of months' time they will no longer want tens or hundreds of thousands of Ukrainians in the United Kingdom.'

I can't know whether the minister's assessment was right or wrong. Undoubtedly denying entry to Ukrainian refugees who wanted to come to the United Kingdom was an act of cruelty to the refugees.

But I also think it was an act of unkindness to us too. It thwarted our need to respond, to show love and compassion. It made us feel helpless, and amplified our feelings of powerlessness and inadequacy.

Maybe it came from a different dashboard, one with no measure for the satisfaction we feel when we overcome a hurdle placed in our way to help a fellow human being. Or maybe it was forgetfulness that caused the Government to overlook how the human spirit warms with an act of kindness to another.

This impulse, to respond to a world that is wanting, to feel some degree of control over our lives, to be more than passengers on a coach trip we never signed up for, you might describe as agency.

What might we do if we got it?

In Chapter Nine I talk about what became the main plank of our work during the pandemic – exposing how ministers took advantage of the desperate scramble to buy PPE to award huge procurement contracts to associates and party donors.

But what was already clear to us was the connection people felt to our work. We tried to find, we wanted and want to be, a vehicle through which others might articulate their desire for things to be different. There is enough in the world that makes us despondent, that leaves us with no way to respond, that fills us with a desire that things be different but gives us no way of achieving it.

The world is long on diagnosis but short on prescription.

I think that our supporters see us – and this is how I want them to see us – as a microphone through which they might speak, as a means by which they might respond to changes happening around them.

One consequence of this connection is the funding to deliver our work.

I have already mentioned that at the start of 2020 we had fewer than 2,000 regular givers and we now have 30,000. Over 60,000 different people gave us money in the 2021/22 financial year.

Of course, without their financial support we could do nothing. It is incredibly important to Good Law Project. But what resonates with me at a personal level are the messages I receive from people who tell me that my voice, and our work, creates space for them to speak their truth.

There's only been one moment in my life where I have looked into the void – and understood how fascism arrives.

It was when the prime minister suspended Parliament. I talk about the case that Good Law Project brought, successfully, to overturn the suspension of Parliament in Chapter Seven. But the truly terrifying thing for me was not the fact of the prime minister having done it – Boris Johnson is a man for whom nothing is unthinkable – but how the media reacted. This was an act that might fairly be described as fascism. A man chosen by some tens of thousands of members of the Conservative Party had asserted an entitlement to suspend as an inconvenience a Parliament elected by tens of millions. If, as was the then orthodox view, this was lawful, what was left of parliamentary democracy? He could suspend Parliament whenever it was convenient to him, and for as long as he liked, and there was nothing that could be done.

But with few exceptions the media reacted with applause or equivocation. A media that had 'both-sided' the proroga-tion, 'balanced' voices who recognised it for what it was with those who sought to justify it, would not condemn any act, be it autocratic, authoritarian, fascistic.

If you live outside the United Kingdom, you might read with surprise the suggestion that much of our domestic media can no longer tell, or will not speak of, the difference between right and wrong.

You might only hear the output of BBC World Service, which has no influence on domestic politics and so, I assume, is not worth Government's time to influence. But to live here is to be in a state of constant surprise at how unmoored from fact our reporting has become. And much that should be say-able, which is right, is rarely spoken in the public square, and certainly not by those who carry an establishment stamp.

So much of Good Law Project's work – certainly during the pandemic and only marginally less so now – is done sitting at a keyboard. We see the data on our supporters but our con-tact with people in real life is all too often mediated through a laptop screen and muffled by the limits of the written word. My real-life interactions with our supporters are infrequent – usually on the streets as I plod homewards from our office.

Perhaps this is why I find them so moving – I still feel thrilled to be approached by a stranger who is anxious to tell me of how she supports our work, and how we have created space for her to speak. To speak – and to respond to events by supporting our work financially. Were we a political party we would rank by income above any bar the Labour and the Con-servative Party and, were you to exclude contributions from big donors and look only at membership income, we would be second only to Labour. We have achieved this in an extraordinarily short period of time. At the time of publication it will be just over three years since we took on our first employee.

We know, because they tell us, that people feel very deeply protective of the work we do and are hugely proud to support us financially. I spend almost as much time encouraging people not to give more than they can comfortably afford as I do soliciting further donations.

These things matter to us and to our supporters – financial support and giving voice. I still have a sense of disbelief about what it means to be trusted by so many people with their money. But I also keenly feel the inadequacy, measured in terms of giving people agency, of what we have been able to do. It is that agency, I believe, that people want.

That we might be an outlet through which our supporters can voice their discontent is one thing. But it is a thin measure of success if what you really want is to give people more agency and enhance their ability to influence the shape their lives take – along with that of their communities.

'I work in a warehouse and I already give you money, what more can I do to help?' This is the question to which I return. What can the law do to help answer this question?

We are developing several programmes of work to try and meet this need.

The first is to devolve – to distribute – the Good Law Project model of litigation to communities across the country. Rather than – or as well as – using the law to hold power to account ourselves, we want to put into the hands of local communities the ability to do it themselves.

The rhythms of campaigning through litigation are difficult and unfamiliar. A traditional campaigning approach identifies an issue, works out how to talk about it in ways that resonate with key audiences, and develops an 'ask' – or call to action – around it.

Almost none of that is possible with litigation. You prioritise areas you want to be active in, and keep your eyes open for unlawful acts by meaningful actors, but you can do no more than that. Without a breach, without an unlawful actor, you have no campaign.

Even when you do spot unlawful conduct in an area you have chosen to be active in, the illegality will not usually coincide with your campaigning messages. Only very rarely is there a close alignment between what offends the public and what offends a judge. So you have to find messaging that bridges the gap between what the legal case is about and the underlying point that might animate your supporters.

The 'ask' is difficult too.

Remember, fewer than one in forty judicial review cases that are initiated succeed. We are sophisticated clients – we can identify what are likely to be good cases more quickly and efficiently than many others and we have access to the best lawyers – but we can never guarantee success and our messaging must always remain mindful of our prospects.

It is also true that the constancy of Government's law-breaking risks creating a dangerous fatigue in the minds of the public. 'They break the law all the time and nothing seems to happen' is a proposition that is put to me frequently. It is a challenge for our model of working – and it is existential for the rule of law and the judges who administer it. What role will be left to it and them if, put bluntly, no one any longer cares?

As I say in Chapter Three, this is principally a problem for the judiciary to confront. Nevertheless, our experience is that campaigning through litigation works. For a community, litigation can be a rallying point. It is a way to respond, with positive action, and a series of sequential steps around which a campaign might be organised. There is a plausible theory of change – successful litigation can change history. And these features create a 'hook' for local journalists, both citizen and professional, to write about how people in their communities are making them better.

Indeed, there are reasons to think campaigning litigation could be even more successful at a local level. Local politics, freed from the deadening ideological hand that steers much national media, can be more volatile and, thus, riskier for incumbent power. And, of course, it's incumbent power, and its abuses, that our litigation challenges.

We don't think we can balance those challenges and opportunities with a platform whose concern is making litigation generally more accessible to the public. But we do plan to create a platform to support particular pieces of litigation.

To understand what this could look like, we commissioned legal advice on the climate emergency declarations entered into by, so far, more than 300 local authorities across the country. A cynic might say that these are relatively easy, and substantially cost-free, pieces of virtue-signalling that give councillors a useful political shield against allegations that they are not doing enough to tackle climate change whilst enabling them to continue to do, well, not enough to tackle climate change.

That advice – which we commissioned from a leading environmental QC – identifies that some of those climate emergency declarations have legal teeth. In the right circumstances, local authorities could be sued for their breach. Imagine 300 local groups threatening – and many of them subsequently bringing – legal actions challenging councillors to match their rhetoric around climate change with action.

The combination of the galvanising effect of the litigation on campaigning with the political peril it created, and the possibility of a humiliating loss in court, would shift the conduct of local authorities. It might not shift the conduct consistently, it might not shift the conduct enough, but it would shift it, across 300 local authorities.

So we can see that it might work, and we would like to try. But how might we enable it?

We hope technology might be the answer.

We are in the early stages of developing a platform through which we might share legal advice, and text that can be used for multiple similar legal actions. We would commission this advice centrally from leading national experts. And we would engage those same experts to continue to provide ongoing advice, which we would share, on issues affecting multiple claimants.

Alongside the legal resources, the platform would host campaigning advice and resources – ready-made forms for crowdfunding, press releases for local media, petitions, details on how to contact councillors and MPs – to spark and support local campaigns.

And, because the project is about fostering a sense of personal agency, a sense of being able to help shape your own destiny, we would also like to create side-by-side a peer-to-peer network so that communities can share their own experiences of what has worked and what hasn't.

Although we envisage that lots of the community groups we hope will form will have a retired or active solicitor amongst them, our plan is that they shouldn't need to. At some stage, when it has become clear what are the leading cases, Good Law Project will step in and offer representation to the claimants in those cases, and have the remainder parked behind their resolution. We would then offer direct, bespoke support to the community that was the litigant in those cases.

We do not envisage we will charge communities for access to the platform. And any legal services they may choose to take from our law firm – Good Law Practice – will be at a price well below market rates. We have established the practice in part to be able to access high-quality legal advice at a low cost and we hope the costs of building and supporting the platform will come from further donations from members of the public.

Although we wanted to imagine how it might work with a specific project – I have mentioned climate emergency declarations – our intention is to build a 'white label' platform. Putting it another way, we intend to build a platform that can be used for lots of different pieces of litigation, across different issues, the objectives of which we support and whose features – a high degree of legal commonality across different local settings and with a strong campaigning pull – are such that the platform might work.

This is obviously an ambitious piece of infrastructure. No one sets out to build something like this without a commercial imperative – why risk the speculative investment without the possibility of profit at the end of it?

But because people choose to back the work we do, we can try these things. We have about forty staff reliant on us for their livelihoods and we cannot be cavalier. But I don't want us ever to confuse the interests of the organisation – to become bigger, more prestigious, comfortably rubbing shoulders with the great and the good – with the importance of impact, and the leveraging of the advantages of our unique model.

Our second route to use the law to enlarge agency involves us lending our infrastructure and expertise to vulnerable communities who might need it.

Once upon a time, communities who were being unlawfully treated would have been able to remedy that treatment through legal aid. After decades of savage cuts, this is no longer meaningfully true. The people most affected by these cuts in legal aid are those who need it most. And they fall into two classes: a social class of those who lack the money to pay lawyers and the social capital to be able to access them without payment; and a political class comprised of minorities the Government finds it politically useful to target with acts of performative cruelty. Heaven help you, because legal aid will not, if you are both.

We know we can be useful to those communities. The law to protect them exists – but what is missing is access to it. We have tended to respond by identifying cases, in consultation with those communities, and sponsoring them ourselves. And we will continue to do this where we need to. Our efforts have been welcomed by the communities we have worked with – but it doesn't give them agency.

We would like, instead, to shift to giving communities more ability to litigate for themselves.

We will need to find philanthropic funding to help us meet our aspirations for the law firm – Good Law Practice – so that communities can litigate for themselves at rates they can afford. We will help them crowdfund for the diminished costs of the cases they want to bring. We will share with them our insights into what a successful media campaign looks like – and use our public-facing channels to amplify their messaging. And we will help them choose the right barristers.

This is, we think, what good allyship looks like. It puts into the hands of those who need them the tools we have made. And they will get to choose how those tools are used.

But it also delivers huge benefits for us. Our work will be even better informed by their needs and it means that when we take on programmes of litigation, we will also know that we will have a place to pass those programmes on. This will mean we can do more work for more communities.

Our third programme is no less ambitious and doesn't involve litigation at all.

As the central contradiction of capitalism – infinite growth on a finite planet – becomes ever more evident, we want to do something to support the growing demand for structures that sit outside it.

How do you as a community buy and hold a piece of local woodland for the common good? How might you convert a farm to support families who wish to have a smallholding? Or allotments? Might a revival of the housing cooperatives movement begin to address the problems posed by high house prices? Would you like to club together with your neighbours to take over ownership of your failing pub? Or start a community store? All of these models exist but none were easy to create or are easy to replicate.

The law should not be the rock upon which the ship of good intentions founders. And yet all too often it is. The legal marketplace is driven by money. If you have some and you want legal advice, it's not so hard to find it. But the logic works both ways. Where there is no money there tend to be few lawyers. Ownership models that sit outside capitalism by definition lack an investment case. So there tends to be less money to spare to pay for legal advice – and consequently less supply with which to meet demand.

In the space of a few years, Good Law Project has become perhaps the biggest consumer-facing legal brand in the country. With the practice we want to work with local communities to create structures that work for them – and then use Good Law Project's reach to offer ready-made answers to people who want answers. And we don't just want to offer that advice reactively to those who have already identified that they have a need. We also hope that by offering ready-made legal structures we might gently place within arm's reach new ways for communities to live and be.

There is no escaping that the world is very, very big and we are, all of us, small. The consequences of this are felt not just by individuals and communities, but by regions and even by nation states. You see this clearly with island nations in the Pacific, whose very existence is threatened by rising sea levels – they don't tend to talk much about national sovereignty. But, as Liz Truss and Kwasi Kwarteng's short spell in Downing Street exposed, it is equally true for the United Kingdom. The very purpose of the sound and fury, the language of Empire and Commonwealth, the pomp and pomposity, is to obscure some basic truths about the limited room for manoeuvre globalisation leaves to a medium-sized economy off the coast of mainland Europe with an ageing population and poor trading relationships.

These things are true; there is no arguing with them. But still, there is much that the law can do to help people respond to the world around them, to help them reshape their lives to their own choices, and to better those of the people around them. If we succeed in giving back agency, we think we might make some people happier, and that will be no small thing.

Speak

In case you are inspired, in case you want to know more, here are some other people and organisations in the United Kingdom whose work has inspired me.

Activists at Just Stop Oil, Insulate Britain and Extinction Rebellion place personal sacrifice at the heart of the work they do. They understand that keeping the existential costs of climate change at the forefront of political debate can require that they sacrifice personal popularity and liberty. And that combatting powerful narratives means becoming unpopular. The sacrifices of their activists inspire me.

Green New Deal Rising speaks clearly of how those who make the rules are often captured by private interests. They tell their stories with power and clarity and are an inclusive and generous movement.

Kwame Kwei-Armah, artistic director at London's Young Vic theatre, does the most powerful type of advocacy that there is: telling stories that quietly and persistently insist on the shared humanity of everyone, whatever the colour of their skin.

I was enormously moved by the quiet defiance of Professor Priyamvada Gopal in the face of the racist onslaught that followed from her pointing out that white lives are valued in ways that black lives are not. And I admire Professor Sunny Singh and Dr Shola Mos-Shogbamimu for their continued defiance: unless you have suffered what our right-wing press metes out to women of colour who will not learn their place you cannot know what courage it takes just to carry on. The UK organisation I know whose work most aligns with their messages is Runnymede Trust.

There are many wonderful grassroots organisations working quietly to improve the lives of LGBT+ people in the UK, but for advocacy and influence Stonewall is beyond compare.

There are many lawyers I admire but the work done for so long by so many in law centres, quietly and out of the limelight, trying to even the tilted scales of justice, is heroic and speaks to a very important vision of what justice really means.

Level Up campaigns for a world where people from all genders are loved and liberated from bodily and systemic violence. And Southall Black Sisters and Rape Crisis work to help women put their lives together again after the experience of physical violence.

United Voices of the World and the Independent Workers Union of Great Britain both do wonderful work protecting the most precarious workers (and, separately, the latter is the staff union at Good Law Project).

This book tells my story and these are organisations I can speak to. There are many more.

Conclusions

The law is not in equal partnership with the Government. The Government can change it in Parliament, bully the judges who administer it, break it without sanction, and place itself beyond its scrutiny. The Government can – and it does.

There are, in the United Kingdom, no ambitious District Attorneys who can wield the power vested uniquely in the State to gather evidence of lawbreaking. Our regulators, raised at the gentle table of the Good Chap, are under-resourced and, at a cultural level, poorly equipped to deal with the more vigorous world in which they now live.

Our judges cannot create law which is resilient against a rampaging executive by interpreting a written constitution as, almost uniquely amongst democracies, the United Kingdom has no written constitution. Indeed, we barely have a constitution at all. We might think we know what is and isn't cricket – but in a winner-takes-all world you need a rulebook. And the United Kingdom today is that vigorous world – with a simple majority in the House of Commons a government can overturn anything judges might do.

And we have no – literally no – human rights protections that are entrenched and cannot be removed.

Even within their province, the fact that judicial power can be removed qualifies how judges confronted by lawbreaking use it. They fear finding against Government. That is what the statistics suggest, it is what anecdote reveals, and it is what the prime minister Rishi Sunak from his own mouth intends.

Our senior judges are drawn from an incredibly narrow section of society. They are the overwhelming beneficiary of the status quo and, the statistics show, went to school and university with those in government whose acts they now judge. Taken as a class, their politics and social outlook are bound to align with those who hold political and cultural power.

But, however bleak things look, I know the law is impactful.

It can embarrass institutions into acting, as with the Uber case. It can open doors for MPs that would otherwise have remained barred, as with the *Wightman* case about the revocability of Article 50. It can shine light into corners that the Government would rather keep dark, as with our litigation exposing the sleaze or corruption of the procurement VIP lanes. And it can protect democracy. With the law, we protected MPs elected by the nation from a prime minister chosen by members of the Conservative Party who sought to suspend their powers (the prorogation case), and we forced that same prime minister to act as Parliament demanded (the Benn Act case).

None of this has made lawyers and judges popular with the right-wing press – or the ministers who do its bidding. Lawyers and judges are explicitly attacked in ways that would have been almost unthinkable before 2016.

'I have the greatest respect for our judiciary and the rule of law in this country,' wrote Rishi Sunak, before proceeding to threaten a new measure 'which he would activate in the event of judicial recidivism'. You can threaten judges who find against you or you can claim respect for the rule of law, but you can't do both.

That press release sent out by Rishi Sunak during his leadership campaign, which mentioned me by name ten times, led to a further series of toxic attacks in national newspapers – one branding me 'Public Enemy Number One'.[1]

I have faced similar challenges from the Home Secretary Suella Braverman, the Foreign Secretary James Cleverly, Michael Gove, and many others in Cabinet too.

Attacks like this, on a private individual who has done no wrong, from the pinnacle of establishment power, are (I think) without precedent in the United Kingdom. What's more, their criticisms, of the law and my use of it, are completely devoid of analytical content.

Lawyers do not make the law. That power rests with those who have a democratic mandate to do so. All lawyers can do is ask others to observe it. We ensure that Parliament's voice speaks.

I have mentioned above that in 1993, William Rees-Mogg, father of the aforementioned Jacob, challenged the Maastricht Treaty in court. His wealth meant he had no need to crowdfund. He lost the case but there was no challenge to his right to bring it. 'We accept without question,' the Court said, 'that Lord Rees-Mogg brings the proceedings because of his sincere concern for constitutional issues.'

The comparison with the work Good Law Project does is telling. It is not what we do that is novel. The novelty is in who we do it for. Not for editors of *The Times*. Not for peers or wealthy businessmen. The cases we bring are funded by – they have to be because we have no other funders – tens of thousands of people, many giving as little as two pounds a month. Our achievement – so objectionable to those accustomed to asserting monopoly power over the law – is to extend the reach of the law to everyday people. To extend to them, to enhance their access to, what good law can do.

Our model – which democratises access to the law – continues to flourish.

Also hard to pin down is the charge that what we do is 'politics by other means'.

For decades, others have sought to use the law to advance their social agenda – charities like Child Poverty Action Group and Public Law Project – and non-charities like Liberty and the Christian Legal Centre. It is absolutely true that our targets are the Government and Big Tech – but if your concern is to hold power to account, who else is there? The Opposition? Seriously? Government lawyers tell us in private that the fact of our existence does much to encourage legal compliance by Government ministers. If, like a criminal, your concern is to not be caught breaking the law, then you benefit from a world which has no one to police it. But what those Government lawyers tell us is that the threat of challenge by Good Law Project forces ministers to engage with the right question: whether they are acting within the limits Parliament has set for them.

It is certainly true that ministers do not enjoy the challenge we provide. In 2021, David Rose, then a senior investigative journalist at the *Daily Mail*, wrote that:

> When the history of this era comes to be written, the role of the Good Law Project in helping to erode what looked like Johnsonian hegemony will be considerable, I think. One thing I do know from talking to the targets of its efforts: they really hate it. That is an accolade.[2]

There is no greater compliment you can be paid by the power you challenge than to force it to speak your name, to breathe into your lungs the air of power, of saliency. And when those who hold power are forced to attack you, repeatedly, it is because they know you are damaging them – and they can no longer ignore what you are saying and what people are hearing.

We cannot restore things to what they should be, but a parallel United Kingdom in which Good Law Project did not exist would, all the evidence suggests, be disfigured by even greater contempt for the rule of the law.

I'm no expert in campaigning theory. I can't claim to have built a social movement. 'Big ideas' about how to change the world that aren't about what you, the reader, can do to make change happen leave me cold. Worse than that, they leave me feeling even more powerless than I did before.

The book I want to read is one that leaves me knowing what *I* can do to make things better. Everything else curdles the milk of human kindness and stunts the will to change.

Unlocking that path from desire to action is, I think, the great challenge for social campaigners. As I explained in Chapter Ten, I think the law has a big part to play – it can shape the world around us – and I want to ensure it does.

Although we have grown very quickly, we have not yet managed to broaden our focus to begin to tackle what has been lost through the removal of legal aid. Lawyers talk about 'access to justice' but what lurks behind that rather bland phrase is a fairly grim reality. The consequence has been to turn the law, all too often, from a tool for ethical levelling up to yet another weapon for the wealthy to raze their opponents to the ground.

We want to begin to address, at least with some signal cases, this unfairness. Using money donated by our tens of thousands of regular givers we have established, and we fund, an independent law firm, Good Law Practice. It has no reason to maximise its income. It exists to meet our legal needs and those of the communities we serve. We can't provide legal support for everyone but we can provide support for some, irrespective of ability to pay.

And we have established a programme to bring the law closer to the communities we hope it will serve. We want to help them access the law to build organisations that will enable them to bridge the gap. Because you don't need to be a lawyer for the law to make a difference. You just need a community around you. It was building this, rather than being a lawyer, that brought Good Law Project into existence.

What You Can Do

When I began my journey away from my practice as a tax lawyer, when I first started a WordPress blog called waitingfortax.com back in June 2013, I had a few hundred followers on Twitter.

I didn't have – I have never had – a platform to speak in the media. Not a newspaper column, or a radio show, or any affiliation to a media outlet. I have, since I started blogging, occasionally written for the mainstream press but this writing came because of the platform I had built.

I created my blog in a few minutes. My writing was just about functional, but I knew what I was writing about.

'Write about what you know' is a golden rule if you are trying to grow your audience. You're going to need a way to win the competition for attention. The world is full of people trying to understand it and who want to feel able to trust someone to explain it to them. If you can be that person you'll find an audience, whatever your area of expertise – teaching, nursing, policing, local government, or pretty much anything else.

But you have to earn that trust. You can lose it by failing to make clear your biases. Or by exposing your lack of expertise by speaking too broadly.

Starting from a position of transparency or independence will also help you be genuinely interesting. So much expert writing is clogged in ways we don't talk about. If you are employed, you will have very little space to write, under your own name at least, in a way that undermines the interests of your employer. If you are reliant on the goodwill of your colleagues, you will have heavy incentives to write with rather than against the grain of consensus.

The fact that so few people write from a place of expertise and impartiality – so few people have the space – makes it easier to succeed if you can cast off those clogs. There were better technical experts than me on some of the tax stuff I wrote about but they had reasons of their own not to talk. Which left the way open for me. Go to where the people aren't.

When waitingfortax.com was in its prime – when I was writing for it most days and attracting a large and influential readership – I was approached by the Global Head of Tax at one of the Big Four global accounting practices who wanted to know whether I might write for them. Professional services firms spend vast sums of money producing content which is barely read, and he saw me as a route by which they might, relatively cheaply, extend their reach. But the truth, as I told him, was that I couldn't succeed inside his tent. What made me interesting to read was that I could write without fear or keeping an eye on the interests of clients – his or mine. I wouldn't be able to replicate that success in a way they would feel comfortable with.

You also have to put your expertise in front of people when they need it. Let's face it, no one is interested in tax in the abstract. Not the sort of people I wanted to reach, anyway. But by keeping a close eye on what was happening in the media and in politics – and trying to anticipate when tax stories would arise – I could write topical stuff from an expert perspective that those with national platforms needed. When there was a news event with a tax element, I would write for a general readership and tweet it at the journalists who were covering the story or who I knew would be writing about it for the newspapers.

Sometimes they would get in contact and I could brief them in more detail. Sometimes they would quote me in the pieces they were writing. And sometimes they would tweet my pieces out and some of their followers would become followers of mine.

My professional community wasn't an important audience for me. Quite understandably, it wasn't interested in what I had to say, not to start with anyway. I was a 'junior' tax barrister and my messages were uncomfortable and lacked real-world impact. But when my blog got noticed outside the world of tax, they began to engage too. And in November 2014, fewer than 18 months after I started writing publicly about tax and politics, and whilst still a 'junior' barrister, I was invited by the Institute of Chartered Accountants in England and Wales, by far the most forward-thinking of the accounting regulators, to give the Hardman Lecture, the most important professional event in the tax calendar.

The attention my blog gathered caused global campaigners to come to me for advice on strategic litigation in the tax field and it built up the online community without which Good Law Project could never have happened. It meant I could speak to hundreds of thousands of people who shared my concerns – and who would help me bear the costs of putting them before a judge.

The other important thing I learned is to expect that change will cost.

There is no way to live in a world that is unjust without finding ways to cushion ourselves against it. But making things better won't happen with uplifting thoughts and organic groceries. Change costs, as Lydia Grant, the dance teacher in the seminal 1980s TV series *Fame!* almost said. Before adding: 'And right here is where you start paying: *in sweat.*'

The forces that have shaped the world as it is, and like it this way, are powerful. They are, by very definition, the winners of the status quo. If they're not complaining, if they are not stiffening their sinews to stop you, it's because you're not posing a risk to how things are.

What we can give – what part of us we feel able to sacrifice to the gods who demand of us that we make the world better – will change as we move through our lives with different burdens of responsibility to our children and to our parents and to ourselves. Sometimes it is a struggle even to get out of bed and what we can do is conditioned by the choices forced on us by our jobs and our income. There's no morality in necessity.

But if you want to write or talk or protest impactfully against the grain of power, you have to sign up to the idea of sacrificing something.

Perhaps you will take risks in leaking documents – we are often told by civil servants of what is happening around them.

But too few of them share the proof. Simply telling might make them feel better, but it certainly doesn't make the world better.

Sometimes it can make it worse.

A senior civil servant at the Department for Communities and Local Government approached us through a trusted intermediary in relation to the then prime minister's so-called 'levelling up' fund. They told us that the supposed criteria for the fund were put together *after* the decision to channel public money to Tory Red Wall seats – the criteria had been retrofitted to justify the pork-barrelling – and that it was a judicial review that we absolutely must take: 'I am sure there is a scandal there,' they said.

We issued proceedings and what came back from Government disclosed nothing of what we had been told happened. I went back to the intermediary. The civil servant reiterated to them that it was true but refused to take any risk by leaking to us the documents that would disrupt the story the Government had prepared for the Court.

We were left with no choice but to withdraw from the litigation – which was costly in financial and reputational terms. And that civil servant – they are the very opposite of an isolated case – stood by whilst ministers appropriated to their party-political purposes huge amounts of public money. They disliked what they saw, they knew it was wrong, but they would not act.

The lives of each of us are different. We all have different constraints. I was lucky to be self-employed and with some financial freedom. But still, I tell this story because it is emblematic of how too much of the world works. People think they want things to be better – but lack the inclination to take even small risks to bring that change about. It is in the accumulation of acts of turning away, of refusing to take personal responsibility, that we create the conditions for bad things to happen and for the world to get worse.

Not all of us will have lives that can accommodate the price that Just Stop Oil or Insulate Britain protestors pay: arrest and imprisonment. But there is always something we can do. And the safest way to know if we are – or merely keeping our consciences at bay – is to ask whether it costs.

'The world is in a bad state,' said Viktor Frankl, 'but everything will become still worse unless each of us does his best.'[3]

No less important is the duty we owe to ourselves – to try and live in ways that make us happy and fulfilled. We each get to make our own choices as to how to find meaning, to express our longing for solidarity and community, in a world that can feel remote and alien.

Gather the evidence, build a community of expertise around you, and what the law can do it will.

Acknowledgements

Thanks to my agent, Antony Topping at Greene & Heaton, and my editor, Jamie Joseph, who together decided I had a book in me. Somewhere. Thanks to Conor Gearty KC, CN Lester, Charlotte Clark and colleagues for help and comments on the manuscript. Thanks to my friend Dave, who has given me the profound gift of enabling me to live the life I choose. And thanks finally to the original dream team at Good Law Project of Rachel Smethers, Siham Bortcosh, Gemma Abbott and Trish Murray, some of whom are still with me and all of whom I adore.

Notes

Chapter One: Getting to Now

1 J. Maugham, 'How Do You Solve a Problem Like Tax Avoidance: What's the Scale of the Problem', Waiting for Tax, 21 June 2013, https://waitingfortax.com/2013/06/21/how-do-you-solve-a-problem-like-tax-avoidance-whats-the-scale-of-the-problem/

2 J. Maugham, 'Weak Transmission Mechanisms – and Boys Who Won't Say No', Waiting for Tax, 7 August 2014, https://waitingfortax.com/2014/08/07/weak-transmission-mechanisms-and-boys-who-wont-say-no/

3 N. Barber, T. Hickman, J. King, 'Pulling the Article 50 "Trigger": Parliament's Indispensable Role', UK Constitutional Law Association, 27 June 2016, https://ukconstitutionallaw.org/2016/06/27/nick-barber-tom-hickman-and-jeff-king-pulling-the-article-50-trigger-parliaments-indispensable-role/

4 J. Read, 'Steve Baker refuses to name person who gave him advice on overspend', *New European*, 31 March 2019, https://www.theneweuropean.co.uk/brexit-news-steve-baker-on-bbc-politics-live-44414/

5 D. Pegg, 'Vote Leave drops appeal against fine for electoral offences', *Guardian*, 29 March 2019, https://www.theguardian.com/politics/2019/mar/29/vote-leave-drops-appeal-against-fine-for-electoral-offences

6 M. Weaver, J. Waterson, 'Leave.EU fined £70,000 over breaches of electoral law', *Guardian*, 11 May 2018, https://www.theguardian.

com/politics/2018/may/11/leaveeu-fined-70k-breaches-of-electoral-law-eu-referendum

7 K. Klarenberg, 'Operation Surprise: leaked emails expose secret intelligence coup to install Boris Johnson', *The Grayzone*, 15 May 2022, https://web.archive.org/web/20221003020600/https://thegrayzone.com/2022/05/15/operation-leaked-emails-intelligence-coup-boris-johnson/

8 C. Cadwalladr, 'Online abuse is a tawdry attempt to limit what we say', *Guardian*, 18 November 2018, https://www.the-guardian.com/commentisfree/2018/nov/18/the-chilling-undertones-of-andrew-neil-mad-cat-woman-tweet

9 A. Widdecombe, 'I refuse to join the witch hunt over the Boxing Day fox killer, says Ann Widdecombe', *Daily Express*, 1 January 2020, https://www.express.co.uk/comment/columnists/ann-widdecombe/1222712/witch-hunt-jolyon-maugham-fox-hunt-boxing-day

10 J. Maugham, tweet: 'Here, for those who do not have access to it, is @RSPCA_Official's Press Statement to which mine refers.', Twitter, accessed on 27 October 2022, https://twitter.com/JolyonMaugham/status/1235554748381741057?s=20&t=sGfxZ5JhrQDqnpVL1rp60Q

11 O. Murphy, '"I felt like I had a ticking clock behind me": How NHS waiting times are leaving trans people bankrupt and on the brink', *Metro*, 23 July 2022, https://metro.co.uk/2022/07/23/in-focus-nhs-waiting-times-leaving-trans-people-broke-and-on-the-brink-17019469/

Chapter Two: Winner Takes All

1 UK Parliament, 'Pariliament's authority, https://www.par-liament.uk/about/how/role/sovereignty/#:~:text=Parlia

mentary%20sovereignty%20is%20a%20principle,that%20
future%20Parliaments%20cannot%20change.

2 M. Kennedy, 'Tributes to Lord Bingham, "the greatest
   judge of our time"', *Guardian*, 12 September 2010, https://
   www.theguardian.com/law/2010/sep/12/tributes-lord-
   bingham-judge-dies

3 T. Bingham, *The Rule of Law*, Penguin, 2011.

4 R. Husain QC, E. Mitchell, J. Pobjoy, T. Gregory, 'Nationality and Borders Bill, Clause 9: Joint Opinion', available at:
   https://docs.google.com/file/d/1t5FQ2MtMb4gWpWW
   uOra-gzJYFYWtwlW6/view

5 B. Stanford, 'Compulsory Voter Identification, Disenfran-
   chisement and Human Rights: Electoral Reform in Great Britain', *European Human Rights Law Review*, vol. 23, no. 1, 2018,
   https://pure.coventry.ac.uk/ws/portalfiles/portal/21624029/
   Binder1.pdf; J. Garland, 'Proposed Voter ID Reforms in the
   UK: The Dangers of "Fraud" Based Regulation', Oxford
   Human Rights Hub, 18 October 2021, https://ohrh.law.ox.
   ac.uk/proposed-voter-id-reforms-in-the-uk-the-dangers-
   of-fraud-based-regulation/; A. Kapoor, 'Voter ID: a disproportionate solution to an invisible problem', Runnymede
   Trust, 9 July 2021, https://www.runnymedetrust.org/blog/
   voter-id-a-disproportionate-solution-to-an-invisible-problem

6 YouGov tracker poll, https://docs.cdn.yougov.com/b7b9e3t-
   put/TheTimes_VI_220616_W.pdf

7 A. Allegretti, 'Tory whips accused of threatening rebels with loss
   of local funding', *Guardian*, 15 September 2021, https://www.
   theguardian.com/politics/2021/sep/15/tory-whips-accused-
   threatening-rebels-loss-local-funding

8 *R (UNISON) v Lord Chancellor* [2017] UKSC 51, https://www.
   bailii.org/uk/cases/UKSC/2017/51.html

9 *R v Lancashire County Council ex parte Huddleston* [1986] 2 All ER 941

10 Good Law Project, 'Public Enemy Number One', 21 August 2022, https://goodlawproject.org/news/public-enemy-number-one/

11 H. Siddique, 'Dramatic fall in successful high court challenges to government policy', *Guardian*, 23 June 2022, https://www.theguardian.com/law/2022/jun/23/dramatic-fall-in-successful-high-court-challenges-to-government-policy

12 A. Gimson, P. Goodman, 'Interview: Braverman says that what may emerge from Russia "is a basis for charges of genocide"', Conservative Home, 20 May 2022, https://conservativehome.com/2022/05/20/interview-braverman-says-that-what-may-emerge-from-russia-is-a-basis-for-charges-of-genocide/

13 E. Casalicchio, 'London Playbook: The gift of freedom – Pull the other one – I'm an ethics adviser, Geidt me outta here', Politico, 17 June 2022, https://www.politico.eu/newsletter/london-playbook/london-playbook-the-gift-of-freedom-pull-the-other-one-im-an-ethics-adviser-geidt-me-outta-here/

14 If you don't believe me, look at sections 7(2)(c), 68(1) and 69(1) of the Constitutional Reform Act 2005.

15 G. Mukherjee, N. Barber, 'Norms & Narratives in the Constitution of the United Kingdom: In Conversation with Nick Barber', Review of Democracy, 25 April 2022, https://revdem.ceu.edu/2022/04/25/norms-narratives-in-the-constitution-of-the-united-kingdom-in-conversation-with-nick-barber/

16 C. Gearty, 'In the Shallow End; Conor Gearty on the UK Supreme Court', *London Review of Books*, 27 January 2022, https://www.lrb.co.uk/the-paper/v44/no2/conor-gearty/in-the-shallow-end

Chapter Three: What the Law Can Do

1 'Coronavirus: "Right" to delay contract transparency in pandemic, says Hancock', BBC News, 21 February 2021, https://www.bbc.co.uk/news/uk-politics-56145490

2 *Marks and Spencer plc v Her Majesty's Commissioners of Customs and Excise* [2005] UKHL 53, https://www.bailii.org/cgi-bin/format.cgi?doc=/uk/cases/UKHL/2005/53.html

3 *R v Foreign Secretary, ex p. Rees-Mogg* [1994] QB 552

4 *R (Good Law Project and others) v Secretary of State for Health and Social Care* [2021] EWHC 346 (Admin), https://www.bailii.org/ew/cases/EWHC/Admin/2021/346.html

5 Good Law Project, 'Civil servants were asked to break the law for the convenience of No. 10 special advisers', 4 February 2021, https://goodlawproject.org/update/civil-servants-break-law-for-no10/

6 Cabinet Office, 'Findings of Second Permanent Secretary's investigation into alleged gatherings on Government premises during Covid restrictions', 25 May 2022, available at: https://assets.publishing.service.gov.uk/government/uploads/system/uploads/attachment_data/file/1078404/2022-05-25_FINAL_FINDINGS_OF_SECOND_PERMANENT_SECRETARY_INTO_ALLEGED_GATHERINGS.pdf

7 Good Law Project, 'NEW: Met Police refusing to investigate No 10 gatherings likely to be unlawful', 17 December 2021, https://goodlawproject.org/news/new-met-police-likely-unlawful/

8 L. Shaw, 'Boris Johnson reveals he's a Tignanello fan', The Drinks Business, 12 July 2019, https://www.thedrinksbusiness.com/2019/07/boris-johnson-reveals-hes-a-tignanello-fan/

9 M. Smith, R. Wearmouth, 'Rishi Sunak to spend £13,000 a year heating new pool – six times average energy bill', *Daily*

Mirror, 23 April 2022, https://www.mirror.co.uk/news/poli-
tics/rishi-sunak-spend-13000-year-26782055

Chapter Four: Judging the Judges

1 *Bell and another v The Tavistock and Portman NHS Foundation Trust
   and others* [2020] EWHC 3274 (Admin), https://www.bailii.
   org/ew/cases/EWHC/Admin/2020/3274.html
2 Endocrine Society, 'Endocrine Society urges policymakers
   to follow science on transgender health', 28 October 2019,
   https://www.endocrine.org/news-and-advocacy/news-
   room/2019/transgender-custody-statement
3 *Gillick v West Norfolk and Wisbech Area Health Authority* [1986]
   AC 112, https://www.bailii.org/uk/cases/UKHL/1985/7.html
4 G. Lavery, '"The Divisional Court Brought to That Decision a
   Series of Preconceptions about Gender": A Conversation with
   Jolyon Maugham, QC', gracelavery.org, 1 April 2021, http://
   www.gracelavery.org/conversation-jolyon-maugham/
5 *Bell and another v The Tavistock and Portman NHS Foundation Trust*
   [2021] EWCA Civ 1363, https://www.bailii.org/ew/cases/
   EWCA/Civ/2021/1363.html
6 J. Maugham, 'Freshly-minted QC defends silk system – and
   bacon buttie picture', Legal Cheek, 18 February 2015, https://
   www.legalcheek.com/2015/02/freshly-minted-qc-defends-
   silk-system-bacon-buttie-picture/
7 *Commissioners for Her Majesty's Revenue and Customs v NCL Investments Ltd and another* [2022] UKSC 9, https://www.bailii.org/
   uk/cases/UKSC/2022/9.html
8 Ministry of Justice, 'Diversity of the judiciary: 2022 statistics',
   14 July 2022, https://www.gov.uk/government/statistics/
   diversity-of-the-judiciary-2022-statistics

9 The Sutton Trust, 'Elitist Britain 2019: The educational backgrounds of Britain's leading people', 24 June 2019, https://www.suttontrust.com/our-research/elitist-britain-2019/

10 Courts and Tribunals Judiciary, 'Judicial Diversity and Inclusion Strategy 2020–2025 launched', 5 November 2020, https://www.judiciary.uk/guidance-and-resources/judicial-diversity-and-inclusion-strategy-2020-2025-launched/

11 'White male lawyers should "think twice before talking about sport at work to avoid excluding women"', *Daily Telegraph*, 21 October 2022, https://www.telegraph.co.uk/news/2022/10/21/white-male-lawyers-should-think-twice-talking-sport-work-avoid/

12 Good Law Project, 'Ground-breaking polling YouGov: trust in the judiciary', 11 November 2022, https://goodlawproject.org/ground-breaking-polling-yougov-trust-in-the-judiciary/

13 C. Phipps, 'British newspapers react to judges' Brexit ruling: "Enemies of the people"', *Guardian*, 4 November 2016, https://www.theguardian.com/politics/2016/nov/04/enemies-of-the-people-british-newspapers-react-judges-brexit-ruling

14 J. Maugham, 'Leaving without a deal will put lives at risk – we're not prepared', CrowdJustice, 2019, https://www.crowdjustice.com/case/not-ready-for-no-deal/

15 J. Shklar, *Political Thought and Political Thinkers*, University of Chicago Press, 1998

Chapter Five: Setting Up Good Law Project

1 J. Burn-Murdoch, 'Britain and the US are poor societies with some very rich people', *Financial Times*, 16 September 2022, https://www.ft.com/content/ef265420-45e8-497b-b308-c951baa68945

2 H. Whitehead, 'Commission clears Runnymede Trust after Conservative MPs complained about its work', Civil Society, 2 September 2021, https://www.civilsociety.co.uk/news/commission-clears-runnymede-trust-after-conservative-mps-complained-about-its-work.html

3 'Five million people in households with children have experienced food insecurity since lockdown started', Food Foundation, 4 May 2020, https://foodfoundation.org.uk/news/five-million-people-households-children-have-experienced-food-insecurity-lockdown-started

4 Dr L. E. Major, 'Why is Social Mobility so low and what can we do about it?', The Sutton Trust, https://www.york.ac.uk/media/educationalstudies/documents/Social%20Mobility%20Public%20Lecture%20York%206.pdf

5 Good Law Project, 'Just how successful are we?', 10 June 2022, https://goodlawproject.org/news/just-how-successful-are-we/

6 Good Law Project, 'Ground-breaking polling YouGov: trust in the judiciary', 11 November 2022, https://goodlawproject.org/ground-breaking-polling-yougov-trust-in-the-judiciary/

7 J. Maugham, 'No, the legal system isn't biased against men – it allows them to rape with near impunity', *New Statesman*, 4 May 2018, https://www.newstatesman.com/politics/2018/05/no-legal-system-isn-t-biased-against-men-it-allows-them-rape-near-impunity

Chapter Six: Taking On the Brexit Goliath

1 House of Commons Briefing Paper Number 07212, 'European Union Referendum Bill 2015–16', House of Commons

Library, 3 June 2015, https://researchbriefings.files.parliament.
uk/documents/CBP-7212/CBP-7212.pdf

2   House of Commons Hansard, 'European Union Referendum
    Bill', 16 June 2015, vol. 597, col. 231, https://hansard.parlia-
    ment.uk/commons/2015-06-16/debates/15061658000001/
    EuropeanUnionReferendumBill

3   *Erlam and others v Rahman and another* [2015] EWHC 1215 (QB),
    https://www.bailii.org/ew/cases/EWHC/QB/2015/1215.html

4   *R (Good Law Project) v Electoral Commission* [2018] EWHC
    2414 (Admin), https://www.bailii.org/ew/cases/EWHC/
    Admin/2018/2414.html

5   Electoral Commission, 'Vote Leave fined and referred to
    the police for breaking electoral law', 17 July 2018, https://
    www.electoralcommission.org.uk/media-centre/vote-
    leave-fined-and-referred-police-breaking-electoral-law

6   See the European Commission for Democracy Through Law
    (Venice Commission) Code of Good Practice on Referendums
    at paragraph 24.

7   J. Elgot, J. Grierson, 'Electoral Commission launches inquiry into
    leave campaign funding', *Guardian*, 21 November 2017, https://
    www.theguardian.com/politics/2017/nov/20/electoral-
    commission-launches-inquiry-into-leave-campaign-funding

8   D. Cummings, 'On the Referendum #6: Exit plans and a second
    referendum', dominiccummings.com, 23 June 2015, https://
    dominiccummings.com/2015/06/23/on-the-referendum-
    6-exit-plans-and-a-second-referendum/

9   House of Commons Hansard, 'Referendums (Scotland and
    Wales) Bill', 22 May 1997, vol. 294, cols. 886–89, https://
    hansard.parliament.uk/commons/2015-06-16/debates/
    15061658000001/EuropeanUnionReferendumBill

10 D. Cummings, 'On the Referendum #6: Exit plans and a second referendum', dominiccummings.com, 23 June 2015, https://dominiccummings.com/2015/06/23/on-the-referendum-6-exit-plans-and-a-second-referendum/

11 'Bagehot's Notebook: An interview with Dominic Cummings', *The Economist*, 21 January 2016, https://www.economist.com/bagehots-notebook/2016/01/21/an-interview-with-dominic-cummings

12 T. Shipman, 'Boris calls for "no" to Europe – then "yes"', *The Times*, 28 June 2015, https://www.thetimes.co.uk/article/boris-calls-for-no-to-europe-then-yes-5hnppo8v2l7

13 BBC Radio 4 *Today*, tweet: 'Cabinet Minister @DLidington on having a 2nd Brexit referendum: "We all told the people in 2016 you're having the final say . . ." [. . .]', Twitter, 14 December 2018, accessed on 3 November 2022, available at: https://twitter.com/BBCr4today/status/1073485380228407296

14 'Reality Check: Has Corbyn changed his mind on Article 50?', BBC News, 22 July 2016, https://www.bbc.co.uk/news/uk-politics-uk-leaves-the-eu-36866170

15 N. Robinson, 'The referendum is over – now the BBC must fight a new Brexit bias', *Radio Times*, 4 April 2017, https://www.radiotimes.com/tv/current-affairs/nick-robinson-the-referendum-is-over-now-the-bbc-must-fight-a-new-brexit-bias/

16 J. Maugham, 'How to Deliver a Second Referendum', Waiting for Tax, 24 June 2016, https://waitingfortax.com/2016/06/24/deliver_second_referendum/

17 N. Barber, T. Hickman, J. King, 'Pulling the Article 50 "Trigger": Parliament's Indispensable Role', UK Constitutional Law Association, 27 June 2016, https://ukconstitutionallaw.org/2016/06/27/nick-barber-tom-hickman-and-jeff-

king-pulling-the-article-50-trigger-parliaments-indispensable-role/

18 *R (Miller) v The Secretary of State for Exiting the European Union* [2016] EWHC 2768 (Admin), https://www.bailii.org/ew/cases/EWHC/Admin/2016/2768.html

19 C. Phipps, 'British newspapers react to judges' Brexit ruling: "Enemies of the people"', *Guardian*, 4 November 2016, https://www.theguardian.com/politics/2016/nov/04/enemies-of-the-people-british-newspapers-react-judges-brexit-ruling

20 'Liz Truss defends judiciary after Brexit ruling criticism', *Guardian*, 5 November 2016, https://www.theguardian.com/law/2016/nov/05/barristers-urge-liz-truss-to-condemn-attacks-on-brexit-ruling-judges

21 E. Shirbon, 'Branded "enemies of the people" over Brexit case, senior UK judges hit back', Reuters, 29 March 2017, https://www.reuters.com/article/us-britain-eu-judges/branded-enemies-of-the-people-over-brexit-case-senior-uk-judges-hit-back-idUSKBN1701BA

22 *R (Miller and another) v Secretary of State for Exiting the European Union* [2017] UKSC 5, https://www.bailii.org/uk/cases/UKSC/2017/5.html

23 Prime Minister's Office, 'PM Speech: The government's negotiating objectives for exiting the EU', 17 January 2017, https://www.gov.uk/government/speeches/the-governments-negotiating-objectives-for-exiting-the-eu-pm-speech

24 'Brexit case "attempt to block will of people" says Sajid Javid', BBC News, 4 November 2016, https://www.bbc.co.uk/news/uk-politics-37866411

25 *Wightman v Secretary of State for Exiting the European Union* [2018] CSIH 62, https://www.bailii.org/scot/cases/ScotCS/2018/[2018]_CSIH_62.html

26 Advocate General's Opinion of 4 December 2018, *Wightman and Others v Secretary of State for Exiting the European Union*, C-621/18, https://curia.europa.eu/juris/document/document.jsf;jsessionid=8548A4C7B0F1C9B3032F040D211BA5A1?text=&docid=208385&pageIndex=0&doclang=EN&mode=lst&dir=&occ=first&part=1&cid=3665789

27 Judgment of 10 December 2018, *Wightman and Others v Secretary of State for Exiting the European Union*, C-621/18, https://curia.europa.eu/juris/document/document.jsf;jsessionid=8548A4C7B0F1C9B3032F040D211BA5A1?text=&docid=208636&pageIndex=0&doclang=EN&mode=lst&dir=&occ=first&part=1&cid=3665789

28 House of Commons Hansard, 'EU: Withdrawal and Future Relationship (Votes)', 27 March 2019, vol. 657, col. 458, https://hansard.parliament.uk/Commons/2019-03-27/debates/23130CF5-9C4C-4C35-835C-0AC5F6B74F89/EUWithdrawalAndFutureRelationship(Votes)

29 House of Commons Hansard, 'EU: Withdrawal and Future Relationship Votes', 27 March 2019, div. 391, https://hansard.parliament.uk/Commons/2019-03-27/division/BFF1E508-0EC1-4AF4-A8B6-EE02E5DD2E62/EUWithdrawalAndFutureRelationshipVotes?outputType=Party

30 House of Commons Hansard, 'EU: Withdrawal and Future Relationship (Votes)', 1 April 2019, div. 400, https://hansard.parliament.uk/Commons/2019-04-01/division/735350BE-2DD5-4E7A-AFF5-8B181DBC743F/EUWithdrawalAndFutureRelationship(Votes)?outputType=Names

Chapter Seven: When the Chips Are Down

1   *R (Miller) v the Prime Minister* [2019] UKSC 41, https://www.bailii.org/uk/cases/UKSC/2019/41.html

2   D. Cummings, 'On the Referendum #6: Exit plans and a second referendum', dominiccummings.com, 23 June 2015, https://dominiccummings.com/2015/06/23/on-the-referendum-6-exit-plans-and-a-second-referendum/

3   B. Rigby, G. Heffer, 'Andrea Leadsom rules out shutting down parliament to push through Brexit', Sky News, 7 June 2019, https://news.sky.com/story/andrea-leadsom-rules-out-shutting-down-parliament-to-push-through-brexit-11736195

4   Matt Hancock MP, tweet: 'Proroguing Parliament undermines parliamentary democracy and risks a general election. I rule it out and call on all candidates to do the same [image]', Twitter, 6 June 2019, accessed 3 November 2022, available at: https://twitter.com/MattHancock/status/1136610833750994951?s=20&t=sjcMAkhGiSlFabDxfpkmBw

5   P. Walker, 'Matt Hancock backs Boris Johnson in Tory leadership race', *Guardian*, 17 June 2019, https://www.theguardian.com/politics/2019/jun/17/matt-hancock-backs-boris-johnson-in-tory-leadership-race

6   D. Chipakupaku, 'U-turn from Matt Hancock as he defends suspending parliament', Sky News, 31 August 2019, https://news.sky.com/story/health-secretary-matt-hancock-u-turns-on-proroguing-parliament-11798608

7   House of Commons Hansard, 'Prorogation (Disclosure of Communications)', 9 September 2019, vol. 664, col. 522, https://hansard.parliament.uk/commons/2019-09-09/debates/ACF1C7B2-087F-46D2-AB69-3520C0675BC8/Prorogatio

n(DisclosureOfCommunications)#contribution-66C7B4D9-
A5E4-4AD5-8EE3-CE8D4051FE71

8   *Best of the Spectator*, podcast: 'Women With Balls: with Nikki da
Costa', 22 October 2021, available at: https://podcasts.apple.
com/us/podcast/women-with-balls-with-nikki-da-costa/
id793236670?i=1000539378220

9   House of Commons Hansard, 'G7 Summit', 3 September 2019, vol. 664, col. 41, https://hansard.parliament.
uk/Commons/2019-09-03/debates/9C6A36DF-1CCF-
4C07-9F81-DD16B8564D0C/G7Summit

10 A. Clark, 'Boris Johnson's prorogation of parliament is lawful,
Scottish court rules', *Guardian*, 4 September 2019, https://www.
theguardian.com/politics/2019/sep/04/boris-johnsons-
prorogation-of-parliament-is-lawful-scottish-court-rules

11 'Lord Sumption on Boris Johnson's prorogation of
parliament', 29 August 2019, *The Times*, https://www.the-
times.co.uk/article/lord-sumption-on-boris-johnson-
s-prorogation-of-parliament-the-legal-case-for-szjqpxoxz

12 S. Coates, 'Boris Johnson called David Cameron "girly swot",
leaked document reveals', Sky News, 7 September 2019,
https://news.sky.com/story/boris-johnson-branded-david-
cameron-girly-swot-leaked-document-reveals-11803807

13 *Joanna Cherry QC MP and others v The Advocate General for Scotland* [2019] CSIH 49, https://www.bailii.org/scot/cases/
ScotCS/2019/2019_CSIH_49.html

14 J. Maugham, tweet: 'This is a quite extraordinary thing for @
bernardjenkin, who Chairs the @CommonsPACAC, to tell a
constituent', Twitter, 16 September 2019, accessed 25 October 2022, available at: https://twitter.com/JolyonMaugham/
status/1173581351204904961

15 G. Rayner, H. Yorke, A. Mikhailova, 'Boris Johnson to make new push for general election after Supreme Court "frustrated the will of the people"', *Daily Telegraph*, 24 September 2019, https://www.telegraph.co.uk/politics/2019/09/24/boris-johnson-make-new-push-general-election-supreme-court-frustrated/

16 N. Watt, 'Scaling back the Supreme Court', BBC News, 20 December 2019, https://www.bbc.co.uk/news/uk-politics-50863138

17 O. Wright, 'Judges could be appointed by politicians', *The Times*, 30 September 2019, https://www.thetimes.co.uk/article/judges-could-be-appointed-by-politicians-x3fgkplcl

18 L. Graham, 'The Reed Court by Numbers: How Shallow is the "Shallow End"?', UK Constitutional Law, 4 April 2022, https://ukconstitutionallaw.org/2022/04/04/lewis-graham-the-reed-court-by-numbers-how-shallow-is-the-shallow-end%EF%BF%BC%EF%BF%BC/

19 H. Stewart, S. Carroll, 'Brexit: Boris Johnson short of options as rebels vow to secure delay', *Guardian*, 7 September 2019, https://www.theguardian.com/politics/2019/sep/06/boris-johnson-short-of-options-as-rebels-vow-to-secure-brexit-delay

20 'Boris Johnson: "I'd rather be dead in a ditch" than ask for Brexit delay', BBC News, 5 September 2019, https://www.bbc.co.uk/news/av/uk-politics-49601128

21 House of Commons Hansard, 'G7 Summit', 3 September 2019, vol. 664, col. 27, https://hansard.parliament.uk/Commons/2019-09-03/debates/9C6A36DF-1CCF-4C07-9F81-DD16B8564D0C/G7Summit

22 'What is the nobile officium?', BBC News, 8 October 2018, https://www.bbc.co.uk/news/uk-scotland-49933273

23 'Boris Johnson "has secret plan" to keep Brexit on track . . . but only three others in Downing Street know what it is', *Daily Mail*, 15 September 2019, https://www.dailymail.co.uk/news/article-7466857/Boris-Johnson-secret-plan-Brexit-track.html

24 J. Maugham, 'The Flaw in the Benn Act', Waiting for Tax, 15 September 2019, https://waitingfortax.com/2019/09/15/the-flaw-in-the-benn-act/

25 T. Shipman, C. Wheeler, 'Gove: Tories will collapse if UK is not out of EU by October 31', *Sunday Times*, 22 September 2019, https://www.thetimes.co.uk/article/gove-tories-will-collapse-if-uk-is-not-out-by-october-31-d2mkbpjj9

26 J, Maugham, tweet: 'In 2013, when I was not a public figure, I gave an interview to a local newspaper about my plans to restore a local heritage asset [. . .]', Twitter, 22 September 2019, accessed 25 October 2022, available at: https://twitter.com/JolyonMaugham/status/1175763311369031680?s=20&t=pQBOwIVjwC6VIZT1WFWsnw

27 A. Hill, 'Supreme court litigant advised to buy stab vest after death threats', *Guardian*, 26 September 2019, https://www.theguardian.com/law/2019/sep/26/supreme-court-litigant-advised-to-buy-stab-vest-after-death-threats

28 *Vince and others v Prime Minister and another* [2019] CSOH 77, https://www.bailii.org/scot/cases/ScotCS/2019/2019_CSOH_77.html

29 *Vince and others v Prime Minister and another* [2019] CSIH 51, https://www.bailii.org/scot/cases/ScotCS/2019/2019_CSIH_51.html

Chapter Eight: Wrestling with Uber

1   *Autoclenz Ltd v Belcher* [2011] UKSC 41, https://www.bailii.
org/uk/cases/UKSC/2011/41.html

2   M. Taibbi, 'The Great American Bubble Machine', *Rolling Stone*,
5 April 2010, https://www.rollingstone.com/politics/politics-
news/the-great-american-bubble-machine-195229/

3   *Aslam & Ors v Uber BV and others* [2016] EW Misc B68
(ET) (28 October 2016), https://www.bailii.org/ew/cases/
Misc/2016/B68.html

4   *Uber BV v Aslam, Farrar, Dawson and others* [2017]
UKEAT/0056/17/DA, https://assets.publishing.service.
gov.uk/media/5a046b06e5274a0ee5a1f171/Uber_B.V._and_
Others_v_Mr_Y_Aslam_and_Others_UKEAT_0056_17_
DA.pdf

5   *Uber BV and others v Aslam and others* [2018] EWCA Civ 2748,
https://www.bailii.org/ew/cases/EWCA/Civ/2018/2748.
html

6   *Uber BV and others v Aslam and others* [2021] UKSC 5, https://
www.bailii.org/uk/cases/UKSC/2021/5.html

7   J. Maugham, 'Uber: HMRC and the Public Accounts Committee', Waiting for Tax, 21 December 2017, https://
waitingfortax.com/2017/12/21/uber-hmrc-and-the-public-
accounts-committee/

8   The Sutton Trust, 'Elitist Britain 2019: The educational backgrounds of Britain's leading people', 24 June 2019, https://
www.suttontrust.com/our-research/elitist-britain-2019/

9   Judgment of 20 December 2017, *Asociación Profesional Elite Taxi
v Uber Systems Spain SL*, C-434/15, https://curia.europa.eu/
juris/document/document.jsf?text=&docid=198047&pageI
ndex=0&doclang=EN&mode=lst&dir=&occ=first&part=
1&cid=3681727

10 Response to Freedom of Information request to Transport for London, 22 January 2018, accessed 25 October 2022, response and attachments available at: https://www.whatdotheyknow.com/request/correspondence_25

11 *R (United Trade Action Group Ltd) v Transport for London* [2021] EWHC 3290 (Admin), https://www.bailii.org/ew/cases/EWHC/Admin/2021/3290.html

12 J. Maugham, 'Don't be too hard on US multinational: Treasury to HMRC', Waiting for Tax, 23 January 2018, https://waitingfor-tax.com/2018/01/23/dont-be-too-hard-on-us-multinational-treasury-to-hmrc/

13 H. Davies, S. Goodley, F. Lawrence, P. Lewis, L. O'Carroll, 'Uber broke laws, duped police and secretly lobbied governments, leak reveals', *Guardian*, 11 July 2022,https://www.theguardian.com/news/2022/jul/10/uber-files-leak-reveals-global-lobbying-campaign

14 Private correspondence between the author and journalists.

15 G. Wells, J. Horwitz, D. Seetharaman, 'Facebook Knows Instagram Is Toxic for Teen Girls, Company Documents Show', *Wall Street Journal*, 14 September 2021, https://www.wsj.com/articles/facebook-knows-instagram-is-toxic-for-teen-girls-company-documents-show-11631620739?mod=article_inline

16 J. Kollewe, 'Uber settles VAT claim with HMRC and posts better than expected results', *Guardian*, 1 November 2022, https://www.theguardian.com/technology/2022/nov/01/uber-settles-vat-claim-with-hmrc-and-post-better-than-expected-results

Chapter Nine: Vampires and Sunlight: The PPE Cases

1 G. Orwell, *Orwell's England*, ed. P. Davison, Penguin Random House, 2020.

2 House of Commons Hansard, 'Engagements', 25 March 2020, vol. 674, col. 337, https://hansard.parliament.uk/Commons/2020-03-25/debates/E02BF9C1-538F-49C0-B79D-3CC56E2B6309/Engagements

3 Department of Health and Social Care, 'PPE procurement in the early pandemic', 17 November 2021, https://www.gov.uk/government/news/ppe-procurement-in-the-early-pandemic

4 J. Croft, J. Pickard, 'UK government "drowning" in PPE contract requests, court told', *Financial Times*, 22 April 2021, https://www.ft.com/content/23792a43-b50f-4e1c-a1a7-700c9f152e09

5 J. Maugham, tweet: 'But civil servants were worried about Ayanda not getting a contract (it "wouldn't be a good outcome") [. . .]', Twitter, 7 September 2022, accessed on 3 November 2022, available at: https://twitter.com/JolyonMaugham/status/1567420344029396992/photo/1

6 Good Law Project, 'Specific disclosure bundle', 29 April 2021, accessed 26 October 2022, available at: https://drive.google.com/file/d/1--50U54imEiHElD9ydP1OZBwoAJz7xCU/view

7 N. Boardman, 'Boardman Report on Cabinet Office Communications Procurement', 8 December 2020, https://www.gov.uk/government/publications/findings-of-the-boardman-review

8 G. Greenwood, B. Kenber, 'Andrew Mills: Adviser behind bungled £250m mask contract hides earnings', *The Times*, 21 January 2021, https://www.thetimes.co.uk/article/andrew-mills-adviser-behind-bungled-250m-mask-contract-hides-earnings-0lwgbxog5

9 A. Bychawski, M. Williams, 'Record profits for firm involved in bungled £250m PPE deal', openDemocracy, 1 October 2021, https://www.opendemocracy.net/en/dark-money-investigations/record-profits-for-firm-involved-in-bungled-250m-ppe-deal/

10 A. Gross, J. Kelly, 'Leaked government email reveals Tory peer's anger at treatment of PPE company', *Financial Times*, 23 November 2021, https://www.ft.com/content/3970a940-c6a3-4fa1-b675-1c20aed3aa3d

11 D. Conn, 'PPE Medpro declines to say how it would repay millions if told to do so', *Guardian*, 25 November 2022, https://www.theguardian.com/uk-news/2022/nov/25/ppe-medpro-declines-to-say-how-it-would-repay-millions-if-told-to-do-so

12 D. Conn, V. Dodd, P. Lewis, K. Rawlinson, 'Michelle Mone's home raided as PPE firm linked to Tory peer investigated', *Guardian*, 29 April 2022, https://www.theguardian.com/uk-news/2022/apr/29/nca-launches-investigation-ppe-firm-linked-to-michelle-mone

13 S. Neville, 'UK squanders £10bn on defective or unsuitable PPE during pandemic', *Financial Times*, 1 February 2022, https://www.ft.com/content/740aa990-9bed-4cd3-b75b-0a5ce50b55c8

14 National Audit Office, 'The supply of personal protective equipment (PPE) during the COVID-19 pandemic', 25 November 2020, https://www.nao.org.uk/reports/supplying-the-nhs-and-adult-social-care-sector-with-personal-protective-equipment-ppe/

15 S. Bright, J. Lubbock, '"Another Shocking Example of Waste": UK Spends At Least £23.4 Million to Dispose of Unused PPE', Byline Times, 8 April 2022, https://

bylinetimes.com/2022/04/08/waste-uk-spends-at-least-23-4-million-to-dispose-of-unused-ppe/

16 J-P. Ford Rojas, '"Shameful and toxic": MPs demand answers over billions of PPE going up in smoke', Sky News, 10 June 2022, https://news.sky.com/story/shameful-and-toxic-mps-demand-answers-over-billions-of-ppe-going-up-in-smoke-12630903

17 Unpublished documents held by the author.

18 J. Corderoy, 'Clearing House: Government admits it's done nothing about "Orwellian" unit', openDemocracy, 20 January 2022, https://www.opendemocracy.net/en/freedom-of-information/clearing-house-government-admits-its-done-nothing-about-orwellian-unit/

19 *R (Good Law Project) v Prime Minister* [2022] EWHC 298 (Admin), https://www.bailii.org/ew/cases/EWHC/Admin/2022/298.html

20 *Cape Intermediate Holdings Ltd v Dring (Asbestos Victims Support Groups Forum UK)* [2019] UKSC 38, https://www.bailii.org/uk/cases/UKSC/2019/38.html

21 National Audit Office, 'Investigation into government procurement during the COVID-19 pandemic', HC 959, 26 November 2020, https://www.nao.org.uk/wp-content/uploads/2020/11/Investigation-into-government-procurement-during-the-COVID-19-pandemic.pdf

22 ibid.

23 J. Maugham, tweet: 'Someone has helpfully leaked documents to Private Eye showing that Mills was paid £32.4m [image]', Twitter, 11 November 2021, accessed 26 October 2022, available at: https://twitter.com/JolyonMaugham/status/1458703032716255235?s=20&t=n2ZJZ9UYiaLI_f1xo4jDqg;

J. Maugham, tweet: 'Private Eye also reveals that another Ayanda director made £11.6m commission on the deal [image]', Twitter, 11 November 2021, accessed 26 October 2022, available at: https://twitter.com/JolyonMaugham/status/1458703608 183234563?s=20&t=n2ZJZ9UYiaLI_f1xo4jDqg

24 D. Bloom, 'Government "wastes" millions on 50million coronavirus masks that won't be used in NHS', *Daily Mirror*, 6 August 2020, https://www.mirror.co.uk/news/politics/ government-wastes-millions-50million-coronavirus-22477733

25 J. Maugham, tweet thread: 'Last night, I said that I was aware of evidence DHSC had been paying higher prices for PPE to connected suppliers. And that I was working to put that evidence into the public domain.[. . .]', Twitter, 12 October 2020, accessed on 26 October 2022, available at: https://twitter. com/JolyonMaugham/status/1315553658671632385?s=20&t =jkT8N4yyVJzAgyZ2YULOhw

26 *Advanced Multi-Technology for Medical Industry and others v Uniserve Ltd* [2022] EWHC 264 (Ch), https://www.bailii.org/ew/ cases/EWHC/Ch/2022/264.html

27 J. Maugham, tweet thread: 'If you want to know how much £££ the favoured few were making from PPE contracts, and you do, then buckle up. [. . .]', Twitter, 8 March 2022, accessed on 26 October 2022, available at: https://twitter. com/JolyonMaugham/status/1501210404650991628?s=2 0&t=Qu9sJZFMLYq-nPePQ2gyeg

28 *R (Good Law Project Limited and another)) v Secretary of State for Health and Social Care* [2022] EWHC 46 (TCC), https://www. bailii.org/ew/cases/EWHC/TCC/2022/46.html

29 National Audit Office, 'Investigation into the management of PPE contracts', 30 March 2022, https://www.nao.

org.uk/press-releases/investigation-into-the-management-of-ppe-contracts/

30 J. Heaf, 'The counterparty puzzle: the curious case of the Miami jewellery designer, the government's PPE scandal and the lawyer on its trail', *GQ*, 27 April 2021, https://www.gq-magazine.co.uk/politics/article/ppe-scandal

31 Government Legal Department's 'Summary Grounds of Resistance', unpublished.

32 'COVID-19: Businessman paid $28m in "lucrative" PPE deal – US court papers', Sky News, 17 November 2020, https://news.sky.com/story/covid-19-businessman-paid-28m-in-lucrative-ppe-deal-us-court-papers-12134943

33 M. Ceberio Belaza, 'El "caso Emperado" destapa una multinacional de la evasión fiscal', *El País*, 23 December 2012, https://elpais.com/politica/2012/12/22/actualidad/1356194869_721251.html

34 'Go-between paid £21m in taxpayer funds for NHS PPE', BBC News, 17 November 2020,https://www.bbc.co.uk/news/uk-54974373

35 Office of the Registrar of Consultant Lobbyists, 'Summary of investigation', 26 September 2022, https://registrarofconsultantlobbyists.org.uk/summary-of-investigation-asj-properties-limited-asjp/

36 J. Maugham, tweet: '7. Now, what about that £5.13 per mask unit price? Some civil servants were concerned about it. It was "well above the average we are currently paying of £2.69 per unit." [. . .]', Twitter, 21 March 2020, accessed on 26 October 2022, available at: https://twitter.com/JolyonMaugham/status/1505820459824295937?s=20&t=oGKZJJ8WeUElqE2OvIVYjA

37 J. Maugham, tweet: 'But that cannot be right because four days earlier another supplier was told "we are no longer looking to purchase" MX2016V FFP3 models [. . .]', Twitter, 25 June 2021, accessed on 26 October 2022, available at: https://twitter.com/JolyonMaugham/status/1408490423203553284?s=20&t=e7Nss7WVyIoe2yFKAL17gw

38 Good Law Project, 'REVEALED: Testing firm awarded government approval after Tory fixer lobbied Matt Hancock', 27 September 2021, https://goodlawproject.org/update/testing-tory-fixer-matt-hancock/

39 A. Wager, T. Bale, P. Cowley, A. Menon, 'The Death of May's Law: Intra- and Inter-Party Value Differences in Britain's Labour and Conservative Parties', *Political Studies* 70(4), 2022, 939–61, https://doi.org/10.1177/00323217211995632

Conclusions

1 J. Walker, D. Williamson, 'Rishi vows to crackdown on activist lawyers – "stop politicising courts"', *Daily Express*, 20 August 2022, https://www.express.co.uk/news/politics/1658086/Rishi-sunak-activist-lawyers-crackdown

2 D. Rose, Tweet: 'When the history of this era comes to be written, the role of the Good Law Project in helping to erode what looked like Johnsonian hegemony will be considerable [. . .]', Twitter, 14 November 2021, accessed on 4 November 2022, available at: https://twitter.com/DavidRoseUK/status/1459860296064020482?s=20&t=F3_esgoHFYFsSZVoLoBWdA

3 V. Frankl, *Man's Search for Meaning*, Penguin, 2013 (first edition published in 1946).

Index